Early Child Care and Education in Finland

C000155064

What is childhood like in Finland? What kind of practical solutions have been created and evaluated that aim at both providing good childhood experiences and supporting children's positive development? What practices aim to prevent child exclusion from regular education and social experiences and to foster children's healthy development in emotional, social, and behavioural terms?

This book considers the reality of childhood in Finland. It discusses the realisation and evaluation of early childhood education and addresses aspects of research and practice concerning children under the age of 10. It examines the growth and development of young children, how learning and teaching are organised, practices of rearing children and the state of child care in Finland.

Contributors represent a variety of universities and sub disciplines in the science of education and focus on perspectives of children's well-being, special viewpoints of early childhood education, care, and research in Finland.

This book was originally published as a special issue of *Early Child Development and Care*.

Kaarina Määttä, PhD, is Deputy Vice-Chancellor and Professor of Educational Psychology in the Faculty of Education at the University of Lapland, Finland. Her research interests include love, attachment, and social relationships during the life span of human beings; early education; guidance on and processes of doctoral theses; and positive psychology and human strengths.

Satu Uusiautti, EdD, is a Specialist in the Faculty of Education at the University of Lapland, Finland. Her research interests include qualitative methods, positive psychology, and happiness, success, and well-being at various phases of life.

Early Child Care and Education in Finland

Edited by
Kaarina Määttä and Satu Uusiautti

Routledge
Taylor & Francis Group

LONDON AND NEW YORK

First published 2013
by Routledge
2 Park Square, Milton Park, Abingdon, Oxfordshire OX14 4RN

Simultaneously published in the USA and Canada
by Routledge
711 Third Avenue, New York, NY 10017

First issued in paperback 2014

Routledge is an imprint of the Taylor and Francis Group, an informa business

British Library Cataloguing in Publication Data
A catalogue record for this book is available from the British Library

ISBN 978-0-415-63591-2 (hbk)

ISBN 978-1-138-84478-0 (pbk)

Typeset in Times New Roman
by Taylor & Francis Books

Publisher's Note
The publisher would like to make readers aware that the chapters in this book may be referred to as articles as they are identical to the articles published in the special issue. The publisher accepts responsibility for any inconsistencies that may have arisen in the course of preparing this volume for print.

Contents

CONTENTS

Citation Information

The chapters in this book were originally published in the *Early Child Development and Care*, volume 182, issue 3-4 (March-April 2012). When citing this material, please use the original page numbering for each article, as follows:

Chapter 1
How do the Finnish family policy and early education system support the well-being, happiness, and success of families and children?
Kaarina Määttä and Satu Uusiautti
Early Child Development and Care, volume 182, issue 3-4 (March-April 2012)
pp. 291-298

Chapter 2
Evaluating the quality of the child care in Finland Eeva Hujala, Elina Fonsén and Janniina Elo
Early Child Development and Care, volume 182, issue 3-4 (March-April 2012)
pp. 299-314

Chapter 3
Individual plans for children in transition to pre-school: a case study in one Finnish day-care centre Tuija A. Turunen
Early Child Development and Care, volume 182, issue 3-4 (March-April 2012)
pp. 315-328

Chapter 4
Sámi education in Finland Pigga Keskitalo, Kaarina Määttä and Satu Uusiautti
Early Child Development and Care, volume 182, issue 3-4 (March-April 2012)
pp. 329-344

Chapter 5
Having, loving, and being: children's narrated well-being in Finnish day care centres
Anna-Maija Puroila, Eila Estola and Leena Syrjälä *Early Child Development and Care*, volume 182, issue 3-4 (March-April 2012)
pp. 345-362

Notes on contributors

Piia M. Björn, PhD, has had a position as Lecturer since 2007 and is currently the head of the Special Education section at the University of Jyväskylä, Finland. Her scientific expertise and interest focuses on family interaction, intervention studies and development of academic skills (especially reading, writing and mathematics) across all age levels.

Mari Broberg is a Postdoctoral Researcher at the University of Turku, Finland. She received her PhD in education from the University of Turku in 2010. Her doctoral dissertation concerned Finnish children's well-being in stepfamilies.

Janniina Elo is a Graduate Student in early childhood education. Elo works as a research assistant in an international research project, focusing on comparative research and quality of ECE.

Eila Estola, PhD, is Adjunct Professor and senior researcher for the Faculty of Education at the University of Oulu in Finland. Her main research interests are in narrative research on teachers, teacher education, and diverse childhood environments.

Elina Fonsén is a PhD candidate in early childhood education. Fonsén works as a project coordinator at the University of Tampere, Finland, in development projects of pedagogical leadership and quality of ECE.

Iiris Happo, EdD, is Principal Lecturer at Oulu University of Applied Sciences, Finland. Previously, she has worked as a teacher, researcher, and expert of early childhood education and pedagogy at Rovaniemi University of Applied Sciences, Finland, and the University of Lapland, Finland, and as an early childhood education teacher.

Anitta Heikkilä, PhD, is a Teacher in Ounasrinne School (Rovaniemi), Finland. She graduated in education from the Faculty of Education, University of Lapland, Finland, in 2008. Her research interests are in clothing and pupils' dressing at school. Her doctoral dissertation "Clothes in the child's life. Clothing of a schoolchild in a countryside village in northern Finland during the years 1909-1939" defined the idea from a historical perspective.

Eeva Hujala is Professor of early childhood education. Hujala's research areas are ECE quality assessment, and cross cultural research on child care, as well as leadership, management and educational development in early childhood education. Hujala's teaching responsibilities are focused on ECE programmes of bachelor, master and doctor levels. Hujala is also the president of the Finnish Association of Early Childhood Education and is involved with many international ECE businesses.

Kosti Joensuu is Master of Social Sciences (M.Soc.Sc) and graduated from the University of Jyväskylä, Finland, in 2004, with philosophy as a major subject. Kosti Joensuu now works at the University of Lapland, in Finland, as a graduate student and a junior researcher, a lecturer of educational psychology and as a student of applied psychology in the master's degree programme of leadership psychology.

Irma Kakkuri, LicEd, is Senior Lecturer at the University of Jyväskylä, Special Education Section, Finland. Her core areas of teaching are related to reading and writing difficulties and higher education students' learning-to-learn skills. She is a member of several research groups aimed at learning, teaching and student well-being.

Pirkko Karvonen, PhD, has been Project Manager in the "Storytellers" project (2006–2009) whose purpose was to create child-oriented, holistic patterns for preventing problems with reading and writing abilities before school age. Linguistic and motor skills were emphasized in the project and also the integration of these skills. She has previously had a long career at the University of Jyväskylä, Finland.

Pigga Keskitalo, EdD, is the Associate Professor at Sámi University College (Sámi allaskuvla) in Kautokeino, Norway. She has written a doctoral thesis about Sámi upbringing, 'Cultural sensitivity in the Sámi School through educational anthropology' (2010) at the Faculty of Education, University of Lapland, Finland (published in Finnish). Pigga Keskitalo is a Sámi woman herself and lives in Enontekiö. She has been working as a teacher educator for several years and has published numerous articles about Sámi education.

Laura Kirves is a PhD student at the University of Helsinki, Finland, in the Department of Teacher Education and Early Childhood Education. Her research interests include bullying in early childhood education, well-being and systems intelligence in day care.

Elina Kontu, PhD, is Adjunct Professor (early childhood education) and a lecturer in the Department of Teacher Education, at the University of Helsinki, Finland. Her research interests include special education and music therapy.

Tiina Lämsä is a Kindergarten Teacher and a PhD candidate. She graduated from the Department of Early Childhood Education and is working on her doctoral research in the Graduate School for Family Studies and as a part of the Palette research project at the Family Research Centre, University of Jyväskylä, Finland. Her doctoral research concerns adults' perceptions of children from the perspective of everyday life.

Paavo H. T. Leppänen, PhD, is Professor of psychology and directs the Developmental and Cognitive Brain Research Laboratory at the Department of Psychology at the University of Jyväskylä, Finland. His research interests include neurocognitive studies of risk factors for learning disabilities, in particular dyslexia, auditory and speech processing, language learning, and training effects.

Kaarina Määttä, PhD, is Deputy Vice-Chancellor and Professor of Educational Psychology in the Faculty of Education at the University of Lapland, Finland. Her research interests include love, attachment, and social relationships during the life span of human beings; early education; guidance on and processes of doctoral theses; and positive psychology and human strengths.

Anna-Maija Puroila, PhD, is Doctoral Researcher for the Faculty of Education at the University of Oulu in Finland. Her research interests deal with early childhood settings and narrative research with children.

Kaisa Malinen received her PhD in psychology in 2011. Her dissertation dealt with spousal relationship in families with young children with a special focus on relationship maintenance and daily life. She is trained as a psychologist and works at the Family Research Centre, University of Jyväskylä, Finland.

Pirjo-Liisa Poikonen, PhD, is Senior Assistant of early childhood education in the Department of Education, University of Jyväskylä, Finland. Her research focuses on collaboration, social interaction and partnership in preschool and school contexts and factors contributing to children's transition from preschool to school.

Jyrki Reunamo is Lecturer in the Department of Teacher Education, University of Helsinki, Finland. His research interests include early childhood, research methods and education for sustainable development.

Anna Rönkä, PhD, is Principal Lecturer at the JAMK University of Applied Sciences, Finland. One of her areas of expertise is the development of mobile-based diary methods to study and support parenting and child well-being.

Nina Sajaniemi is Adjunct Professor, Principal Investigator and a lecturer in the Department of Teacher Education, University of Helsinki, Finland. She has expertise in developmental neuropsychology and her research interests are in intent participation learning, pedagogical sensitivity, stress regulation and early learning.

Eira Suhonen, PhD, is Lecturer (special education) at the University of Helsinki, Finland. Her research focuses on early childhood special education, early identification of children's special needs, day care quality and adult's engagement.

Leena Syrjälä, PhD, is Professor at the Faculty of Education, University of Oulu in Finland. Her main research interests deal with teachers biographical and narrative research, place, and methodology of narrative research.

Tuija A. Turunen is Postdoctoral Research Fellow at the Research Institute for Professional Practice, Learning & Education (RIPPLE), Charles Sturt University, Australia. Her research interests include transitions in early childhood, especially starting school.

Satu Uusiautti, EdD, is a Specialist in the Faculty of Education at the University of Lapland, Finland. Her research interests include qualitative methods, positive psychology, and happiness, success, and well-being at various phases of life.

Introduction

How do the Finnish family policy and early education system support the well-being, happiness, and success of families and children?

Introduction

What is childhood like in Finland? What kind of practical solutions have been created and evaluated – as well as those under development – that aim at both providing good childhood experiences and supporting children's positive development? What practices aim to prevent exclusion from regular education and social experiences and to foster children's healthy development in emotional, social, and behavioural terms? This issue consists of 12 articles that address aspects of research and practice concerning children under the age of 10, including their growth and development, the organisation of learning and teaching, and practices of rearing and child care in Finland. Authors represent a variety of universities and subdisciplines of the science of education. Reports are organised within the following strands: (1) the realisation and evaluation of early childhood education; (2) perspectives on children's well-being; and (3) special viewpoints to early childhood education, care, and research in Finland. In order to give international readers an insight of the situation in Finland, we will next provide an introduction about the Finnish family policy and educational system.

Early child care and education in Finland

Contemporary policy and practice emphasise the need to support parenthood and foster teachers' professionalism and their interaction with those in related professions. These developments pose fascinating challenges within the overall context of a rapidly changing Finnish society. In this article, we provide an introduction on the current state of early childhood and the guidelines of the family policy exercised in Finland: what are the children's and families' rights and benefits and how is the well-being of families and children supported by the state in Finland? The rights and benefits form the basis of all child care and education and exemplify the attitude that we have towards families with children in Finland. Furthermore, we address the issue of early childhood education and care (ECEC) in Finland's Programme for International Student Assessment (PISA) success as it has been the subject of increasing interest during the past few years. All actions should be first and foremost focused on children's well-being.

The Finnish family policy in a nutshell

In Finland, the Ministry of Social Affairs and Health (MSAH) is responsible for main-taining and developing family policy and the welfare of children, youth, and families in collaboration with other government ministries. The MSAH's area of responsibility concerns especially the development of social and health services and income security for families with children. Finnish family policy rests on three pillars: a child-oriented society, thriving families with children, and the prevention of social exclusion (Ministry of Social Affairs and Health [MSAH], 2006).

In services created for families with children, the focus ever since the 1970s has been on developing child-care systems for small children. The MSAH's family policy places an emphasis on the reconciliation of work and family life in order to improve the oppor-tunities for parents to spend more time with their children and to make it easier for women to go to work. In Finland, both parents of the vast majority of families with children under school age are in full-time employment. Under these circumstances, a reliable, safe, and reasonably priced day-care system is of vital importance (MSAH, 2006).

Finland uses the Nordic welfare state principles and methods, which are based on the state's responsibility for its citizens. Thus, welfare services, such as ECEC, are arranged and funded by central and local government (Heinämäki, 2008). Conse-quently, there are a variety of family policy activities, services, and benefits available (see The Social Insurance Institution of Finland, KELA, http://www.kela.fi). Before and after childbirth, mothers (and children) use the services of maternity and child welfare clinics. Mothers start their maternity leave 50 days at the earliest and 30 days at the latest before the expected date of delivery; the leave is funded by KELA to those mothers who live in Finland (covered by the Finnish social security system), whose pregnancy has lasted for at least 154 days, and who have undergone a medical examination at a maternal welfare clinic or at a doctor's office before the end of the fourth month of pregnancy. Maternity allowance is paid for the first 105 days of entitlement, and the amount depends on a mother's salary (if she had a job before becoming pregnant).

Parental leave begins after the maternity leave. During parental leave, KELA pays a parental allowance for 158 working days (a little over half a year). The child will be about nine-month old when the entitlement to the parental allowance ends. The parental leave can be taken either by the mother or the father or it can be shared to enable them to take turns in looking after their child. Both parents cannot be on parental leave at the same time (with the exception of the parents of multiple birth children). In 2009, of the total of the parental allowances, 91% was paid to mothers (Official Statistics of Finland, 2009; Statistical Yearbook of the Social Insurance Institution, 2009).

In addition to parental allowances, fathers can take between 1 and 18 days of pater-nity leave after childbirth in order to look after their child at home together with the mother. The paternity leave can be taken at any time after the birth of a child while maternity or parental allowance is being paid and it can be divided into up to four sep-arate periods. KELA pays the paternity allowance during the leave. In addition to a paternity leave after childbirth, fathers can take a supplementary full month of paternity leave. This is referred to as 'Daddy Month'. Fathers who take the last 12 working days in the parental allowance period get 1–24 additional working days of leave. The Daddy Month can be between 13 and 36 weekdays (excluding Sundays).

After parental allowance or extended paternity allowance, parents can take a child-care leave with full employment security to look after a child under the age of 3, although both parents cannot be on full-time leave at the same time. In addition, a child benefit is paid for children under 17 who are living in Finland. Its amount depends on the number of eligible children in the household.

Parents can choose to place their child in a day-care centre run by the municipality, look after their child while receiving child home care allowance, or choose a private day-care allowance and make their own arrangements for child care. The allowances are payable from the end of the parental allowance period (or any extended paternity leave) until the time the child starts school. For children within the extended compulsory education system, this right to choose ends at the end of July of the year in which the child reaches the age of 7. Parents (or other guardians) can place their child in a municipal day-care centre or with a family child-care provider.

It is worth remembering that state services are based on taxation. Finland changed over from family-based taxation to individual taxation in 1976. The change to individual taxation and the removal of family-based deductions has made taxation simpler and clearer. In Finland, the shift to individual taxation caused an increase in the number of married women in paid employment (MSAH, 2006).

The Finnish educational system

In Finland, education is a public service, and general education, vocational education, and higher education are free of charge (see the chart of the Finnish Education System, http://www.minedu.fi/export/sites/default/OPM/Koulutus/koulutusjaerjestelmae/liittee t/finnish_education.pdf). Basic education, upper secondary education, and vocational education are financed by the state and local authorities. General education and vocational education are provided by local authorities. Universities are autonomous and financed by the government. Furthermore, there are also liberal studies for adults who are economically supported by the government.

Municipalities (local authorities) are the providers of education. Providers of education and schools set up their own curricula on the basis of the national core curriculum. In curricula, local needs can be taken into consideration. Schools can have their own profiles, such as science or music education (Jakku-Sihvonen & Niemi, 2006).

According to the Finnish Education Act (628/1998), all children in Finland have to go to school at the age of 7. Primary school begins at the beginning of the autumn semester. Basic education lasts nine years. At the comprehensive schools, classroom teachers are mainly responsible for classes 1–6, and most of the subjects are taught by subject teachers in grades 7–9 (Jakku-Sihvonen & Niemi, 2007).

Preschool education starts at the age of 6. Finnish children have the right to participate in voluntary and free preschool education during the year preceding compulsory education, and nearly all six-year-old children (96% of this age group; see Eurydice, 2009) do so. In Finland, children go to day care before going to school, and they attend actual preschool education for one year, which consists of learning social skills and the basics of reading and writing.

Early childhood and preschool education and care in Finland

Day-care services

Day-care services are open to every child – in other words, all children below school age are entitled to receive municipal day care. Day-care costs are calculated according to the family size and income and range between €23 and €254 a month (MSAH). There are also private day-care services available for which the family can have governmental private day-care allowance to cover part of the costs (Heinämäki, 2008). The above-mentioned services are important as the female labour force participation in Finland is 72% of women (15−64 years), only 18.2% of whom are in part-time employment. Furthermore, the labour force participation rate of women with a child or children under six years is 49.6% of whom 8% work part time (OECD, 2006).

Day-care staff

The official documents of early childhood education (MSAH, 2002; Official Statistics of Finland, 2009) define early childhood education as an educational interaction that takes place within small children's living surroundings and is aimed at promoting children's balanced and healthy growth, development, and learning. Early education is organised and controlled by society and comprises the wholeness of care, education, and teaching (Act on Children's Day Care, 36/1973, 304/1983).

Adult−child ratios in day-care services are the following: one adult per seven children, aged between three and six years; one adult per four children up to the age of 3. In day-care centres, all staff must have at least secondary-level education from the field and one-third of staff must have a post-secondary-level university degree (i.e. Bachelor of Education, Master of Education, Bachelor of Social Sciences) (Heinämäki, 2008).

Basically, the aim of kindergarten teacher education in Finnish universities is to educate experts in early education. The degree qualifies graduates to work both as kindergarten teachers in children's day-care and pre-primary education as well as in various professions requiring expertise in early education, such as posts in public administration, which may require an applicable higher education degree. During their studies, students will become familiar with, among other things, childhood and the growth of children, the development of personality and learning, and the aims, content, and methods of public early and pre-primary education. In addition, students will gain competence in the analysis, critical evaluation, and research-based evaluation of their own work (Happo, Määttä, & Uusiautti, 2012, this special issue).

Day care and Finnish PISA success

The question whether there is a connection between Finland's PISA success and early childhood education is interesting. Although Finland's PISA success and its connection to early childhood education is less studied, some features can perhaps be named as effective behind the success. Finnish early education typifies the EDUCARE model, which means the interconnectedness of education and care as well as learning as the foundation of pedagogical action. This pedagogical action has been connected to full-time early education and has been recognised and commended in the Organisation for Economic Co-operation and Development (OECD) reports (Kronqvist & Kumpulainen, 2011).

Finland, like other Nordic countries, differs from most countries participating in PISA in the pace in which children enter academic life. Finnish children begin school only the year they turn seven, and there is very little stress placed on academics in a child's life before that (Kupiainen, Hautamäki, & Karjalainen, 2009; see also Kiiveri & Määttä, 2011). The one-year preschool or kindergarten class for six-year-olds, established in 1998 to help transition from home or day care to school, is attended by nearly the whole age cohort. The curriculum for all early education stresses the salient role of play in fostering children's physical, cognitive, social, and emotional development, with even the preschool year aimed at just preparing children for reading and mathematics through age-appropriate preparatory activities instead of outright teaching (Kupiainen et al., 2009; see also Turunen, 2012, this special issue).

The preschool year, basic education, and both strands of upper secondary education are free of charge for everyone, and in all levels, except general upper secondary education, text books and other requisites are also provided by the school. Daily school meals are provided for all in both basic and upper secondary schools without charge. Children have the right to attend their geographically nearest basic school but can also apply for a place in any other school with vacant places in their municipality (Kupiainen et al., 2009).

In pre-primary and basic education, pupils are entitled to any welfare services they might need for full engagement in their respective educational programmes, including general health and dental care for all students. All pupils are also entitled to special education when necessary. Before school age and especially during the lower grades, at-risk children and students are screened for possible learning problems to allow for early intervention. Any student with learning or adjustment problems is entitled to remedial teaching. When feasible, this is realised by inclusion but can also be arranged through a special education class in regular schools or in a school for students with special needs. An individual teaching and learning plan is made for each student with special needs (Kupiainen et al., 2009).

Providing all students with equal educational opportunities and removing obstacles to learning, especially among the least successful students, have been the leading principles in Finnish educational policy since the twentieth century. In light of the PISA findings, Finland seems to have managed extraordinarily well in combining these two principles – although there are still issues to be reconsidered and improved, for example, concerning education for national minorities (see also Keskitalo, Määttä, & Uusiautti, 2012, this special issue).

As a token of equal educational opportunities, the differences found between schools in Finland have been shown to be among the smallest in the OECD. This is largely due to the non-selective education system where all students are provided with the same kind of comprehensive schooling. In contrast, variation between schools tends to be more pronounced in countries where students are enrolled in different kinds of schools at an early age. In addition, the differences in PISA found among schools between the different regions as well as among the urban and rural areas of Finland have been shown to be relatively unimportant. In Finland, it is thus of little consequence where students live and which school they go to. Students come to school from widely differing family backgrounds in both Finland and the other PISA countries, and family background, as shown by the results of PISA, still has an impact on student performance. In Finland, however, this influence is less marked than the average across OECD countries (Välijärvi et al., 2007).

However, good performance is usually backed up by a network of dozens of factors, which include students' own interests, attitudes, and learning strategies; students' gender and background; learning opportunities offered by home and school; and expectations of parents and schools (e.g. Bajaras & Pierce, 2001; Diaz, 2003; Dumais, 2002; Farkas, Grobe, Sheehan, & Shuan, 1990; Wößmann, 2003). Therefore, in view of the significance, PISA has attained at both the international and national levels of education policy since the release of the first PISA results in 2001, a wider discussion might be warranted regarding the making of (too) far-reaching conclusions for national education policies based on just one type of study, covering only one dimension among the multitude of objectives each country has set for their education systems (see, e.g. Jakku-Sihvonen, Tissari, Ots, & Uusiautti, 2011). The current empirical evidence, combined with the moral argument for educational equality, still speaks strongly for a comprehensive school with high national standards and well-functioning student support (Kupiainen et al., 2009).

Conclusions: children's well-being at the core of the matter

We live our lives with other people and choose and feel in relation to other people and events, in other words, acknowledging human interdependency. Storh (2009) has combined love with the idea of 'minding others' business'. She explains that we might be morally required to intervene in someone's life in order to promote that person's own happiness. Storh (2009, p. 136) concludes: 'My flourishing depends on the flourishing of others. That makes it all the more important to permit wise intervention in others' affairs, for in minding others' business, we are also often minding our own'. Transmitting this kind of an attitude in our children could be the main guideline in upbringing. This is what love fundamentally is, and children will learn to use it if we – as educators, parents, and other significant people in children's life – set an example by directing our mindful and loving action in children and other people as well (see also Määttä & Uusiautti, 2011, forthcoming; Uusiautti & Määttä, 2011). Children's well-being thus is the responsibility of those people who live with and live close to children, such as parents, other immediate caregivers, teachers, and friends (Ambert, 1994; Arendell, 1997).

Worldwide statistics show how the number of working mothers of young children has risen over the past few decades as has the use of child care (Ebbeck & Hoi Yin, 2009). A day-care centre is not just any place where children spend their day while parents are working (Kyrönlampi-Kylmänen & Määttä, 2010). ECEC lays the foundation for success in later life.

The core of education – not only in Finland but across the world – should be on enhancing children's well-being as today's main emphases seem to be in efficiency, competitiveness, and individualism that can lead to increasing insecurity in a constantly changing world. Indeed, the ethics of caring concerns teaching and education (Gilligan, 1982). In fact, caring has been argued to be the central aim and method of education (see Burns & Rathbone, 2010; Noddings, 1988). The child-care provider is one of the most important elements in quality child care, and therefore, it is not unimportant what kind of surroundings day care or school or other institution provides for children's development and growth (e.g. Boshcee & Jacobs, 1997; Hagegull & Bohlin, 1995) in addition to home (Määttä, 2007; Sheridan & Burt, 2009). Caring about our children means a genuine will to understand and make an effort for their protection, support, and development by cherishing their authentic selfhood (see Joensuu, 2012, this special issue).

In this special issue, Finnish ECEC is studied from various points of view. Rigorous research and constant development are the basic means through which the system can secure the well-being and success of families and children.

References

Ambert, A.-M. (1994). An international perspective on parenting: Social change and social constructs. *Journal of Marriage and the Family, 56,* 529–543.

Arendell, T. (1997). *Contemporary parenting. Challenges and issues. Understanding families.* London: Sage.

Bajaras, H.L., & Pierce, J.L. (2001). The significance of race and gender in school success among Latinas and Latinos in college. *Gender and Society, 15*(6), 859–878.

Boshcee, M.A., & Jacobs, G. (1997). *Ingredients for quality child care.* National Network for Child Care. Retrieved from http://www.nncc.org/choose.quality.care/ingredients.html#anchor143569

Burns, D.P., & Rathbone, N. (2010). The relationship of narrative, virtue education, and an ethic of care in teaching practice. *In Education, 16*(2). Retrieved from http://ineducation.ca/article/relationship-narrative-virtue-education-and-ethic-care-teaching-practice

Diaz, A.L. (2003). Personal, family, and academic factors affecting low achievement in secondary school. *Electronic Journal of Research in Educational Psychology, 1*(1), 43–66.

Dumais, S.A. (2002). Cultural capital, gender, and school success: The role of habitus. *Sociology of Education, 75*(1), 44–68.

Ebbeck, M., & Hoi Yin, B.Y. (2009). Rethinking attachment: Fostering positive relationships between infants, toddlers and their primary caregivers. *Early Child Development and Care, 179*(7), 899–909.

Eurydice. (2009). *National summary sheets on education systems in Europe and ongoing reforms.* Finland: European Commission.

Farkas, G., Grobe, R.P., Sheehan, D., & Shuan, Y. (1990). Cultural resources and school success: Gender, ethnicity, and poverty groups within an urban school district. *American Sociological Review, 55*(1), 127–142.

Gilligan, C. (1982). *In a different voice. Psychological theory and women's development.* Cambridge: Harvard University Press.

Hagegull, B., & Bohlin, G. (1995). Day care quality, family and child characteristics and socio-emotional development. *Early Childhood Research Quarterly, 10,* 505–526.

Happo, I., Määttä, K., & Uusiautti, S. (2012). Experts or good educators – or both? The development of early childhood educators' expertise in Finland. *Early Child Development and Care, 182*(3–4), 487–504.

Heinämäki, L. (2008). *Early childhood education in Finland.* Potsdam: Liberales Institut. Retrieved from http://pro-kopf.de/fileadmin/Downloads/OC_39-Heinaemaeki-ECE_in_Finland.pdf

Jakku-Sihvonen, R., & Niemi, H. (2006). Introduction to the Finnish education system and teachers' work. In R. Jakku-Sihvonen & H. Niemi (Eds.), *Research-based teacher education in Finland – reflections by Finnish teacher educators* (pp. 7–16). Turku: Finnish Educational Research Association.

Jakku-Sihvonen, R., & Niemi, H. (2007). Introduction. In R. Jakku-Sihvonen & H. Niemi (Eds.), *Education as societal contributor* (pp. 9–20). Frankfurt am Main: Peter Lang.

Jakku-Sihvonen, R., Tissari, V., Ots, A., & Uusiautti, S. (2011). Teacher education curricula after the Bologna process – a comparative analysis of written curricula in Finland and Estonia. *Scandinavian Journal of Educational Research.* Advance online publication. DOI:10.1080/00313831.2011.581687

Joensuu, K. (2012). Care for the other's selfhood: A view on child care and education through Heidegger's analytic of Dasein. *Early Child Development and Care, 182*(3–4), 417–434.

Keskitalo, P., Määttä, K., & Uusiautti, S. (2012). Sámi education in Finland. *Early Child Education and Care, 182*(3–4), 329–343.

Kiiveri, K., & Määttä, K. (2011). Children's opinions about learning to read. *Early Childhood Education and Care,* Advance online publication. DOI: 10.1080/03004430.2011.579737

Kronqvist, E.-L., & Kumpulainen, K. (2011). *Lapsuuden oppimisympäristöt. Eheä polku varhaiskasvatuksesta kouluun* [Childhood learning environments. Harmonious path from early education to school]. Helsinki: WSOYpro.

Kupiainen, S., Hautamäki, J., & Karjalainen, T. (2009). *The Finnish education system and PISA* (Ministry of Education Publications, No. 46). Finland: Ministry of Education. Retrieved from http://www.pisa2006.helsinki.fi/files/The_Finnish_education_system_and_PISA.pdf

Kyrönlampi-Kylmänen, T., & Määttä, K. (2010). What do the children really think about a day-care centre – the 5 to 7-year-old Finnish children speak out. *Early Child Development and Care.* Advance online publication. DOI: 10.1080/03004430.2011.557861

Ministry of Social Affairs and Health. (2006). *Finland's family policy*. Helsinki: Author. Retrieved from http://www.stm.fi/en/publications/publication/_julkaisu/1058023#en

Määttä, K. (2007). Vanhempainrakkaus – suurin kaikista [Parental love – the greatest love]. In K. Määttä (Ed.), *Helposti särkyvää. Nuoren kasvun turvaaminen* [Fragile – Securing youngsters' growth]. Helsinki: Kirjapaja.

Määttä, K., & Uusiautti, S. (2011). Pedagogical love and good teacherhood. *In Education, 17*(2). Retrieved from http://ineducation.ca/article/pedagogical-love-and-good-teacherhood

Määttä, K., & Uusiautti, S. (Forthcoming). Pedagogical love and pedagogical authority – connected or incompatible? *International Journal of Whole Schooling.*

Noddings, N. (1988). An ethic of caring and its implications for instructional arrangements. *American Journal of Education, 96*(2), 215–231.

Official Statistics of Finland. (2009). *Helsinki: The Social Insurance Institution.* Retrieved from http://www.kela.fi/it/kelasto/kelasto.nsf/alias/Perhe_09_pdf/$File/Perhe_09.pdf?Open Element

Organisation for Economic Co-operation and Development (OECD). (2006). *Starting Strong II: Early childhood education and care.* Retrieved from http://www.oecd.org/dataoecd/16/2/ 37423404.pdf

Sheridan, S.M., & Burt, J.D. (2009). Family-centered positive psychology. In S.J. Lopez & C.R. Snyder (Eds.), *Oxford handbook of positive psychology* (pp. 551–559). Oxford, NY: Oxford University Press.

Statistical Yearbook of the Social Insurance Institution. (2009). *Helsinki: The Social Insurance Institution.* Retrieved from http://www.kela.fi/it/kelasto/kelasto.nsf/alias/Yearbook_09_pdf/ $File/Yearbook_09.pdf?OpenElement

Storh, K. (2009). Minding others' business. *Pacific Philosophical Quarterly, 90,* 116–139.

Turunen, T.A. (2012). Individual plans for children in transition to pre-school: A case study in one Finnish Day-care centre. *Early Child Development and Care, 182*(3–4), 315–328.

Uusiautti, S., & Määttä, K. (2011). The ability to love – a virtue-based approach. *British Journal of Educational Research, 2*(1), 1–19.

Välijärvi, J., Kupari, P., Linnakylä, P., Reinikainen, P., Sulkunen, S., Törnroos, J., & Arffman, I. (2007). *The Finnish success in PISA – and some reasons behind it 2. PISA 2003.* Jyväskylä: Institute for Educational Research.

Wößmann, L. (2003). Schooling resources, educational institutions and student performance: The international evidence. *Oxford Bulletin of Economics and Statistics, 65*(2), 117–170.

Kaarina Määttä and Satu Uusiautti
Faculty of Education, University of Lapland, Rovaniemi, Finland

Evaluating the quality of the child care in Finland

Eeva Hujala, Elina Fonsén and Janniina Elo

In this study we examine parents' and teachers' perceptions of the early childhood education and care (ECEC) quality in Finland. The study is based on the paradigm of inclusionary quality and the assessment is based on the quality evaluation model. The parents and teachers assess the quality to be good. The strength of the quality was the effect factor assessed by the parents, and the intermediate factor assessed by the teachers. The curriculum content and pedagogy of learning were assessed with lower ratings by both groups. The assessments of the factors differed significantly between the respondent groups, except for the intermediate factor. The high standard deviation in quality variables indicates that there is variation in quality among ECEC organisations. The results show that there is a demand for creating a national quality evaluation system to guarantee equal child-care services everywhere in Finland.

Introduction

The purpose of the study is to describe the quality of early childhood education and care (ECEC) by using data collected from Finnish child-care centres during the twenty-first century. The assessment of the ECEC quality has been implemented child-specifically by both parents and teachers. The aim of the study is to provide knowledge of the strengths and weaknesses of Finnish ECEC. The differences of the parents' and teachers' quality assessments will be analysed, and the factors connected to them will be discussed. The quality of ECEC in Finland has been steered with the information guidance. No nationally guided quality evaluation has been carried out so far. Questions have been raised as regards the variation of the quality of the early childhood education. While the number of decentralised ECEC organisations is increasing in Finland, there is a growing need for quality management and for pedagogical leadership. In addition, the ECEC quality needs to be evaluated, because the number of pedagogically trained professionals has decreased. Based on the results of this study, theory-based quality evaluation and its importance as a tool for professional reflection will be discussed.

Research on quality evaluation

Quality research in ECEC was initiated from the USA in the 1970s (Greenman & Fuqua, 1984; Pence & Pacini-Ketchabaw, 2008; Phillips, 1987), and reached Finnish child care in the 1990s (Hujala-Huttunen, 1995; Niiranen, 1987; Tauriainen, 2000). The European Commission Network on Childcare, and especially their publication 'Quality Targets in Services for Young Children' (1996), was one of the impulses that started the leadership discussion to enhance quality management in Finland.

The ongoing debate on quality has faced some important changes in the past decades. In the 1970s, the quality research focused on the comparisons of maternal and non-maternal care without considering the substantive nature of the functions of child care. During the 1980s, child-care studies tended to define the quality and variety of child-care settings and children's individual responses to the different forms of care (Clarke-Stewart, 1987; Scarr & Eisenberg, 1993).

In the 1980s and 1990s, the research interest was more comprehensive and contextually orientated than before, and in addition to the proximal influences of child care it examined the distal influences as well (Phillips, 1987; Scarr & Eisenberg, 1993). The individual differences of children and their families were also considered, as well as the variance in the quality of the child-care settings.

Due to the increased quality research, a wide range of quality paradigms have emerged. Some researchers argue that quality is something that can be evaluated, but only based on the objectives of child care (Andersen, 1993). According to others (Dahlberg, Moss, & Pence, 2007), quality is a totally subjective matter which cannot be defined or evaluated. The more traditional viewpoint sees quality as an objective concept that can be scientifically and systematically measured and rationalised. Criticising the objective concept of quality, European quality researchers now identify quality as a subjective, value-based, relative and dynamic concept. Quality when seen as a subjective matter is dependent on time and context (Dahlberg et al., 2007; Moss & Pence, 1994; Parrila, 2004; Weiss, 1994).

According to the paradigm of professional quality evaluation, the definitions of quality and evaluation are based on the knowledge of professionals, research and on theory in early education (Kärrby & Giota, 1994; Phillips, 1987; Scarr & Eisenberg, 1993; Sheridan, 2007; Sylva, 2010). Theory and research enhance the understanding of the phenomenon of childhood, and what good ECEC is. With knowledge gained from theory and research, the educational practices can be further developed, and the foundations for high-quality early education can be formed.

The inclusionary (Pence & Moss, 1994) and participatory (Tauriainen, 2000) paradigm invites the previous quality research into a dialog by revising the former concepts of quality. The inclusionary approach simultaneously takes into consideration the objectives of child-care services, information of the experts, as well as the cultural context and the subjectivity of quality (Dahlberg et al., 2007; Hujala et al., 1999; Parrila, 2004; Pence & Moss, 1994; Tauriainen, 2000). The inclusionary approach emphasises the importance of the stakeholders' subjective views and experiences of quality. The present quality research sees the input gained especially from children to be important. Scott (2008) points out that children are reliable sources of information while considering issues connected to their own life. Ebbeck and Waniganayake (2004) acknowledge children's perspectives in quality matters when bringing out the primary 'user perspective'.

Dahlberg and Åsén (1994) as well as Jones and Pound (2008) emphasise that quality evaluation determines what is valued in the early childhood education. They point out that what is evaluated implies what is considered important. Rodd (2006) highlights the importance of research in enhancing the valuation of ECEC professionalism. Well-organised research and evaluation give the possibility to bring out concerns from the field to the administrative level. Pinch (2009) suggests that well-designed evaluation research can contribute to the future research best when the premises of the study as well as the methodological approaches have been theoretically justified. She warns against using the results of the evaluation for just repeating the dominant culture or the prevailing course of action. Instead, the importance of evaluation comes up, however, only when it acts as a catalyst for professional learning.

The Early Childhood Environment Rating Scale (ECERS), its localised versions and related additional measuring tools such as the ECERS-R and the ECERS-E have been widely used methods for assessing the quality of ECEC (Aboud, 2006; Harms & Clifford, 1980; Kalkan & Akman, 2009; Sheridan, 2007; Sheridan, Giota, Han, & Kwon, 2009). Sheridan (2001) describes the pedagogical quality of child-care services using four ECERS-based empirical studies and their meta-analysis. Sheridan's research showed that the most essential elements in quality are teachers' attitude, competence and possibility for competence development, co-operation with parents and leadership. Sheridan (2007) describes how research indicates that evaluation of pedagogical quality differs between external and self-evaluations. High-quality ECEC provider evaluates his/her own quality more critically than low-quality provider. Providers evaluated as being of low quality seem to find problems in external resources while providers evaluated as being of high quality find their own educational practices and methods as areas for improvement. In high-quality groups, children were invited to participate and the atmosphere was more open for children's ideas than in low-quality groups.

The research conducted by Fukkink and Lont (2007) shows that both teachers' education level and in-service training are correlated to high quality and good interaction between the child and the teacher. Some other research findings (Harrist, Thompson, & Norris, 2007; Leseman, 2009) also indicate the key factor of quality to be the pedagogical aspect and especially the relationship between the child and the teacher. In focus group interviews with the owners and directors of child-care centres, parents, teachers and political decision-makers Harrist et al. (2007) found following quality components: communication and rapport, educational practices, teachers' characteristics, resources and finances, professionalism and visibility, and participation. The researchers stress the crucial role of the directors as the maintainers of interaction and communication between different stakeholders in quality management.

Kalkan and Akman (2009) compared the quality of ECEC provided by public and private services in Turkey. The results indicated that there is no statistical difference between the service providers, but in general the quality of ECEC appeared to be low. Tobin (2005) considers the fading of the contextual aspects and the dominating position of the values of western societies over national values to be a problem in international research. Tobin emphasises that the quality standards must be created in a dialogue with the local practitioners. The problem is demonstrated, for instance, in the quality evaluation of the child–teacher ratio based on the American quality standard: in France and in Japan ECEC is evaluated to be of a lower quality than in the USA. In these countries, cultural values appreciate more collective aspects than taking care of an individual child as in the USA.

When conducting research on evaluation, it is important to declare the ontological and epistemological assumptions, and also the values – visible or latent – of the evaluation model. At best, the model is able to capture different characteristics of quality, to visualise pedagogical processes, to control the standards of quality and to improve quality (Sheridan, 2007).

Conducting research

Research task

The purpose of the study is to provide knowledge and to describe the quality of ECEC in Finland. In the research, the quality has been examined based on the theoretical quality evaluation model of ECEC. Quality as a phenomenon has been conceptualised as structural, intermediate, process and effect factors. The focus is on the parents' and teachers' perceptions of ECEC quality. Their views of different quality factors are being compared and analysed.

The research questions in this study are:

- What is the perceived quality of ECEC in the Finnish child-care centres and family day care?
- What are the differences of the quality assessments by parents and teachers?
- What are the perceived strengths and weaknesses of Finnish child care?

Methods

Quality evaluation model of ECEC in the study

The quality instrument used in the study is based on the quality evaluation model of ECEC (Figure 1). The theoretical framework of developing the instrument is based on the contextual theory of the child's growth (Hujala, 1999), which has its foundation in Bronfenbrenner's (1979) ecological psychology, and also in the constructivist conception of learning.

According to the contextual growth theory (Hujala, 1999), quality is being reviewed from the point of view of different actors and factors. The quality factors of ECEC are defined as structural, intermediate, process and effect factor (Hujala-Huttunen, 1995; Hujala et al., 1999). In order to emphasise the present Finnish values of ECEC, the instrument has been updated according to National Curriculum Guidelines on Early Childhood Education and Care in Finland (2005). In the renewed model, the questions about the curriculum content and pedagogy of learning are separated from the process factor into its own factor (Hujala & Fonsén, 2010).

In the process of constructing the instrument, the quality criteria were compiled. The operationalised variables, i.e. the questions, were developed on the basis of the

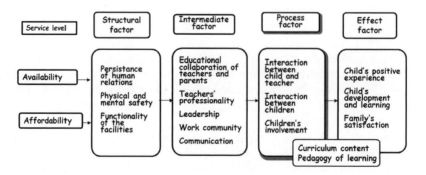

Figure 1. The quality evaluation model of ECEC (Hujala-Huttunen, 1995; Hujala & Fonsén, 2010; Hujala et al., 1999).

12

research as well as the views of the professional experts and the customers. The assessed variables, in all except one factor, are the same for parents and teachers. In the curriculum content and pedagogy of learning teachers' and parents' evaluation perspectives are different. The teachers assess the curriculum content and the pedagogy of learning as a process factor, i.e. how little children are being taught. The parents evaluate it as an effect factor, i.e. what the children have learned.

The quality factors presented in the model are supposed to be interdependent so that good-quality effects require a good-quality process which is directed by factors with indirect effects and ultimately more or less regulated by the framework factors. The premises of the child-care quality evaluation lie on the level of service, and especially on its adequacy and availability. ECEC is based on the structural factor, which is also the fundamental quality. The operational quality is regulated by the intermediate and process factors, and the curriculum content and the pedagogy of learning. The process factor represents the actual 'education and care' process. The customer perspective can be detected by examining the effect factor. Together the theory-based quality factors form a comprehensive framework for quality assessment.

The *structural factor* regulates the physical and psychological conditions of the ECEC activities. The quality evaluation instrument contains items, or as we later on refer to as questions, such as 'Child-care facilities provide children with opportunities for group activities and privacy to be alone'. *The intermediate factor* aims to assess the guidance of the child's educational process and the ensurance of the factors related to the teachers' skills. These are measured with questions such as 'An individual ECEC plan is drawn up for the child in collaboration with the teachers and the parents'. *The process factor* aims to assess the implementation of the educational process and the quality of the interaction between the child and the teacher with questions such as 'Child's suggestions and independent decisions are taken into account in child care'.

The curriculum content and pedagogy of learning variables measure the implementation and the effectiveness of the mathematical and linguistic skills, as well as the contents of natural science as an ECEC quality factor. The questions related to the *effect factor* assess children's and parents' satisfaction with the child care, and its perceived quality. The effect factor is measured with questions such as 'Child has enjoyed and been a willing participant in manual skills, e.g. sewing, pottery and woodworking'.

Data collection

The context for data collection is Finnish child-care programmes, including the ECEC programmes for 1–5-year-old children and the pre-primary class for 6-year-olds. The ECEC programmes are mainly publicly provided in child-care centres and in home-based or group-based family child care. In this research, the public child-care centres cover up to 98% of the programmes and private child-care centres 2%. In every Finnish child-care group, there are at least one qualified teacher with BA-level education, and two assistant teachers who are usually child-care nurses. In this study all staff members responsible for the children, and at the same time responsible of the quality, are referred to as *teachers*.

The current study is based on empirical data ($N = 22,948$) that has been collected cumulatively during the years 2000–2010 within research projects in Finnish municipalities. The sampling can be described as convenience sampling, referring to the voluntariness of municipalities to take part in the quality research. The participants have been duly informed of the research as well as the voluntary nature of it, and their consent to participate was elicited. The data consist of quality assessment material from both public and private child-care programmes from a total of 394 child-care programmes from 32 municipalities. The response rates have varied between 38% and −100%.

The assessments of child-care quality are based on the evaluators' views of the ECEC. In the beginning, the empirical data were collected from the parents and teachers using paper questionnaires and later on electronically. The assessments have been conducted child specifically; the parents assess the quality from the point of view of their own child, and the teachers assess the quality of the programme implementation according to every child in the group. In the ECEC quality evaluation, the child perspective is brought out by the assessment of parents and teachers.

There are instructions in the questionnaire for both parents and teachers which determine how the questions should be assessed. Every question has to be assessed according to the source of information defined in the questionnaire: observation, written documents, interviews and information from the child. The response options in the questionnaires are in five-point Likert scales, where option 1 stands for the lowest quality level and 5 stands for the highest quality level. There were also two open-ended questions which are: 'In addition to the previous questions, what other factors have enhanced or reduced the quality of your child's care in your opinion?' and 'A proposal for improving the quality of education in child care'.

Analysing the data

In data analysis we used mainly quantitative methods and included qualitative analysis in reporting the results. The paradigm of mixed methods was applied slightly. Mixed methods examine the research questions in a multiple methodological way, and it aims to broaden the perspective of the social phenomena of the research focus (Tashakkori and Creswell 2008). Qualitative analysis in this study extends the viewpoint of the quality in the research, and increases the validity and the accuracy of the quantitative results.

The quality factors were based on the theoretical Quality Evaluation Model (Figure 1). The different quality factors in ECEC were used to form their own sum score of means. In addition to that, the sum scores of the mean values were formed of the parents' and teachers' responses. The reliability indexes of the quality factors examined by Cronbach's alpha (α) varied from 0.58 to 0.90. In this study the reliability indexes were high and therefore gave a reliable basis for using the sum variable values in the data analysis.

In quantitative analysis, the statistical significance between the assessments of the respondent groups was tested. The normal distributions of the factors were tested with the Kolmogorov−Smirnov test before analysing the data. The test (Kolmogorov−Smirnov = 0.021−0.259, $p < 0.001$) indicated that the distributions of the factors were skewed and therefore non-parametric tests were chosen. The differences in the parents' and teachers' assessments were tested by using the Mann−Whitney U-test.

Both quantitative and qualitative results are reported in a dialog with the theory, research and present researchers. The responses to the open-ended questions were analysed by a content analysis. The quotations reported reflect the authentic voices of the informants, and with this we want to be in a dialog with the respondents.

Results

Quality of Finnish ECEC

The quality of Finnish child-care programmes was examined based on the respondents' overall view. The data consisted of 22,948 child-specific quality assessments by parents and teachers. The parents' and teachers' assessments of all variables were summed and the obtained mean was 4.22. It can be considered very good in demonstrating the overall quality of Finnish child-care services as perceived by parents and teachers.

When the factors are examined separately according to the parents' and teachers' assessments (Figure 2), the differences between the groups can be seen although they are minor ones. The *structural factor* was assessed with quite low-quality scores in both respondent groups. However, parents assessed the structural factor slightly higher than the teachers. The teachers gave the highest quality ratings to the *intermediate factor*. The teachers' assessment of the intermediate factor was higher than the parents'. The same pattern can be detected in the *curriculum content and pedagogy of learning*. The quality ratings of the curriculum content and pedagogy of learning received the lowest scores of all factors in both groups. As for the *process factor*, the parents' and teachers' quality assessments differed only slightly. Both groups agreed on the quality of the process factor as being good. The parents rated the *effect factor* of ECEC with the highest scores of all quality factors.

These results indicate that the strengths of Finnish ECEC are the parents' satisfaction with the effectiveness of ECEC and the teachers' satisfaction with the intermediate quality factor. Both respondent groups perceived the quality of the process factor to be good. However, there are pedagogical challenges in implementing the curriculum content and pedagogy of learning.

The differences of the assessments by both groups were tested with the Mann–Whitney U-test. The test proved that the assessments differ significantly in every factor excluding the intermediate factor. The values showed the statistically significant ($p < 0.001$) difference in the structural factor ($U = 5.643E7$), process factor ($U = 6.180E7$), curriculum content and pedagogy of learning ($U = 3.341E7$), and in the

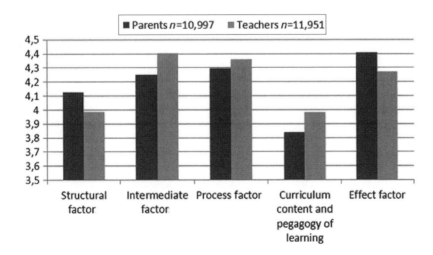

Figure 2.   Means of the quality factors assessed by parents and teachers.

effect factor ($U = 5.360E7$). Because the differences in the quality factors between the groups are statistically significant, the parents' and teachers' quality assessments were examined by variables, except for the intermediate factor where no statistically significant difference existed between the groups.

Quality of the structural factor in ECEC

In investigating the individual variables, a more specific analysis of the assessments conducted by the parents and teachers can be formulated. Table 1 shows that both parents and teachers agree on the highest ratings in question (Q) number 1 'The child was admitted to the requested child-care centre' (parents = P 4.75, teachers = T 4.83), although the standard deviation is high. This shows that the child's unconditional and universal right to child care, as well as the principle of local services, are present in Finnish ECEC. Interestingly, 'The child-care centre's reliable back-up system for absent employees' (Q 2) receives the lowest scores from both groups (P 3.53, T 3.50). In this issue the standard deviations are highest (1.28; 1.09). It seems that the creation of a reliable back-up system is a big challenge in many ECEC institutions. An efficient system for substitutes is poorly implemented compared with the other quality issues.

The facilities of Finnish child-care centres have a good reputation, yet there is a remarkable difference in teachers' and parents' evaluations. The parents rated the *safety of the facilities* (Q 3, 4) higher than the teachers. The difference of opinions between the groups is greatest in question 5 concerning the *pedagogical functionality of the facilities*, which is poorly assessed especially by the teachers (P 3.81, T 3.51). It can be assumed that the pedagogical goals set by the teachers are so high that the facilities are perceived to restrict the implementation of the high-quality pedagogy. However, in this assessment the high standard deviation indicates that there is a lot of disagreement in the opinions.

Quality of the process factor in ECEC

Table 2, concerning the *process factor*, shows that there are interesting differences between parents' and teachers' assessments, for example, in the question that deals with parent–teacher partnership. 'Children are personally welcomed and told goodbye' (Q 19) scored the highest of all of the process factors from the teachers

Table 1. Parents' and teachers' assessments of the variables in the structural factor.

Structural factor of ECEC	Parents		Teachers	
	M	SD	*M*	SD
1. The child was admitted to the child-care center at parents' request	4.75	0.96	4.83	0.80
2. The child-care center has a reliable back-up child-care system or substitutes for absent employees	3.53	1.28	3.50	1.09
3. Indoor facilities are safe for children	4.40	0.69	4.21	0.72
4. Outdoor facilities are safe for children	4.12	0.84	3.97	0.82
5. Child-care facilities provide children opportunities for group activities and privacy to be alone	3.81	0.99	3.51	1.11

Table 2. The variables of the process factor assessed by the parents and teachers.

Process factor of ECEC	Parents		Teachers	
	M	SD	M	SD
18. Parents are told about the news and the events of the day when the child is picked up from the child care	4.24	0.86	4.55	0.61
19. Children are personally welcomed and told goodbye	4.51	0.73	4.80	0.42
20. A child's need to play is addressed during everyday activities in the child care	4.49	0.65	4.49	0.60
21. Children's sportiness and need to exercise takes place in everyday life in the child care	4.37	0.70	4.25	0.68
22. Children's questions and thoughts are responded in everyday life	4.31	0.67	4.38	0.63
23. Children's play materials and toys are available to the children	4.37	0.66	4.32	0.66
24. Children's suggestions and independent decisions are taken into account in the child care	4.07	0.74	4.02	0.71
25. Children are cuddled, cherished and personally paid attention to	4.10	0.84	4.40	0.66
26. Children are praised for trying. Children gain successful experiences and joy of learning	4.36	0.67	4.61	0.54
27. Children's various emotions are accepted; children are helped to stand disappointments, comforted in sorrow and their joys are shared	4.35	0.68	4.60	0.54
28. Children are helped to solve conflict situations	4.31	0.67	4.52	0.61
29. Adults are helping the child to follow through child's own play and activity ideas	4.21	0.70	4.22	0.69
30. Children participate in everyday life activities and duties	4.08	0.82	3.60	0.91
31. Children have the opportunity to continue a play for long period of time, even many days in the child care	3.77	0.94	3.25	1.05
32. Children are accepted the way they are	4.53	0.66	4.71	0.49
33. The individuality of the child and the dissimilarity between families are respected and recognised in the child care	4.33	0.72	4.56	0.56
34. The child has friends in the child care centre	4.60	0.62	4.54	0.63
35. Children's friendships are supported	4.32	0.70	4.65	0.52

(4.80) compared with the assessments from the parents (4.51). Do the parents' and teachers' different assessments mean that the parents have higher expectations? Do the parents expect more individual attention, or do they just experience the situation differently?

An acceptance of children's individuality (Q 32–33) and *children's social needs and interaction with peers* (Q 34–35) were perceived to be of a high quality by both groups. In Finnish child care the child-centred pedagogy is highly valued, which can be related to an emphasis on individuality (National Curriculum Guidelines on Early Childhood Education and Care in Finland, 2005). The finding concerning social needs indicates that in Finnish child care the social relationships between children are highly valued. The IEA Pre Primary Project (Ojala, 1999) reported similar findings. In Hujala's (2004) longitudinal study, both parents and teachers have defined for decades that the most important goal of Finnish child care is to support the children's social development. In the questions measuring the more *traditional group-based pedagogy* (Q 20–23), the parents and teachers assessed the quality similarly.

In these questions, teachers are core informants for many parents. Also, it is presumable that in the questions not engaged with emotional perspective, the parents assess quality from the point of view of a group more than their own child.

The most negative assessments given by the parents and teachers were related to the *children's involvement in ECEC* (Q 24, 30–31). These questions were poorly assessed by both groups, but received remarkably low scores from the teachers. According to the overall findings of the study, the parents and teachers are generally satisfied with the child care except with the children's *involvement*. Based on these results, it can be assumed that the children's participation in daily activities does not occur as expected. Does this indicate that the daily schedule defines the pedagogy of ECEC, in which case the children's play and participation are subordinate to the schedule? The teachers seem to assent this, but the inconsistency can be detected from the assessments. Is the tradition of the daily schedule so strong that the teachers feel it is unchangeable? The teachers seem to value the children's participation, but the implementation has not succeeded.

The greatest difference between the assessments of the two groups is in the questions measuring *pedagogy that supports the children's emotional security* (Q 25–28). Although the parental evaluations score high, the teachers' evaluations score systematically higher. The differences in the assessments might indicate the respondents' different assessment perspectives. The parents assess quality from the point of view of their child, whereas the teachers' evaluations are based on a group perspective.

All in all the results lead to the conclusion that the *children's individuality and social needs* as well as the *parent–teacher partnership* are assessed to be of a good quality. These issues are considered to be important in Finnish ECEC, and they both have been implemented with a high quality.

The quality of the curriculum content and the pedagogy of learning in ECEC

The curriculum content and the pedagogy of learning aspects assess the mathematical, linguistic and science content areas and their implementation and effectiveness. The teachers assess the curriculum content from the point of view of the pedagogy, in other words how the children are taught, whereas the parents assess the effectiveness of the curriculum content, i.e. what the children have learned. The questions concerning the curriculum content and the pedagogy of learning scored the lowest of all of the quality factors (Table 3) by both respondent groups.

Table 3.   Parents' and teachers' assessments of the curriculum content and pedagogy of learning in ECEC.

Curriculum content and pedagogy of learning in early childhood education	Parents		Teachers	
	M	SD	M	SD
36. The child's linguistic skills are developed in the child care	3.86	0.95	4.22	0.75
37. Mathematical skills which are practiced/which children have learned through play in everyday life situations in the child care	3.68	1.03	3.86	0.87
38. The children become acquainted with nature and natural phenomena in everyday life situations in the child care	3.93	0.93	3.96	0.80
39. The children become acquainted with the immediate surroundings, for example, through trips, in the child care	3.91	1.02	3.88	0.90

The analysis revealed that the teachers assessed the pedagogy of linguistic (Q 36) and mathematical skills (Q 37) which have been carried out better than what the parents assessed the children have actually learned. The teachers scored 4.22 in the development of linguistic skills, whereas the parents scored notably lower, 3.86. The lowest quality rating given by the parents was the development of mathematical skills (3.68). The teachers' assessments were also low (3.86) for providing the contents of mathematics.

> Our child is able to read and count very well. This has become a challenge to preschool, because the assignments seem too easy and boring for her. As a parent I wish that there were additional tasks for children like mine. (Parent)

The results suggest that the teaching of linguistic skills is the pedagogical strength of the Finnish child care. The weakness of the pedagogy of learning is connected to parents' perceptions about the children's mathematical learning. Also, questions 38 and 39 related to the natural sciences scored quite low from both respondent groups. It seems that the curriculum content and pedagogy of learning are challenges in developing the quality of Finnish child care.

Quality of the effect factor in ECEC

Out of all the quality factors, the parents are the most satisfied with the quality of the effect factor. The teachers' assessments on the effect factor are also high, but not as high as assessed by the parents (Table 4). The strength of the quality of the effect factor seems to be the children's happiness with the programme. Question 40 'Children are enthusiastic, happy and satisfied with their lives in the child-care centre' (P 4.49; T 4.47) and question 42 'The child is happy to come to the child care' (P 4.42; T 4.48) scored the highest by both groups. The question 46, 'The child has enjoyed and been a willing participant in manual skills (e.g. sewing, pottery and woodworking)' receives lower scores than other questions. The teachers score even lower (3.96) than the parents (4.11).

Table 4. Parents' and teachers' assessments of the effect factor.

Effect factor of ECEC	Parents		Teachers	
	M	SD	M	SD
40. Children are enthusiastic, happy and satisfied with their lives in the child-care centre	4.49	0.65	4.47	0.59
41. Child-care practice meets the views and hopes of the child and the parents	4.40	0.71	4.33	0.61
42. The child is happy to come to the child care	4.42	0.72	4.48	0.61
43. The child enjoys music (e.g. playing instruments, singing, creative sport and dancing)	4.36	0.80	4.24	0.79
44. The child enjoys visual arts (e.g. drawing, painting and designing)	4.37	0.76	4.18	0.82
45. The child enjoys stories, children's literature and acting	4.25	0.77	4.17	0.79
46. The child enjoys manual skills (e.g. sewing, pottery and woodworking)	4.11	0.95	3.96	0.94
47. The child enjoys physical exercise (e.g. games, gymnastic, various sports)	4.35	0.81	4.18	0.87

In parents' views the children enjoy more and participate more intensively in the ECEC activities than what the teachers seem to think. The parents' assessments are based on the feedback from their children, whereas the teachers base their knowledge on the everyday situations in the child care. This could indicate that the children's experiences of the child care are so positive and this has been conveyed to the parents as well. In any case, both respondent groups feel the effectiveness of the programme to be of a high quality.

In Finland, the customer-orientated programme is emphasised. There are also strong attempts to operate according to the wishes of the children and their families. Although differences between the assessments within certain items appear, the results of the effect factor indicate that the child care has succeeded in reaching the co-operative aims. As both parents and teachers assess with good ratings 'The child-care practice meets the views and hopes of the child and the parents'.

> I wish the teachers all the best and thank you for the good care. Our family is very satisfied with the child care. It is so nice to come in the mornings when the staff welcomes us warmly. (Parent)

Discussion

The purpose of this research was to describe the quality of Finnish child care as perceived by the parents and teachers, and analyse the differences in assessments between the groups. The quality instrument used in the study has a theoretical and cultural foundation. To be theoretically and culturally appropriate, it has been constructed by researchers and professionals in the child-care field. The purpose of the cumulatively collected empirical data is to produce a reference file when developing ECEC. It offers Finnish municipalities, child-care centres and groups reference for *finding* the strengths and the weaknesses to develop ECEC in the programmes. Theory-based quality evaluation gives foundation for ensuring teachers' professional development. Reflection on one's own work enables professionalism, but that process requires valid tools.

Variation in the quality of the programmes

The quality of Finnish child care is perceived to be very good. Because it is known that the ratings of the customer satisfaction surveys are commonly on a high level (Johnson, Shavitt, & Holbrook, 2011), we were sensitive even for the minor differences in the assessments. We consider the lower assessments in the quality profile as a challenge in developing child-care practices.

High standard deviations (SD = 0.42–1.90) in the variables of the quality assessments within the respondent groups indicate that the quality varies considerably in Finnish child care. This research reinforces the results of previous studies indicating that Finnish child care is generally of a high quality but the quality varies among the programmes (Kalliala, 2008). The variation indicates that today's strategy of steering the quality management by information steering is inadequate for ensuring equality and professional development.

The results related to the children's quite low involvement in ECEC also indicate that perceiving children as active subjects in play and other situations requires improvement. According to Heikka, Hujala, and Turja (2009), procedures in child care appeared to be constructed by effortless practice more than the child's needs or wishes. The teachers' theoretical knowledge is on a high level, but this theoretical knowledge is not steering practice. The meaning of play and child-centredness are emphasised in the curriculum but they have not yet been implemented properly.

One essential aim in developing ECEC is to strengthen the pedagogy of learning and the curriculum contents. This result leads us to ponder on whether the implementation of the curriculum needs to be reconsidered. Is it so that the focusing on parent–teacher partnership in Finnish child care has compromised the primary function of ECEC: To support the child's learning process. The integration of an individual ECEC plan and the curriculum is a new and challenging task which according to this research, should be improved. Taking the child's participation in the programme into account, and the integration of the child observations and curriculum contents are considerable improvement challenges.

The teachers' higher-quality ratings in the questions concerning the process factor and the educational practices evoke a question of the relationship between the parents' expectations and the educational practices of teachers. The results can also be interpreted from the point of view that the parents are not aware enough of the child's day in the child care. According to this interpretation, the improvement of communication and making the educational practices visible enable the parents to have a better understanding of the pedagogy of learning, contents of practice and the quality of the child–teacher interaction in the child care. The parents' opportunity to participate and to become acquainted with the child's everyday life in the child care should be defined in the individual ECEC plan. Rivas and Sobrino (2011) emphasise that strengthening the communication between teachers and parents is an appropriate way in solving problems encountered in responding to the expectations of parents and the provided education.

Quality management

In Finland, the existence of the qualified professionals is considered to guarantee the high quality of ECEC. The recent trend shows that the number of pedagogically trained professionals has decreased, which is a matter of great concern. The expansion of the child-care centres into decentralised organisations (Halttunen, 2009) and reducing the pedagogically trained personnel in the child-care centres set a growing pressure on the pedagogical quality management. Kalliala (2008) claims that differences in quality can be found in an adult's sensitivity in interaction with a child. The international quality research emphasises unanimously that the strengths and variation of quality in ECEC must be visible and the quality management needs to be supported (i.e. Barros & Aguiar, 2010; Gol-Guven, 2009; Paiva, Shneider, Mahchado, & Perinazzo, 2009; Pence & Pacini-Ketchabaw, 2008; Rivas & Sobrino, 2011). Rohacek, Adams, and Kisker (2010) highlight the importance of leadership style in maintaining the quality of ECEC. The director's high level of confidence in the staff and also high expectations for teachers' competence and professionalism were connected to the high quality of ECEC. As a result of this study, it seems that in Finland a national quality management system would be needed in order to ensure high-quality child care. However, the selection of the quality evaluation instrument needs to be carefully considered. According to Fenech, Sumsion, and Goodfellow (2008), the external quality standardisation of ECEC may even weaken the pedagogical quality. The inclusive quality evaluation, which is based on the discipline of early childhood education, should lay the premises for the systematic development of practices, and serve as a pedagogical tool for leadership.

References

Aboud, F.E. (2006). Evaluation of an early childhood and preschool program in rural Bangladesh. *Early Childhood Research Quarterly, 21,* 46–60.

Andersen, J. (1993). *Quality in early childhood education.* Copenhagen: BULP.

Barros, S., & Aguiar, C. (2010). Assessing the quality of Portuguese child care programs for toddlers. *Early Childhood Research Quarterly, 25,* 527–535.

Bronfenbrenner, U. (1979). *The ecology of human development.* Cambridge: Harvard University Press.

Clarke-Stewart, A. (1987). In search of consistencies in child care research. In D. Phillips (Ed.), *Quality in child care: What does research tell us* (pp. 105–120). Washington, DC: NAEYC.

Dahlberg, G., & Åsén, G. (1994). Evaluation and regulation: A question of empowerment. In P. Moss & A. Pence (Eds.), *Valuing quality in early childhood services* (pp. 157–171). London: Chapman.

Dahlberg, G., Moss, P., & Pence, A. (2007). *Beyond quality in early childhood education and care. Languages of evaluation* (2nd ed.). London: Routledge.

Ebbeck, M., & Waniganayake, M. (2004). *Early childhood professionals: Leading today and tomorrow.* Sydney: Maclennan & Petty.

Fenech, M., Sumsion, J., & Goodfellow, J. (2008). Regulation and risk: Early childhood education and care services as sites where the 'laugh of Foucault' resounds. *Journal of Educational Policy, 23,* 35–48.

Fukkink, R.G., & Lont, A. (2007). Does training matter? A meta-analysis and review of caregiver training studies. *Early Childhood Research Quarterly, 22,* 290–311.

Gol-Guven, M. (2009). Evaluation of the quality of early childhood classrooms in Turkey. *Early Childhood Development and Care, 179,* 437–451.

Greenman, J.T., & Fuqua, R.W. (1984). *Making day care better: Training, evaluation, and the process of change.* New York: Teachers College Press.

Halttunen, L. (2009). *Päivähoitotyö ja johtajuus hajautetussa organisaatiossa* [Child care work and leadership in decentralized organization]. Jyväskylä Studies of education, psychology and social research 375. Retrieved from https://jyx.jyu.fi/dspace/handle/123456789/22480

Harms, T., & Clifford, R. (1980). *The early childhood environmental rating scale.* New York: Teachers College, Columbia University.

Harrist, A., Thompson, S., & Norris, D. (2007). Defining quality child care: Multiple stakeholder perspectives. *Early Education and Development, 18,* 305–336.

Heikka, J., Hujala, E., & Turja, L. (2009). *Arvioinnista opiksi. Havainnointi, arviointi ja suunnittelu varhaispedagogiikassa* [Learned from the evaluation. Observation, evaluation and planning in the early childhood education]. Vantaa: Printel.

Hujala, E. (1999). Challenges for a childhood in a changing society. In H.K. Chiam (Ed.), *Towards excellence in early childhood education* (pp. 135–154). Kuala Lumpur: University of Malaya.

Hujala, E. (2004). Early childhood education and care in a changing society – international reflections. In M. Lundkvist & C. Öhberg (Eds.), *Det synliga barnet. Praktiska och teoretiska perspektiv på pedagogiken. Festkrifg tillägnad Marita Lindahl* (pp. 119–130, Rapport 9/2004). Vasa: Åbo Akademi.

Hujala, E., & Fonsén, E. (2010). Varhaiskasvatuksen laadun vahvuudet ja kehittämiskohteet [The strengths and development areas in quality of early childhood education]. *Lastentarha, 2,* 8–10.

Hujala, E., Parrila, S., Lindberg, P., Nivala, V., Tauriainen, L., & Vartiainen, P. (1999). *Laadunhallinta varhaiskasvatuksessa* [Quality management in early childhood education]. Oulun yliopisto: Varhaiskasvatuskeskus.

Hujala-Huttunen, E. (1995). Varhaiskasvatuksen laadunarviointi [Early childhood education quality assessment]. In E. Hujala-Huttunen & E. Estola (Eds.), *Näkökulmia varhaiskasvatukseen* (pp. 69–82). Oulun: lastentarhanopettajaopistonjulkaisuja.

Johnson, T.P., Shavitt, S., & Holbrook, A.L. (2011). Survey response styles across cultures. In D. Matsumoto & F.J.R. Van De Vijver (Eds.), *Cross-cultural research methods in psychology* (pp. 130–178). New York: Cambridge University Press.

Jones, C., & Pound, L. (2008). *Leadership and management in the early years. From principles to practice.* Maidenhead: Open University Press.

Kalkan, E., & Akman, B. (2009). Examining preschools' quality in terms of physical conditions. *Procedia – Social and Behavioral Sciences, 1,* 1573–1577.

Kalliala, M. (2008). *Kato mua! Kohtaako aikuinen lapsen päivähoidossa?* [Look at me! Face the adult child's in child care?]. Helsinki: Gaudeamus Helsinki University Press.

Kärrby, G., & Giota, J. (1994). Dimensions of quality in Swedish day care centers: An analysis of early childhood environment rating scale. *Early Child Development and Care, 104,* 1–22.

Leseman, P. (2009). The impact of high quality education and care on the development of young children: Review of the literature. *Early childhood education and care in Europe: Tacking social and cultural inequalities* (pp. 17–49). Brussels: Education, Audiovisual and Culture Executive Agency P9 Eurydice.

Moss, P., & Pence, A. (Eds.). (1994). *Valuing quality on early childhood services.* London: Paul Chapman Publishing Ltd.

National Curriculum Guidelines on Early Childhood Education and Care in Finland. (2005). Stakes 56. Retrieved from http://www.thl.fi/thl-client/pdfs/267671cb-0ec0-4039-b97b-7ac6ce6b9c10

Niiranen, P. (1987). *Mikä on laatua päivähoidossa?* [What is quality in child care?]. Helsinki: Sosiaalihallituksen julkaisu 17.

Ojala, M. (1999). Sosiaalis-kulttuurinen lapsen kehittymisen ja oppimisen analyysi: IEA Preprimary-projekti [The analysis of the child's socio-cultural development and learning: IEA Preprimary Project]. In I. Ruoppila, E. Hujala, K. Karila, J. Kinos, P. Niiranen, & M. Ojala (Eds.), *Varhaiskasvatuksen tutkimusmenetelmiä* (pp. 404–423). Jyväskylä: PS-kustannus ja Atena.

Paiva, M.G.C., Shneider, A., Mahchado, M.L.S., & Perinazzo, P.V.D. (2009). A new look on early child care and education (ECCE) as joint responsibility. *Current Issues in Comparative Education, 11,* 33–41. Retrieved from http://www.tc.columbia.edu/cice/Current/11/11_Brazil_JR.html

Parrila, S. (2004). Laatu päivähoitoa koskevassa varhaiskasvatustutkimuksessa [Quality in early childhood education research in child care]. In R. Ruokolainen & K. Alila (Eds.), *Varhaiskasvatuksen laatu on osaamista ja vuorovaikutusta. Varhaiskasvatuksen laadunhallinnan ja ohjauksen kehittämishankkeen julkaisu. Sosiaali- ja terveysministeriön julkaisuja, 6* (pp. 69–79). Retrieved from http://www.stm.fi/c/document_library/get_file?folderId=28707&name=DLFE-3644.pdf

Pence, A., & Moss, P. (1994). Towards an inclusionary approach in defining quality. In P. Moss & A. Pence (Eds.), *Valuing quality on early childhood services* (pp. 172–179). London: Paul Chapman Publishing Ltd.

Pence, A., & Pacini-Ketchabaw, V. (2008). Discourses on quality care: The investigating 'quality' project and the Canadian experience. *Contemporary Issues in Early Childhood*, *9*, 241–255.

Phillips, D.A. (Ed.). (1987). *Quality in child care: What does research tell us?* Washington, DC: National Association for the Education of Young Children.

Pinch, K.J. (2009). Seer 2008 keynote address: The importance of evaluation research. *Journal of Experiential Education 2009*, *31*, 390–394.

Quality Targets in Services for Young Children. (1996). *European Commission Network on Childcare and other measures to reconcile the employment and family responsibilities of men and women*. Retrieved from http://childcarecanada.org/sites/childcarecanada.org/files/Qualitypaperthree.pdf

Rivas, S., & Sobrino, A. (2011). Determining quality of early childhood education programmes in Spain: A case study. *Revista de Educatión*, *355, Mayo-agosto* 2011, 257–283.

Rodd, J. (2006). *Leadership in early childhood* (3rd ed.). Maidenhead: Open University Press.

Rohacek, M., Adams, G., & Kisker, E. (2010). *Understanding quality in context: Child care centers, communities, markets, and public policy*. Washington, DC: Urban Institute. Retrieved from http://www.urban.org/uploadedpdf/412191-understand-quality.pdf

Scarr, S., & Eisenberg, M. (1993). Child care research: Issues, perspectives, and results. *Annual Review Psychology*, *44*, 613–644.

Scott, J. (2008). Children as respondents. The challenge for quantitative methods. In P. Christensen & A. James (Eds.), *Research with children. Perspectives and practices* (2nd ed., pp. 98–119). New York: Routledge.

Sheridan, S. (2001). *Pedagogical quality in preschool. An issue of perspectives*. Göteborg: Acta Universitatis Gothoburgensis.

Sheridan, S. (2007). Dimension of pedagogical quality in preschool. *International Journal of Early Years Education*, *15*, 197–217. Retrieved from http://gupea.ub.gu.se/bitstream/2077/19111/1/gupea_2077_19111_1.pdf

Sheridan, S., Giota, J., Han, Y.-M., & Kwon, J.-Y. (2009). A cross-cultural study of preschool quality in South Korea and Sweden: ECERS evaluations. *Early Childhood Research Quarterly*, *24*, 142–156.

Sylva, K. (2010). Quality in early childhood settings. In K. Sylva, E. Melhuish, P. Sammons, I. Siraj-Blatchford, & B. Taggart (Eds.), *Early childhood matters. Evidence from the effective pre-school and primary education project* (pp. 70–91). London: Routledge.

Tashakkori, A., & Creswell, J.W. (2008). Editorial: Mixed methodology across disciplines. *Journal of Mixed Methods Research*, *2*, 3–6.

Tauriainen, L. (2000). *Kohti yhtenäistä laatua. Henkilökunnan. Vanhempien ja lasten laatukäsitykset päiväkodin integroidussa lapsiryhmässä*, Jyväskylä Studies in Education, Psychology and Social Research 165.

Tobin, J. (2005). Quality in early childhood education: An anthropologist's perspective. *Early Education & Development*, *16*, 421–434.

Weiss, S. (1994). *Quality in child-care institutions and the relationship between care and education in Denmark*. Copenhagen: BULP.

Individual plans for children in transition to pre-school: a case study in one Finnish day-care centre

Tuija A. Turunen

This paper outlines a case study on teachers' and parents' perspectives on children's individual plans in transition from early childhood education to pre-school in Finland. The study was based on the importance of continuity as a part of positive educational transition experiences. The national curricula, educators' interpretations and parents' perspectives were investigated in one day-care centre. Individual planning is mandatory in early childhood, but there is little information about using the plans in transition to pre-school. At the local level, individual planning occurred in discussions with parents and various planning forms. Familiarity and good relationships between the educators and the parents were important. The educators and the parents had different perceptions of the usefulness and use of individual planning. On the basis of this study, individual planning can be recommended as an appropriate tool to strengthen continuity in transition, but more discussion between parents and educators is needed to build a shared understanding about it.

Introduction

In Finland, the period of pre-school education[1] is a transition year to primary school for six-year-old children, a year before they start primary school. Since 2001, local authorities have provided free pre-school education for all children, but participation is voluntary for families (*Laki perusopetuslain muuttamisesta*, 1999). Most families choose pre-school education for their children; in 2007, 99% of six-year-olds were enrolled in pre-school (Eurydice, 2009). Pre-school education is mostly provided in day-care centres and many children continue with their pre-school education in the same day-care centre they had attended previously (Finnish Ministry of Education, 2004; Siniharju, 2007). Although pre-school education in Finland is play based, starting pre-school is a transition from play-oriented early childhood education to more structured and target-oriented pre-school, which is often provided in separate pre-school groups (Finnish Ministry of Education, 2004). In other sectors of early childhood education, the children are usually in mixed-age groups of three- to five-year-olds.

Individual planning based on a child's strengths and needs is an important part of Finnish early childhood education. Educators and parents together draw up an individual plan for each child (*Laki sosiaalihuollon*, 2000; *National curriculum guidelines*, 2004). Alasuutari and Karila (Alasuutari, 2007; Alasuutari & Karila, 2010; Karila, 2005) have previously studied children's individual planning and co-operation between parents and educators in Finnish early childhood education. Alasuutari and Karila (2010) analysed individual planning forms at the municipal level, Alasuutari (2007) studied partnerships in early childhood education from the educator's point of view, and Karila (2005) analysed the discussions between parents and educators. In this paper, I continue the research on individual planning processes in Finnish early childhood education and consider them in the context of transition from early childhood education to pre-school. This study was conducted in a public Finnish day-care centre and individual planning was studied from three perspectives: national curricula, educators' interpretations and parents' experiences.

Educational transitions in early childhood

Rogoff (2003) described developmental transitions in early childhood as phases of changing relationships and roles in community. Elder and Shanahan (2006) defined transitions as substantial times of changes in one's life course. Dockett and Perry (2007, p. 5) talked about starting school as a turning point which marks 'a significant change in the ways a child participates in the family and community'. Transition experiences across the life course are cumulative: the experiences of earlier transitions impact on later life transitions and transitions in early childhood can impact on how future transitions are experienced (Elder, 1998). The importance of positive transition experiences in early childhood is evident in many studies (Dockett & Perry, 2007; Einarsdottir, 2010; Entwisle & Alexander, 1998; Fabian & Dunlop, 2002). Such positive experiences help build children's 'transition capital' (Dunlop, 2007). With this capital, children draw on the success of earlier transitions as they approach, engage and then move on into future transitions.

Educational transitions in early childhood, including starting pre-school, mean changes in culture, roles, identity and daily experiences of everyone involved (Dunlop, 2007; Educational Transitions and Change [ETC] Research Group, 2011). Changes are characteristic elements of transitions, but they are also a potential source of stress, tension and anxiety (Brostrom, 2002; Griebel & Niesel, 2003). Changes can be marked as discontinuities between settings. To smooth the transition, the changes should be understood and minimalised if possible (Griebel & Niesel, 2003). One way to decrease discontinuities is to build on a child's existing knowledge and strengths and listen to and respect parents and other educators. This requires interaction and the development of respectful relationships (Educational Transitions and Change [ETC] Research Group, 2011). As Rimm-Kaufman and Pianta (2000, p. 492) said, 'These relationships either support or challenge children's adjustment into day-care centre and predict children's subsequent relationships in school'.

Educational transitions in early childhood occur in a context of developing interactions between individuals, groups and institutions (Rimm-Kaufman & Pianta, 2000). In his ecological theory, Bronfenbrenner (1986) described different contexts as systems which influence families as the context of a child's development. Microsystems are the places where a child is personally involved, such as home and school (Bronfenbrenner, 1979). In transition to pre-school, early childhood education, pre-school and home encounter and form a mesosystem in which different contexts are intertwined in a child's life (Bronfenbrenner, 1979). In this mesosystem, the continuity between the microsystems is built on shared responsibility for a child's development and well-being (Parke & Buriel, 2006). Interaction between the microsystems links them and offers educators and parents possibilities to provide the child with the care and education which meets his/her individual needs. Based on the ecological framework, respectful relationships between educators and parents in early childhood education are regarded as important supporting elements in a child's development (Bronfenbrenner, 1979, 1986; Bronfenbrenner & Evans, 2000).

Methodology

In this paper, I consider how children's individual plans were used in transition from early childhood education to pre-school in one day-care centre. I argue that the individual plans can be a valuable tool in building continuity in the transition process and thus promote a positive transition experience and the first steps in building transition capital. Individual planning was studied at three levels: national curricula, educators' interpretations and parents' experiences.

The research questions were as follows:

(1) National curricula:
   (a) What is the content of individual plans?
   (b) What is the process of individual planning?
   (c) How is the transition taken into account in the documents?
(2) Educators' interpretations of individual planning:
   (a) What are the content and process of individual planning in the setting?
   (b) How is the continuity of a child's well-being, development and learning supported by the individual planning during the transition?
(3) Parents' experiences of individual planning:
   (a) How parents see their role in individual planning for their child?
   (b) How individual planning helps parents to see the continuity of their child's well-being, learning and development during the transition?

This study is a descriptive, qualitative case study conducted in one Finnish day-care centre. The data were gathered in May and June 2006, when starting pre-school in the following August was topical in the setting. The day-care centre consisted of four groups: two for three- to five-year-olds and two for six-year-olds. Altogether about 50 children and 10 staff members attended the centre. The day-care centre was located in a suburb of a middle-sized town in Finland. The children lived in the nearby, mostly middle-class, neighbourhoods. The day-care centre was located in a home-like building with shared areas, separated rooms for each group, a gymnasium and a big outdoor area with a small forest. The outdoor area was used in turns during the day and shared in the afternoons. When the children started pre-school, they moved to another room in the familiar premises.

I aimed to gain a holistic and in-depth picture of individual planning in one setting and the case-study approach allowed me to study individual planning in a context of one setting at the time when the educators and parents had started to plan the transition (Gerring, 2006; Simons, 2009; Yin, 2003, 2009). To do this, I gathered various data sets. The *National curriculum guidelines on early childhood education and care in Finland* and the *Core curriculum for pre-school education in Finland 2000* represented the official curriculum and were analysed to the extent that was related to individual planning and continuity between early childhood education and pre-school education. To capture the local perspective, I looked at six individual planning forms used in the setting and interviewed six educators. Three educators were early childhood teachers with university degrees. Two teachers worked with pre-school groups and one with younger children. Three other educators were nurses with secondary-level education; one of them worked with pre-schoolers and two with younger children. Parents' experiences were pursued in interviews with 11 parents (nine mothers alone and one interview with the mother and the father) in 10 interviews.

The quality of this study can be considered as construct and internal validity (Cohen, Manion, & Morrison, 2011; Yin, 2009). To ensure the validity, I based the study on the previous research on transitions in early childhood and the importance of continuity during the transitions. The data were gathered from multiple sources and were a representative sample inside the case. Nearly all the parents of five-year-olds and nearly all staff members participated in the interviews. The curricula and forms related to individual planning processes were gathered extensively. The results of one case cannot be generalised as such, but they can help to gain a better understanding of the processes, benefits and challenges of individual planning in the transition to pre-school in similar settings (Gerring, 2006; Yin, 2009).

The interviews followed an interview guide, with themes about which I wanted the interviewees to talk. According to Bogdan and Biklen (2007), this kind of semi-structured interview can produce comparable data from the participants. The educators were interviewed in a group because I wanted to promote discussion and gain diverse opinions and perspectives. Following Vaughn, Schumm, and Sinagub (1996, p. 16), the goal was to 'conduct an interactive discussion that can elicit a greater, more in-depth understanding of perceptions, beliefs, attitudes, and experiences from multiple points of view'. The educators' interview lasted for about an hour and was audio- and video-recorded. The video-recording was only used to identify the speaker, which, in a group interview, can otherwise be complicated. The parents were interviewed individually at a time and place convenient for them. Some parents wanted to be interviewed in the day-care centre, some invited me to their homes and one mother came to the university. The interviews lasted from 20 to 50 minutes and were audio-recorded.

The data were analysed using qualitative content analysis with the emphasis on abductive inference (Krippendorff, 2004). Following Peirce's (Peirce & Lång, 2001) thinking about the role of concepts in human thinking and interpretations, the analysis was led by theory-based concepts outlining the phenomenon (Bertilsson & Christiansen, 2001; Josephson & Josephson, 1996). This approach assisted in delimiting the analysis and focusing on essential issues in the theoretical framework. The data were analysed by using the following codes: the content of individual plans, how the individual planning was drawn up and who participated in it, and continuity in transition to pre-school.

Results

Individual planning in national curricula

According to the legislation, individual planning is mandatory in Finnish early childhood education (*Laki sosiaalihuollon*, 2000). The *National curriculum guidelines* (2004) instruct that

> The early education and care of an individual child is based on the individual ECEC [early childhood education and care] plan drawn up jointly by the staff and the child's parents at

the start of the care relationship. The plan aims to take account of the child's individuality and parent's views in arranging the child's care. (p. 29)

In the curriculum, a child and his/her family's individual needs formed the base of the early childhood education provided. Individual plans were to be made for every child and parents were to play an important role in their development. The relationship between parents and educators was referred to as a partnership requiring mutual, continuous and committed interaction (*National curriculum guidelines*, 2004). Individual planning continued in pre-school, but it was not compulsory.

In the initial phase of pre-school education, the teacher *may* draw up the child's pre-school education plan in co-operation with parents. (*Core curriculum*, 2000, emphasis added)

Although not compulsory, an individual pre-school education plan is widely used in pre-school education. According to a review on pre-school education in Finland, 69% of pre-school teachers used children's individual plans a lot when planning everyday activities (Finnish Ministry of Education, 2004).

In the *National curriculum guidelines on early childhood education and care in Finland* (2004), the content of the individual plan was described as follows:

The individual ECEC plan takes into consideration the child's experiences, current needs and future perspectives, interests and strengths, and individual needs for support and guidance. In discussions with the parents, attention should be drawn to positive aspects that foster the child's development. (p. 29)

In the *Core curriculum for pre-school education in Finland 2000*, the content of a child's pre-school education plan was defined as follows:

The plans shall focus on factors essential to individual development, such as the objectives to be set for the child's growth and development and the assessment of the child's strengths and weaknesses. (p. 16)

Officially, pre-school education was not as strength based and family oriented as early childhood education. The processes and the contents of individual plans also differed at each level. Despite these discontinuities, the *National curriculum guidelines on early childhood education and care in Finland* instructed educators to build continuity in individual planning between early childhood education and pre-school education:

The staff should ensure that the individual ECEC [early childhood education and care] plan and the individual pre-school education plan form a functioning whole. (p. 30)

The continuity between early childhood education, pre-school education and primary school education was also addressed in the *Core curriculum for pre-school education in Finland 2000*. The curriculum instructed that education should form an entity that allows consistency and continuity of a child's development and education.

Educators' perspective: interpretations at the local level

In the day-care centre, the national documentation was interpreted at the local level and translated into practice and became an actual curriculum, a reality of the setting (Alasuutari & Karila, 2010; Kelly, 2004). The educators and the context of the setting influenced the interpretations and translation processes and curriculum became a lived experience situated in a real-life context (Pinar, Reynolds, Slattery, & Taubman, 2004; Turunen, 2008). In the group interview, the educators explained how individual planning was interpreted and carried out.

In the day-care centre, individual planning occurred during the discussions between an educator and parents. The educator met families, mostly mothers, at least twice during the year. The first meeting was in September or October.

> Educator 4 (nurse, three- to five-year-olds): For me it is like, with the kids I already know, I can talk with their parents even in the beginning of September. But with a child who is new, I need to work for a while with him/her before I am ready to talk with the parents about the targets for the coming year. I need some basis for the discussion.
> Educator 3 (early childhood teacher, pre-school): In the pre-school group we have had the discussions in September.

In May, the educators met the parents again. If the parents wanted, there were more discussions during the year. The intensity of co-operation depended on a child's individual needs and parents' wishes. If a child had special needs, the special education early childhood teacher, therapists working with the child and the family, and the pre-school teacher were involved in individual planning.

The individual planning required various forms which the parents and educators completed either beforehand or during the discussions. When their child started in the day-care centre, the parents filled a form called 'Information about the Child'. The child's perspective was captured in 'My Own Plan'. For example, the *My Own Plan* form included the statement

> The child participates in his/her individual planning in accordance to his/her capabilities.

There was also a form for parents to complete: 'My Family Tells'.

> At the day-care centre, the care and education is planned together with the parents according to individual needs and personal characteristics of every child. The information from the parents is very important to the child's immediate educators. To complete this form, the parents are asked to write down some information about their child, when he/she starts in the day-care centre or proceeds from a group to another.

The educators told that using these forms, the individual plans were drawn up by the educators and the parents at the beginning of the year. The parents were always involved in completing the individual plan.

> Educator 4 (nurse, three- to five-year-olds): And there is this individual ECEC plan which is done with the parents. Here it is also asked how it will be evaluated and what kind of co-operation the parents would like to have.
> Educator 3 (early childhood teacher, pre-school): Do you give the form to the parents beforehand?
> Educator 6 (early childhood teacher, three- to five-year-olds): I have not given it automatically. Some parents want it and then I have given it, but not automatically.
> Educator 4: And in addition to that, there is an observation form for overall development for the kids who will go to a child health clinic for 5-year-olds health check. We fill it in here at day-care centre. It is usually given to parents so that they can have a look and then we have filled it in here. The parents then take it with them to the clinic.
> Educator 2 (early childhood teacher, pre-school): It is done for all five-year-olds.
> Educator 5 (nurse, three- to five-year-olds): And the three-year-olds have a similar thing.

There were different forms for the plans in early childhood education and pre-school education. Early childhood education plans included the areas of basic care and daily routines; conception of self and emotional life; social, motor and cognitive skills; linguistic development; perception of environment; working habits; self-expression; music/rhythm and play. It also had a section for co-operation and partnership between home and the day-care centre. The individual plan in pre-school education started with a personal section, where information about family, friends, child's favourite activities, personal characteristics and strengths, hobbies, and the needs for support and guidance were recorded. This was followed by a section on the pre-school content areas from the *Core curriculum for pre-school education in Finland 2000*. The last section was about parents' wishes and expectations of the pre-school year, co-operation with the day-care centre, and ways of assessing their child's progress in pre-school.

The individual planning forms encouraged the educators and the parents to record their shared targets and to monitor and evaluate them. The educators aimed to write down concrete targets and evaluation in consultation with the parents.

Tuija: So, what do you write down in those plans?
Educator 3 (early childhood teacher, pre-school): It does, you know, very much depend on the child, and what kind of person the child is. What are the targets for the child. And those targets that we are aiming for, they are not so utopian, but everyday things we are aiming for with the child; concrete things we think are achievable and helpful for the child.
Educator 2 (early childhood teacher, pre-school): That was a good word, the concrete things
Educator 5 (nurse, three- to five-year-olds): At least I, when we fill it together, we have talked, section by section, and I have asked [the parents], what in this section is the thing that we can write down as a target. I have thrown the ball to the parents. Or if there is a concern which we have already talked about, and if the parents do not, then I can put it forward that maybe this is something we can write down as a target. So that we can look at it, for example, in the middle or at the end of the year. Parents are really good at it [with the targets], and they are concrete.
Educator 3: Yes, the parents know their child.

The forms did not contain anything about continuity between early childhood education and pre-school education, and according to the group interview, the practices of individual planning differed in early childhood education and pre-school education and depended also on the educator working with the family. In the discussions in May, the parents of five-year-olds could ask questions about pre-school:

Educator 6 (early childhood teacher, three- to five-year-olds): I have with the parents' of five-year-olds, in the evaluation discussions, I have told them a little about pre-school, and that it is not such a peculiar thing. I told them that it is quite a bit like this daycare, but they do more pre-school things. It is very much about learning social skills and being with other kids and they don't have to be nervous about the pre-school.
Educator 2 (early childhood teacher, pre-school): But there were some parents, I remember, who asked if the children need a backpack and a pencil case, books and pens and...
Educator 4 (nurse, three- to five-year-olds): And can the children be absent from pre-school and
Educator 2: And what pre-school activities you have during the absence. For example if a child spends a week with his/her grandparents, is he/she left behind or...
Educator 4: And is there a written form to apply a leave of absence in pre-school.

Alasuutari and Karila's (2010) study indicated that individual plans in Finland are dominated by developmental psychology, constructing a child as a minor who needs care and positioning parents more as objects than as subjects in their child's education.

As Alasuutari and Karila pointed out, planning forms do not explain how individual planning works in day-care centres. This study broadens the view of individual planning and how the limited guidance at the national level is translated into practice. From the educators' group interview, individual planning appeared to be familiar in discussions with the parents and in the various forms they completed with the parents. The forms guided the discussion in many ways. They tuned the parents and framed the topics of the discussions. They also tuned the educators, not only in the discussion with the parents but also in their daily activities with the child.

Transition and continuity were not part of the forms, but were part of the practices: the educators reported that, in addition to the individual plan, some drawings and other artefacts were collected for a child's portfolio, which was then given to the pre-school teacher. The pre-school teacher then looked at the entire portfolio, not just at the individual plan. Because continuity was a non-visible item in the written documents, it was also a variable, which could change yearly and depended on the educator working with the child and the family. Familiarity with the premises, staff and other children and shared activities with the other groups were considered as important parts of continuity. It was also important that the educators knew the parents. For all these reasons, the transition was not regarded by the educators as a big issue for the children or the families.

Parents' experiences

The parents experienced the educators' interpretations of individual planning in the discussions and through the forms. The interview with the parents started with a question 'Does your child have an individual plan?' Based on the legislation, curricula and discussions with the headmistress, I assumed that this would be an easy opening for the interview, more rhetoric than a real interview question. In 4 of the 10 interviews, the answer to this question was no.

Tuija: Does your child have an individual plan in the day-care centre?
Mother 5: No he doesn't.
Tuija: Have you had a discussion about your child with the staff?
Mother 5: Yes, in the autumn we had the beginning discussion and now in the spring was the final discussion
Tuija: Did someone write down the things?
Mother 5: Yes

Tuija: Does your child have an individual plan?
Mother 1: No I don't think so, the only thing is, these discussions and other things.

All parents recalled the discussion sessions with the educator, but they had not always interpreted it as an individual planning session with an individual plan as an outcome. According to Karila (2005), the partnership between the parents and educators means open communication, shared decision-making and expertise, and clearly with some parents, this had not happened. The intent of the discussion had not been explicitly explained to these parents. Despite this, the discussions were mainly positive experiences for the parents and they felt that they had had an influence on setting the targets for their child. Most of the parents agreed that the discussions formed the basis of the individual support for their child.

Mother 1: It [the discussion] is good so that we know how things are. My son, I think that he is different than he is at home. Because of the more unfamiliar people. It is nice to know, for example about putting on his clothes and other things. Because at home, it is always mother.

Mother 8: The parents are listened to very well and things are written down. And I have the feeling that the things have been put into practice too. So that the staff has clearly shared the things among themselves and everyone knows about our wishes and where we think the support is needed.

The parents had great confidence in the educators. They felt that the educators always had time for parents and the family's wishes and needs had been taken into account.

Mother 5: [after talking about her son's special needs] And it was nice too, I wondered if this can be possible, but yes it can because he needs it. I thought that it is great how individual this can be. She [the educator] said that some other kids might have something else … So this kind of thing, there are plenty of them. [explains how a special requirement of her son was taken into account during the outdoor activities] So, I always notice that. They have paid attention and took it into account. They [the educators] are so good at it.

One parent expressed a critical comment:

Father 6: Actually the paper was filled mechanically, and if I think about it afterwards, I just wonder, what was the purpose of it and the outcome. It remained blurry, at least for me, if I think backwards. So we just filled the paper but I don't know what kind of strengths he has, what should be increased and supported. That remained unclear.

In addition to the discussions, the portfolio was important to the parents. It was a folder or a box that contained their child's drawings and other artefacts the child had made and the individual planning forms. The parents thought that the portfolio could be a good tool for the educators to gain a more comprehensive picture about their child, especially in transition. However, they did not know how the information in the portfolio was used in the day-care centre. Eight parents talked about the portfolio, two parents did not know what was in it and one parent did not think that there was one for her child.

Mother 8: Yes, there is, it is not a folder but a box where the artifacts are collected. It is a kind of a box of growth.
Tuija: Have you seen it, what does it contain?
Mother 8: No I haven't, I don't know what's in it.

Mother 6: I think it [the portfolio] was there [in the discussion], but we didn't look at it. I think that the idea is that it will be given to us now in the spring.

The parents had no or weak knowledge about the usage of the individual planning procedures during the transition. They thought that the individual information about their child could be a good starting point for the pre-school teacher. It could give a basis for individual support for their child also in pre-school, and the parents hoped that the educators had time to read their child's papers and look at the portfolio.

Tuija: Your daughter has this individual plan that has been written down. Do you know how it is used in the transition to pre-school?
Mother 3: No, actually I don't know.
Tuija: How would you like it to be used?
Mother 3: So that the educators from the pre-school group could talk about it and the educators from this present group could tell what we have talked about. So it might be useful.

Tuija: How are the discussions and other things used in this transition to pre-school? Do you know?
Mother 4: I don't know, but I think that the information should go there automatically. So that they [educators in pre-school group] can read it. I think that the folder [portfolio] goes with the child here in the day-care centre.

As for the educators, familiarity was an important element of continuity for the parents. It helped that the building and other children were familiar, and the educators knew the child and the family.

Mother 10: You know, the day-care centre teacher who is in pre-school, she is familiar. She certainly has been with my son already, not very much though, but she knows ... She has the basic information and she knows my son.

Mother 2: But it is so great because it [pre-school] is in the same premises. They [the children] have played with pre-schoolers. So it is familiar.

A personal contact and relationship with the educators strengthened the parents' experience of continuity. They had a feeling of respectful and mutual relationships with the educators (Educational Transitions and Change [ETC] Research Group, 2011; Rimm-Kaufman & Pianta, 2000). From the parents' perspective, personal, face-to-face contacts and familiarity gave good foundations for their child's education. They could count on that. Other individual planning procedures and how they were used in transition were either blurry or unclear for the parents. In particular, the individual plan seemed to remain remote. One parent said that

Mother 6: Actually, we don't have that form. It could be good thing to copy it to the parents.

Discussion

According to this study, individual planning was important in the national curricula, at the local level in the educators' talk and in the forms used in the day-care centre. How their child's individual needs and personal characteristic were taken into account was important to the parents. At national and local levels, parents' involvement in individual planning was emphasised and was reflected in the parents' positive experiences of the discussions. The active participation of the parents is an important factor for continuity and support in transitions. Family involvement benefits the child in many ways (Dockett & Perry, 2007; Henderson & Mapp, 2002). In this study, the parents felt that they had been listened to and their perspectives and wishes had been taken seriously and put into action with their child. This reflects Alasuutari's (2003) results, which show that Finnish parents trust early childhood educators and their professional skills. According to Henderson and Mapp (2002), the continuity of family involvement provides protection for children. The results of this study indicated that the parents were involved and felt that they had been listened to in the early childhood education, but not so much in the transition to pre-school.

In this setting, familiarity and trust were important parts of continuity. Both parents and educators emphasised the value of knowing each other and having personal relationships. The importance of strong, positive relationships between educators and parents in early childhood education has been documented in previous studies (Dockett & Perry, 2007; Griebel & Niesel, 2002; Shpancer, 2002). Instead, the individual planning had little to do with the transition to pre-school. National curricula instructed the educators to ensure consistency and continuity, but this aspect was not present in the forms or the discussions. Consequently, the parents' knowledge about the usage of the individual plan in transition to pre-school was minimal. Griebel and Niesel (2002) suggested that the preparation for transition is needed not only for the children but for the parents as well. In this study, the familiar setting and personal relationships seemed to serve an important role in the preparation for pre-school education, but the meaning of the individual planning remained blurry.

Although the parents were generally satisfied with how they were listened to, there were some issues. This study showed how the national documentation on individual planning was first translated into practices of one day-care centre and then experienced by the parents. In this process, the curriculum changed. The experienced curriculum differed from the official curriculum and the educators' interpretation of it (Kelly, 2004; Turunen, 2008). The distinction between the educators' interpretations and the parents' experiences was evident in some areas. The educators and the parents had different perceptions of the usefulness and use of individual planning. Some parents were not aware that there actually was an individual plan for their child and none of the parents knew how the plans were used in transition to pre-school. This reflects results that are parallel to those of Johansson's (2002) study, in which the majority of the parents were satisfied with the information they had received, but one-third would have liked to receive more information. It might be that the information is available in early childhood settings, but for some reason, it does not reach all families.

In her study, Karila (2005) found that the discussions between educators and parents are often built on educators' professional perspectives. Educators define the themes and use more time in the discussions. Power is with the educator. It might mean that parents do not have space to ask for information. In this study, the discussions were based on the forms, with readymade themes, and parents' voice was limited. To clarify the individual planning and transition processes to the parents, more open and mutual discussion between educators and parents is needed. The educators should reflect on the positioning of themselves and the parents. They should actively endeavour to build respectful relationships, where the parents have time and space to show interests in the discussion and ask the questions they might have. The other important issue is the taken-for-granted nature of many practicalities in day-care centres: they are so self-evident to the educators that they do not remember that the parents may not know them. I agree with Alasuutari (2007) that the idea of partnership in early childhood education challenges the traditional ways of doing things.

This study revealed transition practices in a setting which is typical in Finland (Finnish Ministry of Education, 2004; Siniharju, 2007), but it does not discuss these processes in other situations such as transition to pre-school from home or when pre-school is part of primary school. More research is needed to build a more comprehensive picture about individual planning processes in the various contexts of transition to pre-school. Since this study was conducted, a new core curriculum for pre-school education has been introduced. As its precursor, it contains the idea of building continuity between early childhood education, pre-school education and primary school education. In the curriculum, individual planning is an important part of pre-school education, especially with children with special needs, but there is no advice regarding how these individual plans should support the continuity in transitions (Finnish National Board of Education, 2010). Based on this study, I suggest that the continuity in individual planning should be more explicit at national and local levels and in practices with families. It can be recommended as an appropriate tool in transition to pre-school, but more discussion between parents and educators is needed to build a shared understanding of it.

Note

1. Pre-school education is part of early childhood education and care in Finland, but has its own core curriculum and legislation. In this paper, early childhood education is used to describe the services for children before they start pre-school education.

References

Alasuutari, M. (2003). *Kuka lasta kasvattaa? Vanhemmuuden ja yhteiskunnallisen kasvatuksen suhde vanhempien puheessa* [Who is raising the child? Mothers and fathers constructing the role of parents and professionals in child development]. Helsinki: Gaudeamus.

Alasuutari, M. (2007). Kumppanuus ja asiantuntijuus varhaiskasvatuksessa [Partnership and its challenge to expertise: Early childhood education as a case example]. *Psykologia, 42*(6), 422–434.

Alasuutari, M., & Karila, K. (2010). Framing the picture of the child. *Children & Society, 24*(2), 100–111.

Bertilsson, T.M., & Christiansen, P.W. (2001). Jalkisanat [Epilogue]. In C.S. Peirce & M. Lång (Eds.), *Johdatus tieteen logiikkaan ja muita kirjoituksia. Valinnut ja suomentanut Markus Lång* [Introduction to the logic of science and other writings. Selected and translated by Markus Lång] (pp. 443–473). Tampere: Vastapaino.

Bogdan, R.C., & Biklen, S.K. (2007). *Qualitative research for education. An introduction to theories and methods* (5th ed.). Boston, MA: Pearson.

Bronfenbrenner, U. (1979). *The ecology of human development: Experiments by nature and design*. Cambridge, MA: Harvard University Press.

Bronfenbrenner, U. (1986). Ecology of the family as a context for human development: Research perspectives. *Developmental Psychology, 22*(6), 723–742.

Bronfenbrenner, U., & Evans, G.W. (2000). Developmental science in the 21st century: Emerging questions, theoretical models, research designs and empirical findings. *Social Development, 9*(1), 115–125.

Brostrom, S. (2002). Communication and continuity in the transition from kindergarten to school. In H. Fabian & A.-W. Dunlop (Eds.), *Transitions in the early years. Debating continuity and progression for children in early years* (pp. 52–63). London: RoutledgeFalmer.

Cohen, L., Manion, L., & Morrison, K. (2011). *Research methods in education* (7th ed.). London: Routledge.

Core curriculum for pre-school education in Finland 2000. (2000). Helsinki: Finnish National Board of Education.

Dockett, S., & Perry, B. (2007). *Transitions to school: Perceptions, expectations, experiences.* Sydney: University of New South Wales Press.

Dunlop, A.-W. (2007). Bridging research, policy and practice. In A.-W. Dunlop & H. Fabian (Eds.), *Informing transitions in the early years. Research, policy and practice* (pp. 151–168). Maidenhead: Open University Press.

Educational Transitions and Change (ETC) Research Group. (2011). *Transition to school: Position statement.* Albury-Wodonga: Research Institute for Professional Practice, Learning and Education, Charles Sturt University.

Einarsdottir, J. (2010). Children's experiences of the first year of primary school. *European Early Childhood Education Research Journal, 18*(2), 163–180.

Elder, J.G.H. (1998). The life course as developmental theory. *Child Development, 69*(1), 1–12.

Elder, J.G.H., & Shanahan, M.J. (2006). The life course and human development. In W. Damon & R.M. Lerner (Eds.), *Handbook of child psychology: Vol. 1. Theoretical models of human development* (6th ed., pp. 665–715). Hoboken, NJ: John Wiley & Sons.

Entwisle, D.R., & Alexander, K.L. (1998). Facilitating the transition to first grade: The nature of transition and research on factors affecting it. *Elementary School Journal, 98*(4), 351–364.

Eurydice. (2009). *National summary sheets on education systems in Europe and ongoing reforms*. Finland. Retrieved May 31, 2010, from European Commission http://eacea.ec.europa.eu/education/eurydice/documents/eurybase/national_summary_sheets/047_FI_EN.pdf

Fabian, H., & Dunlop, A.-W. (2002). Introduction. In H. Fabian & A.-W. Dunlop (Eds.), *Transitions in the early years. Debating continuity and progression for children in early education* (pp. 1–7). London: RoutledgeFalmer.

Finnish Ministry of Education. (2004). *Esiopetuksen tila Suomessa* [Pre-school education in Finland]. Helsinki: Opetusministerio.

Finnish National Board of Education (2010). *Esiopetuksen opetussuunnitelman perusteet 2010* [Core curriculum for pre-school education 2010]. Helsinki: Opetushallitus.

Gerring, J. (2006). *Case study research: Principles and practices*. Retrieved from http://CSUAU.eblib.com/patron/FullRecord.aspx?p=288451

Griebel, W., & Niesel, R. (2002). Co-consturcting transition into kindergarten and school by children, parents and teachers. In H. Fabian & A.-W. Dunlop (Eds.), *Transitions in the early years* (pp. 64–75). London: Routledge.

Griebel, W., & Niesel, R. (2003). Successful transitions: Social competencies help pave the way to kindergarten and school. *European Early Childhood Education Research Journal*, Themed Monograph Series No. 1, 25–33.

Henderson, A.T., & Mapp, K.L. (2002). *A new wave of evidence. The impact of school, family, and community connections on student achievement*. Austin, TX: National Center for Family and Community Connections with Schools.

Johansson, I. (2002). Parents' views of transition to school and their influence in this process. In H. Fabian & A.-W. Dunlop (Eds.), *Transitions in the early years. Debating continuity and progression for children in early education* (pp. 76–86). London: RoutledgeFalmer.

Josephson, J.R., & Josephson, S.G. (1996). *Abductive inference: Computation, philosophy, technology*. Cambridge University Press.

Karila, K. (2005). Vanhempien ja paivahoidon henkiloston keskustelut kasvastuskumppanuuden areenoina [Discussions between parents and day-care staff as arenas of educational partnership]. *Kasvatus, 36*(2), 285–298.

Kelly, A.V. (2004). *The curriculum: Theory and practice* (5th ed.). London: SAGE.

Krippendorff, K. (2004). *Content analysis: An introduction to it's methodology*. London: Sage.

Laki perusopetuslain muuttamisesta [An act to change the basic education act]. (1999). 1288/1999 Finnish acts and degrees. Retrieved from http://www.finlex.fi/fi/laki/kokoelma/1999/19990152.pdf

Laki sosiaalihuollon asemasta ja oikeuksista [The act of the status and rights of social welfare clients]. (2000). 812/2000 Finnish acts and degrees. Retrieved from http://www.finlex.fi/fi/laki/kokoelma/2000/20000113.pdf

National curriculum guidelines on early childhood education and care in Finland. (2004). Helsinki: STAKES.

Parke, R.D., & Buriel, R. (2006). Socialization in the family: Ethnic and ecological perspectives. In W. Damon & R.M. Lerner (Eds.), *Handbook of child psychology: Social, emotional, and personality development* (pp. 429–504). Hoboken: John Wiley & Sons.

Peirce, C.S., & Lång, M. (2001). *Johdatus tieteen logiikkaan ja muita kirjoituksia. Valinnut ja suomentanut Markus Lång* [Introduction to the logic of science and other writings. Selected and translated by Markus Lång] (M. Lång, Trans.). Tampere: Vastapaino.

Pinar, W.F., Reynolds, W.M., Slattery, P., & Taubman, P.M. (2004). *Understanding curriculum*. New York, NY: Peter Lang.

Rimm-Kaufman, S.E., & Pianta, R.C. (2000). An ecological perspective on the transition to kindergarten: A theoretical framework to guide empirical research. *Journal of Applied Developmental Psychology, 21*(5), 491–511.

Rogoff, B. (2003). *The cultural nature of human development*. New York, NY: Oxford University Press.

Shpancer, N. (2002). The home-daycare link: Mapping children's new world order. *Early Childhood Research Quarterly, 17*(3), 374–392.

Simons, H. (2009). *Case study research in practice.* London: Sage.

Siniharju, M. (2007). *Esiopetuksen laatu ja merkitys. Vanhempien ja perusopetuksen ensimmaisen vuosiluokan opettajien arvioimana* [The quality and meaning of pre-school education. The evaluation of parents and year one teachers]. Helsinki: Opetushallitus [The Finnish National Board of Education].

Turunen, T.A. (2008). *Mista on esiopetussuunnitelmat tehty? Esiopetuksen opetussuunnitelman perusteiden 1996 ja 2000 diskurssianalyyttinen tutkimus* [What are pre-school curricula made of? A discourse analysis of core curricula for pre-school education in Finland 1996 and 2000]. Rovaniemi: Lapin yliopistokustannus.

Vaughn, S., Schumm, J.S., & Sinagub, J. (1996). *Focus group interviews in education and psychology.* London: Sage.

Yin, R.K. (2003). *Case study research: Design and methods.* London: Sage.

Yin, R.K. (2009). *Case study research. Design and methods* (4th ed.). London: Sage.

Sámi education in Finland

Pigga Keskitalo, Kaarina Määttä and Satu Uusiautti

The purpose of this article is, first, to describe Sámi children's education and its status in the Finnish education system and, secondly, to contemplate its development in Finland. The core of the article is intertwined with issues concerning the status, language, and culture of indigenous peoples. According to the article, the western school dominates instruction and teaching and is spirally connected to the assimilation, power relations, and socialisation process that the Sámi have experienced. The practical framework for Sámi education (based on the earlier findings of the authors) which would direct teaching arrangements and comprehensive pedagogy drawn from the own premises of the Sámi people is reviewed. The Sámi world-view and Sámi values and culture should occupy a central position in teaching, but also in the curriculum.

Dán artihkkala ulbmilin lea govvidit sámi mánáid skuvlendilálašvuođa Suomas. Artihkkalis buktojuvvo ovdan maiddái sámiid gielalaš ja kultuvrralaš dilli álgoálbmogin. Deháleamos čuoččuhus dán čállosis lea dat, ahte oarjemáilmmi skuvlavuogádat báidná sámi oahpahusa. Dát ilbmanupmi lea oktavuođas assimileremii, váldeoktavuođaide ja sosialiserenproseassaide, maiguin sámit leamašan dahkamušas juo jahkečuđiid ja deaivvadit ain otná beaivve. Čálliid ovddit gávnnahemiid vuođul lea hutkojuvvon sámeoahpahusa geavatlaš málle. Dát málle galgá veahkehit lágidit oahpahusa nu, ahte oahpahusa vuolggasadjin livčče sámiid iežaset dárbbut: Sámi máilmmigovva, árvvut ja kultuvra galggašedje leat oahpahusa ja oahppoplánaid guovddážis.

Introduction

Sápmelaččat or the Sámi form the only indigenous people within the area of the European Union. The Sámi's status as an indigenous people is based on their unique world-view, their own history, livelihoods and language. Nowadays, this special nature is ratified with national legislation and international agreements (*The Encyclopaedia of*

Saami Culture [Saamelaiskulttuurin ensyklopedia], 2003). Indigenous peoples can be defined in a variety of ways. According to the International Labour Organization (ILO) convention on indigenous peoples' rights, peoples who live in independent nations are considered indigenous people if they are descended from a population that lived in the country at the time the country was colonised or inhabited or when a modern national state was established. Secondly, indigenous peoples have been greatly independent of the state that governs the region and held on to their linguistic, cultural, and communal features at least as partly separate from the ones of the dominant culture (International Labour Organization, 1996/2011, Convention No. 169). These kinds of definitions are, however, interpretative. The Sámi are recognised as an indigenous people in Finland and Norway and as a people in Sweden. The Constitution of Russian Federation from the year 1993 includes a decree that concerns the protection of indigenous peoples (Nordic Sámi Convention, 2005, p. 99; *The Constitution of the Russian Federation*, 1993). Norway is the only country of the ones populated by the Sámi that has ratified the ILO declaration on the Rights of Indigenous Peoples. Declaration on the Right of Indigenous Peoples was adopted by the General Assembly 13 September 2007 (United Nations, 2007).

The UN's special rapporteur on indigenous rights James Anaya has paid attention to the ruinous effects of the Second World War to the Sámi education and language. Because of the War, the Sámi were left without education in any language for several years which affected harmfully their literacy and ability to hand down their language to future generation. In addition, the present circumstances affect the extinction of the Sámi languages; for example, the facts that in most regions people do not speak Sámi outside their homes at all and that the Sámi-speaking people have sprawled in a geographically wide area (Anaya, 2011). These kinds of things take place although the Sámi's situation has improved. The special rapporteur Anaya pays particular attention to Sámi self-determination at the national level and efforts to revitalise Sámi languages and provide Sámi children and youth with culturally appropriate education (Anaya, 2011).

In addition, more attention should be paid on the availability of teaching. Therefore, in this article, we want to dissect Sámi education in Finland by focusing on cultural-sensitivity (Keskitalo, 2010; Keskitalo & Määttä, in press-a) and school culture (Bishop & Glynn, 1999; Cuban, 1993/1984; Schein, 1992) within which the Sámi teachers act at schools.

In this article, we focus on the following two questions: (1) What is the status of Sámi education in Finland; (2) What are the challenges of Sámi education in Finland; and (3) How could Sámi education be developed in Finland? First, we introduce the main characteristics of the Sámi culture that are relevant to understanding the special position of the Sámi culture in today's Finland and how it affects children's lives and schooling. Furthermore, we analyse the situation through a practical framework designed for developing Sámi education (Keskitalo, Määttä, & Uusiautti, 2011): what kinds of issues have to be taken into consideration in the macro- and micro-level.

The Sámi as indigenous people

The Sámi region and the position of the Sámi in Finland

Sápmi, the region inhabited by the Sámi, expands from Central Norway and Sweden over the northern part of Finland to the Kola Peninsula in Russia and thus, Sápmi is located in four countries. In the northernmost municipalities of Lapland province in Finland, the Sámi have self-government concerning their own language and culture according to the definitions in the Act on the Sámi Parliament and other legislations (*Act on the Sámi Parliament*, 1995/974).

The Sámi's position was written into the Constitution of Finland in 1995 (*The Constitution of Finland*, 731/1999, section 17):

> the Sami, as an indigenous people, as well as the Roma and other groups, have the right to maintain and develop their own language and culture. Provisions on the right of the Sami to use the Sami language before the authorities are laid down by an Act.

The Sámi language Act and the first general decrees concerning the Sámi language came into effect in 1992. The language act was revised in 2003. The Sámi language act includes the Sámi's rights to use their native language in court and with other authorities in state and municipal agencies in the public utilities, and offices. The language act is effective in municipal organs Sámi Domicile Area, Sámi's main residential districts (Saamen kielilaki [The Sámi Language Act], 1086/2003). The purpose of the law is to guarantee the Sámi the right to fair legal proceedings and good administration as well as execution of the Sámi's linguistic rights without having to invoke the law separately. Regulations on the Sámi's linguistic rights are written in the legislation of the school and education system (e.g. *Basic Education Act*, 628/1998) and social welfare and health care (e.g. Act on Children's Day Care, 1973/36). In addition, the Sámi Language Act has to be applied by authorities when adapting the law on patients' position and rights (785/1992) and social welfare customers' position and rights (812/2000) (Vuolab-Lohi, 2007).

Securing this legal position has not come true in practice mostly because of the municipal and state authorities' insufficient knowledge of the Sámi language and multiculturalism. In 2010, a language revitalisation programme was launched in Finland based on the Council of State report on Finland's human rights policy (VNS, 2009). The goal is to carry out more comprehensive and long-span action to secure the survival and development of the Sámi language (Pautamo, 2010).

There are about 9500 Sámi people in Finland. More than 60% of them live outside their home district which makes new kinds of demands on teaching, services, and communication in the Sámi language. Around 70% of under-10-year-old Sámi children live outside of the designed areas. It has been estimated that altogether, there are approximately 75,000–100,000 Sámi in different countries, depending on the method of assessment. Norway has the biggest Sámi population.

Special features of Sámi culture

To the Sámi, Sáminess means a special cultural expression as an ethnic group as certain cultural features and language define the group (Carpelan, 2003). The Sámi culture is not one coherent entity, but covers several cultures and languages. Both spiritual and material sides belong to the Sámi culture. Nature is considered the material base of Sámi culture, including the concepts of scenery, nature, and snow that describe flora and fauna. The Sámi identity, life style, tradition, and more form the spiritual side of culture. In addition to the present, the past belongs to the features that illustrate the societal and social life. The situation of Sámi culture can be seen as resulting from the combination of the special Sámi language, history, mythology, folklore, literature, music, economy, nature, livelihoods, media, rights, education, art, and the factors that explain their societal conditions. In this article, we will review these factors from the children's perspective: what factors most affect and mould children's life and socialisation into the culture.

According to Asta Balto, *sámi bajásgeassin*, the traditional Sámi upbringing consists of learning through work and play. Thus, indirect rearing epitomises Sámi upbringing as Sámi children learn – as it were unobserved – to take responsibility for their actions and living together with their families and surrounding people. The purpose of various approaches, such as *nárrideapmi* (pulling someone's leg), is to increase children's tolerance and sensitivity when communicating with people and simultaneously teach certain roles. Other indirect ways of rearing are, among others, *sollen*, arresting children's attention to other things in an unpleasant situation and addressing them in the third person. Furthermore, *máinnasteapmi*, narration or storytelling is an essential part of Sámi upbringing and means of teaching, sharing and transmitting cultural knowledge (Balto, 1997).

The Sámi languages in Finland

Sámi languages are the closest cognate languages of Finno-Ugric languages (such as Finnish, Hungarian, and Estonian). The Sámi languages are spoken in Finland, Sweden, Norway, and Russia. Many Sámi people have lost their original language under the pressure of the official policy by the states.

The assimilation policy started already in the seventeenth century launched by the church, strengthened at the end of nineteenth century and escalated after the Second World War (Aikio, 1988). Anna-Riitta Lindgren (2000) has brought out the Sámi's reactions to often quite traumatic childhood experiences which varied from the most intensive Sámi activism to the total abandonment of the Sámi language and culture. Ethnic awakening starting from the 1960s has lead to the conscious protection of the Sámi language and various revitalisation actions. Since the mid-1970s, the revised and renewed school laws have improved the Sámi's situation. Despite the positive development, the Sámi languages are categorised endangered. The Sámi languages still hold such a position that the process of changing the language continues regardless of the language revitalisation aspirations.

Three Sámi languages are spoken in Finland: North Sámi (*davvisámegiella*), Inari Sámi (*anarâškielâ*), and Skolt Sámi (*sää'mǩiõll*). Furthermore, there are dialects that vary by region. The North Sámi is the biggest language group and approximately 20,000 people speak it in Finland, Norway, and Sweden, of whom 2000 live in Finland. About 300 people speak Inari Sámi and Skolt Sámi in Finland; mainly in the municipality of Inari which is the only four-lingual municipality in Finland with the official languages of Finnish language and three Sámi languages. The figures are estimations because, for example, in Finland, they are based on people's own declarations built on their subjective assessment on their language proficiency. The members of an assimilated people may regard their language proficiency so low that they declare the dominant language as their native language. Yet, if we were to adopt Tove Skutnabb-Kangas's (2008) idea, one's first language marked in the population register can be the Sámi language even if one had lost it or has only passive knowledge of it.

Livelihoods

The traditional Sámi natural sources of livelihood are collecting natural products, hunting and fishing, reindeer herding, small-scale farming, and handicraft. Nature, seasons, the ecology of game animals and useful plants and the production of biomass have determined life styles in Lappish villages. The traditional life style has been based on multi-economy and seasonal moving from a place to another and therefore, Sámi communities remained small. The changes in the life style and the balance of nature and people going to paid work have also diminished the meaning of natural products in Sámi households. Still in the 1960s, half of the Sámi population in Finland earned their keep from natural sources of livelihood (Lehtola, 2011). Natural sources of livelihood are not just livelihoods or occupations, but part of the Sámi's peculiar life style. Today, the Sámi ply traditional sources of livelihood together with, for example, tourism and other service industries (The Sámi Parliament, 2008).

Duodji, Sámi handicraft, was formed according to the moving and nature-preserving life style. Sámi handicraft refers to hand-made utility articles such as clothes, tools, hunting and fishing equipment, and ornaments made of material such as horns, bone, tin, leather, and fabric. Handicraft skill is an important cultural factor and livelihood for the Sámi. During the past decades, it has started to resemble artistic handicraft. Products are unique both for their production methods and design. Beautiful and decorated items were not made for art but beauty and practicality have always belonged together. *Gákti*, the Sámi national costume, is the Sámi's most visible national and identity symbol that bears the Sámi history. The decorations and entity of the costume tell where the person is from – even the marital status and ancestry for the most discerning beholders (The Sámi Parliament, 2008).

Schools and the boarding house system affected especially youngsters' clothing. Owing to the change in school laws in 1946, compulsory education also concerned children who lived in remote districts. Because of the poor travelling possibilities in northern Finland, most of the Sámi generation spent their schooling in boarding houses at least for a part of the year. The Finnish culture and language dominated in the school and boarding house world, and children were taught only the Finnish handicraft tradition. Thus, many Sámi's natural contact with the traditional Sámi handicraft disappeared and Sámi children grew away from their own culture, language and the costume tradition (Lehtola, 2011; see Rasmus, 2006).

Other cultural expressions

The most famous form of Sámi music is *luohti*, yoiking. Its characteristic features are special voice control, rich rhythmic, improvising, unaccompanied singing, the use of expletives, and the firm relationship with culture. Other traditional forms of Sámi music in Finland are Inari Sámi *livđe* and Skolt Sámi *leúdd* – both are in danger of extinction. Of the instruments that the Sámi use, the most important is the magic drum, *goavddis*, which was a shaman's salient ritual gear. In addition, the Sámi use a 3–5-hole whistle, *fádnobiipa*, made of a sprout of angelica archangelica as well as rattles. In the 1960s, Sámi music started to follow the modern trends. Today, rock, pop, ethnic, heavy metal, dance, techno, rap and children's music as well as hymns are composed in the Sámi languages (The Sámi Parliament, 2008).

The early Sámi settlement was connected with the season-based hunting and fishing culture and nomad life style that lasted until the end of the seventeenth century. At that time, reindeer herding became common among the Sámi and only the minority of the mountain Sámi continued the occupation as a season-based nomadic culture. Other Sámi life styles were not that transient any longer. Until that, the Sámi lived in peat-covered wooden tepees in the middle of which they had a stone-ringed hearth. Later on, the Sámís winter villages consisted of four-cornered log houses that were afterwards used in spring, summer, and autumns villages as well. In addition, the so-called Lappish house typifies the Sámi dwelling culture: on the both sides of a cold porch, there are lounges. Small log or peat-covered outbuildings are situated widely around the unpainted and unsealed main buildings because of the shape of the terrain and to avoid gathering too much snow and to retain the free view from the main building as far as possible (Finnish Environmental Administration, 2011).

The official premises of Sámi education and teaching in the Sámi language

The Sámi language has been officially taught at school since the beginning of comprehensive school in Finland – although already in existence during 1740–1780, teaching took place in turn in the Sámi and Finnish languages. Teaching in the Sámi language started in Utsjoki and Inari in the mid-1970s. Since 1975, comprehensive schools in the Sámi Dominicile Area started to get additional teacher positions in order to start education and teaching in the Sámi language (Lassila, 2001).

According to the current law, pupils can have most of their basic education in the Sámi language if they wanted. The position of the Sámi language is secured in the Sámi Domicile Area by the Finnish Act on Basic Education. The teaching language of the Sámi pupils who live in Sámi's home districts can be the Sámi language. When the pupil is able to study in both Finnish and Sámi languages, the pupil's guardian can choose the teaching language. The pupil may study the Sámi language as the subject of mother tongue and the Finnish language can be used according to the definitions of the curriculum (see *Basic Education Act*, 1983/476.)

Teaching is controlled by the decision of Ministry of Education and Culture (2004/132/428) that concerns the case of allowing state subsidy for the complimentary teaching of immigrants and, for example, Sámi-speaking pupils outside the home district. There are no such regulations on teaching outside the Sámi home district in Finland that would guarantee equally wide rights to study the Sámi language than in the Sámi's home district. The subsidy for complimentary teaching grounds on the maximum of two hours of teaching a week per one teaching group. In practice, the two-hour limitation means that it is not possible to follow the contents and objectives defined in the curriculum or the time allocation defined for the teaching of the mother tongue and foreign languages in the decree of time allocation and therefore, the Sámi language teaching is provided as an optional subject also for native Sámi-speaking pupils (Aikio-Puoskari, 2007; Keskitalo & Määttä, in press-b).

Some of the teaching is provided as virtual teaching. Every comprehensive school and college located in the Sámi Domicile Area provides education in the Sámi language. It has been possible to take the matriculation examination of the first language in the North Sámi language since 1994 and in the Inari Sámi language since 1998 (Matriculation Examination Board of Finland, 2002). Furthermore, after a long wait since 2012, it will be possible to take the matriculation examination of the first language in the Skolt Sámi language as well (Sanila-Aikio, 2011).

According to the national curriculum, the central aim of the education of Sámi-speaking pupils is to support their growth towards active bilingualism and multiculturalism. All subjects support the development of pupils' proficiency in the first language in education in the Sámi language. Education should support pupils' identification with their national cultural heritage and bonding with the Sámi who lives in different countries (Finnish National Board of Education, 2004).

Education should provide pupils with the conditions that support the development of healthy self-esteem without losing their Sámi identity or assimilating into the dominant population. National goals and educational contents are followed in education – yet, by noticing the special features of the Sámi culture and the situation of the Sámi language. Especially, the Sámi's own history and present community, traditional livelihoods as well as the knowledge of traditional music *luohti/livđe/leúdd*, storytelling *máinnasteapmi* (story telling narration and Sámi handicrafts *duodji* are emphasised in education). Pupils should get positive experiences of their own culture through play, narration, action, and participation. The school has to collaborate with the home so that the Sámi rearing and teaching traditions become noticed. Within the realms of possibility, education should be adjusted to the seasonal rhythm of the local Sámi community and the traditional season-based work and changes in nature (Finnish National Board of Education, 2004).

The actual cultural-sensitivity of Sámi education in Finland

Next we will use Pigga Keskitalo et al.'s (2011) practical framework of Sámi education to analyse how Sámi education could be developed in Finland in a cultural-sensitive manner. The model is divided into wider outer factors that provide the background and inner factors that are at the core of developing Sámi education (Figure 1). In culturally sensitive schools, pupils' background and experiences are the starting point of education (Keskitalo, 2010). The research has suggested that indigenous peoples' education has to be built on their own cultural premises and values (Bishop & Glynn, 1999; Cajete, 1994).

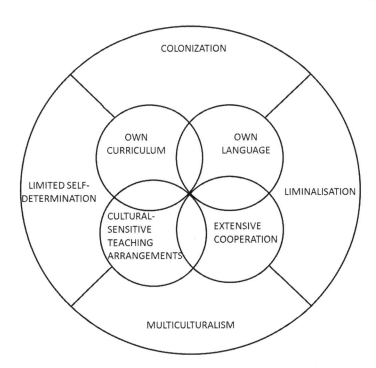

Figure 1. The practical framework of Sámi education (Keskitalo et al., 2011).

In Finland, education in Sámi Domicile Area is divided into Finnish and Sámi-speaking classes. Sámi education takes place at the Sámi classes, including pupils who are Sámi according to their active first mother tongue but, at the beginning of first grades at school, passive Sámi speakers as well are included if the school, teachers and parents agree upon the arrangement. According to our research data, in practice, a pupil group, who has passive knowledge of the Sámi language, may confront the so-called doorman phenomenon when it comes to the striving of language revitalisation. It means that the community, school, teachers, or parents together or separately do not make the restoration of children's Sámi language proficiency possible. The various ethnical backgrounds of the pupils and personnel at some municipalities and schools may have caused uncertainty of how the multicultural school with diverse values could be executed. Furthermore, because of multiculturalism and the fast changes in modern demands and the learning content, the school has to renew its practices constantly. On the other hand, the Sámi culture has reached a transitional period which poses the danger of losing the traditional skills and knowledge. This point of view places challenges for Sámi teaching.

Norway has the best premises to carry out the Sámi education as secured by law and because of the Sámi curriculum and the special Sámi School system. According to Vuokko Hirvonen's (2003/2004) research, multiculturalism in Sámi Schools in Norway can be dissected through James Banks' (1997/1989) model of multicultural teaching where the first level represents the smallest and the fourth level the highest variation. Sámi Schools are at different levels when it comes to the fact how they have reached the special nature of a multicultural school. Some of the Sámi Schools represent the first level as the Sámi myths, holidays, and separate elements of the culture act as the sorts of spices in teaching. These kinds of schools carry on with the assimilation. According to Hirvonen (2003/2004), none of the Sámi Schools has reached the fourth or the highest level, the multicultural Sámi school. The reasons for it are the socio-economic, linguistic, and ethno-political problems (see Ventsel & Dudeck, 1995). Studies have shown that the same phenomenon can be seen in many other indigenous peoples' schools as well (Bartels & Bartels, 1995; Darnell & Hoëm, 1996; Keskitalo, 2003; Lipka, Mohatt, & the Ciulistet Group, 1998).

The school system has a significant role in the colonisation of indigenous peoples (Darnell & Hoëm, 1996). The colonisation of the Sámi means that the national states govern the Sámi's life, including education. As the Sámi live in four countries, they have to follow teaching practices from four different countries. Western School dominates instruction in Sámi education and is spirally connected with the assimilation, power relations, and the socialisation process that the Sámi had experienced (Keskitalo, 2010). The way the school organises teaching is connected with the historical task of the school. The problem in Sámi teaching is mainly that pedagogical arrangements and curricula are similar to the mainstream schools. Students are not socialised into their own culture as deeply as preferred because the Sámi teaching is organised and based on the prevailing values of Western education.

According to Keskitalo's (2010) research, there are difficulties in combining the western school culture with Sámi culture at school. However, the question is not only about the collision of cultures because the problematic issues are always linked with power relations as well (see also Keskitalo & Määttä, in press-a; Kuokkanen, 2009) – and Sámi education lacks self-determination leading to a situation where the Sámi do not have much control over the macro-level framework of education. In ideal circumstances, teaching would be based on the values of the surrounding community (see Hollins, 2008). Yet, it seems that the Sámi's real participation in national curriculum planning and defining the standards is limited.

In many cases, the school systems ignore indigenous peoples when it comes to decision-making, curriculum design, selecting teachers and learning materials as well as defining the standards. In addition, learning materials do not usually provide correct and accurate information about the cultures of indigenous peoples (King & Schiermann, 2004).

Developing and strengthening Sámi education in Finland

As the previous chapter showed, Sámi education is coloured by colonisation, acts in a liminal position or in interfaces, in the field of multiculturalism, and within limited self-determination. Four inner factors appear salient for developing Sámi – and other indigenous peoples' education: creating the indigenous peoples' own curriculum based on own values and the knowledge system; strengthening the position of the indigenous peoples' own language; creating cultural-sensitive teaching arrangements; and diversifying the extensive cooperation.

When developing Sámi education, it is important to know what kind of cultural-historical phases it is premised on. Given the colonised school history of the Sámi teaching and the influence of the western school culture, it can be stated that Sámi education and research function on a variety of frontiers. They can be seen both as physical, geographical and mental frontiers (cf. Anzaldúa, 1999/1987). In the practical pedagogy of Sámi education, both the tradition of western upbringing and science of education and the indigenous people's rearing culture can be seen in operation on the frontiers. The question is whether the school culture is similar with the one pupils have become used to at home, whether pupils make themselves at home when at school and whether different things are valued at home than at school. Otherness mirrors the repressive society and culture and it manifests itself in teacher–pupil interaction so that individuals repeat the macro-level practices in an institutional education situation (Ellsworth, 1997). Instead of assimilating learners to the societal practices, teachers should guide them to break the boundaries related to, for example, social class, gender, or ethnicity (hooks, 1994).

The task of the school has changed as the school history proves. The increasing understanding about the challenges of diversity increases the need for analysing the content of education and knowledge. Awareness of the threatening factors of colonisation and globalisation affects in the background (Singh, Kenway, & Apple, 2005). According to Aimo Aikio, the solution to changing Sámi teaching is in multiculturalism. It requires the realisation of cultural and linguistic equality and everyone in a multicultural society should be polyglot and receptive to multiculturalism (Aikio, 2003). Multiculturalism derives from the need to establish rigorous and respectful dialogues between different forms of thinking and knowledge stemming from indigenous peoples and western experiences in a manner that makes it possible to come up with a synthesis of the way of thinking (see Chacón, Yanez, & Larriva, 2010).

The phase and extent in which the Sámi have been able to affect the planning of Sámi education in reality have been criticised (Hirvonen & Balto, 2008). Indeed, it is recommended that they would fully participate in curriculum planning (see King & Schiermann, 2004). Just the demand to be heard is not enough if authorities and decision-makers do not take into consideration the results of these hearings in their final decisions (Hirvonen & Balto, 2008). Giving the Sámi self-determination concerning education would require political effort and becoming more aware of the matter than before also in education. In order to undergo a transformation, Sámi education has to be considered as one of the factors that construct the society as a part of the welfare state. The legacy of assimilation should be turned into a new kind of future with decolonisation (Smith, 1999) and empowerment (Bishop & Glynn, 1999).

Developing the practices of Sámi education necessitates the creating of a pedagogy that leans on Sámi culture (Keskitalo & Määttä, 2011). In order to make Sámi education cultural-sensitive, it has to perceive the meaning of the socialisation task of the school organisation. Therefore, it should also be considered what kind of cultural well-being Sámi education constructs (see also Yosso's (2006) model of communal and cultural well-being). The curriculum that leans on Sámi conception of time, place, and knowledge should provide such a learning environment, teaching activity, and didactics that it is not bound to a specific subject (Keskitalo, 2010; Keskitalo et al., 2011). It is important to develop the Sámi's own curriculum, strengthen the position of their own language, create cultural-sensitive teaching arrangements, and diversify the extensive cooperation. All this aims at improving the indigenous people's overall well-being and equality as the curriculum supports teaching by having indigenous peoples' culture, knowledge, and information in the centre. Such a curriculum which combines the indigenous people's knowledge and western way of thinking should be developed in active cooperation with the indigenous people's community (see also Darnell & Hoëm, 1996).

In the old culture, the conception of time was sun-centred and bound to observe the nature (Helander & Kailo, 1999). That is not the case in today's schools and therefore, schedules, physical spaces, and working methods are important if we want to develop teaching (Cuban, 1993/1984). For example, Sámi education should be organised in a more flexible way by giving up the 45-minute scheduling. In addition, the Sámi's eight seasons should be utilised (Rasmus, 2004). Furthermore, the Sámi conception of space is not bound to square feet, but is merely circular (see Fjellström, 1985). In teaching arrangements, the Sámi conception of space could be brought out by heading outside to the surrounding society and nature to explore interdependency of people and nature instead of staying in the classroom. Gregory Cajete argues that indigenous peoples' education should pay attention to the cultural foundation of teaching and learning where educational processes are based on traditional values. Adapting the ideas of modern science of education with the traditional idea is complicated and necessitates cooperation with various directions (Cajete, 1994).

The diversity and cultural value of the learning materials that are included in the curriculum should be paid attention to (King & Schiermann, 2004; see also Hoppers, 2002; Macfarlane, 2004). Well-functioning education of indigenous peoples advances the indigenous peoples' language usage, but also supports the proficiency of national and international languages to support intercultural understanding and tolerance. Learning materials in indigenous peoples' language should be produced and tested locally and the whole teaching and especially teaching reading skills should focus on the indigenous children's own language at the initial phase of education. Native speakers of indigenous peoples' languages should be hired as teachers (King & Schiermann, 2004).

One of the biggest challenges is to help pupils become independent and active learners. Information technology has to be put to use in teaching. In addition, children have to be provided opportunities to search for information and to learn not only within the classroom walls but also outside the classroom. Teachers have to adapt new roles as the instructors of learning in such situations where pupils would take more responsibility on learning events. It is difficult also for pupils. However, the question is only about practicing and getting used to the new methods. When adapting the traditional Sámi upbringing and knowledge at the Sámi teaching, teaching should lean on the ideas of social constructivism and reform pedagogy more powerfully. Jan Henry Keskitalo (2009) refers to it with the term '*sámi skuvlamáhttu*' (Sámi school knowledge).

Developing the school is an all-round happening that concerns the whole personnel and pupils as well as requires cooperation with families, the community and society. Comprehensive development helps and supports teachers' work. Teachers' efficient work demands inner motivation and commitment to the class and the school. External change in the administrative structures does not solely guarantee efficient learning; nor does the reconstruction of education change the way of working in the classroom. The new kind of thinking and new working methods have to be adopted before action can change for good. The change takes place as teachers' pedagogical skills develop. Teachers' mastery over the subject contents and pedagogical thinking and action are important when the goal is to improve the efficiency of teaching. To guarantee the quality of teaching, the focus has to be on the improvement of an individual teacher's skills and motivation; but at the same time, the inner structures of school have to be developed so that they support good teaching. The shared value basis at school and mutual support among the personnel are crucial factors.

Discussion

Already back to the 1910s, author Johan Turi questioned the content of Sámi education:

> Five-year-long education is good for the poor Sámi because children can spend their time at school the time they are not yet capable of working for their keep. And that is good too, that children learn to read and write and count, so that traders cannot cheat them everywhere as well as landowners who have deceived in accounting and by giving people a drink earlier. But school does, indeed, mutilate Lappish children. They are well educated, though, but at the same time, they learn plenty of unnecessary information. The worst thing is that they adopt the landowner's nature to a great extent: they are obliged to go away from among the Sámi when in the best learning age and so they learn landowner's life and fail to learn the Sámi life. And their nature change as well: the Sámi nature disappears and landowner's nature is adopted. And many children at the crown's school have trouble with bosom. But there are not any schools in the Sámi's own homes; they have to put their children where the schools are, although it does not feel good. (Turi, 1910, p. 34)

Turi's text can be understood as a criticism towards the school system although he also realises the meaning of school in the modernising and diversifying world. Turi also mentions the role of the school in the colonisation of the Sámi. Turi's perceptions give motivation to look for an answer to the question of how the modern school meets the need of Sámi children and their upbringing. Is the school capable of exploiting the traditional model of Sámi upbringing and Sámi thinking by combining the disciplines of western science of education and thus find solutions and models for organising Sámi education?

Obviously, there is no turning back. Given the cultural and linguistic reality at school (see Bailey, 1991), the starting point for the challenge of developing Sámi education is the need for paradigmatic change (Kuokkanen, 2000). Graham Smith uses the term 'conscientization'. According to Smith, in decolonisation, the colonisers and the history of colonisation are placed in the centre. It is necessary to improve indigenous peoples' situation through conscientisation so that capacity-building, curriculum development, growing both horizontally and vertically, reclaiming equity definitions, putting equity emphasis and accountability on access, participation, retention, and success for indigenous students are considered. Conscientisation functions as transformative action and resistance in a lineal progression (Smith, 2003).

References

Act on Children's Day Care. (1973/36). Ministry of Justice, Finland. Retrieved February 2, 2012, from Finlex data base http://www.finlex.fi/fi/laki/alkup/1973/19730036

Act on the Sámi Parliament. (1995/974). Ministry of Justice, Finland. Retrieved June 7, 2011, from Finlex data base http://www.finlex.fi/fi/laki/kaannokset/1995/en19950974.pdf

Aikio, M. (1988). *Saamelaiset kielenvaihdon kierteessä. Kielisosiologinen tutkimus viiden saa-melaiskylän kielenvaihdosta 1920–1980* [The Sámi in the vortex of language exchange. A language-sociological research on language exchange in five Sámi villages between 1920 and 1980]. Helsinki: Finnish Literature Society.

Aikio, A. (2003). Sámi skuvla – máŋggakultuvrralaš servodaga skuvla. In V. Hirvonen (Ed.), *Sámi áddejupmi ja sámi skuvla* [Sami understanding and Sami education] (pp. 66–70). Nordic Sami Educational Research Conference Kautokeino in November 7th–9th 2001. SUC Report 1-(2003). Guovdageaidnu: Sámi allaskuvla/Samisk høgskole.

Aikio-Puoskari, U. (2007). Saamelaisopetus osana suomalaista peruskoulua – kielenvaihdoksen vai revitalisaation edistäjä? [Sámi teaching as a part of Finnish primary school – contributor to language shift or revitalization?]. In J. Ylikoski & A. Aikio (Eds.), *Sámit, sánit, sátnehá-mit. Riepmočála Pekka Sammallahtii miesseménu 21. beaivve 2007* [Sámis, words, phrases. A Festschrift for Pekka Sammallahti on the occasion of his 60th birthday on May 21, 2007] (pp. 73–84). (Mémoires de la Société Finno-Ougrienne No. 253). Helsinki: The Finno-Ugric Society.

Anaya, J. (2011). *Report of the Special Rapporteur on the situation of human rights and funda-mental freedoms of indigenous people.* New York, NY: United Nations. Retrieved June 28, 2011, from http://unsr.jamesanaya.org/country-reports/the-situation-of-the-sami-people-in-the-sapmi-region-of-norway-sweden-and-finland-2011

Anzaldúa, G. (1999/1987). *Borderlands – La frontera.* San Francisco, CA: Aunt Lute Books.

Bailey, C. (1991). *Start-up multiculturalism. Integrate the Canadian cultural reality in your classroom!* Ontario: Pembroke Publishers.

Balto, A. (1997). *Sámi mánáidbajásgeassin nuppástuvvá* [Sámi childrearing in change]. Oslo: ad Notam Gyldendal.

Banks, J.A. (1997/1989). Approaches to multicultural curriculum reform. In J.A. Banks & C.A. McGee Banks (Eds.), *Multicultural education. Issues and perspectives* (pp. 229–250). Needham Heights, MA: Allyn & Bacon.

Bartels, D.A., & Bartels, A.L. (1995). *When the North was red. Aboriginal education in Soviet Siberia*. Montreal: McGill-Queen's University Press.

Basic Education Act. (1983/476). Retrieved July 6, 2011, from Finlex database http://www. finlex.fi/fi/laki/alkup/1983/19830476

Bishop, R., & Glynn, T. (1999). *Culture counts. Changing power relations in education.* Palmerston North: Dunmore Press.

Cajete, G. (1994). *Look to the mountain: An ecology of indigenous education.* Durango, CO: Kivaki Press.

Carpelan, C. (2003). *Saamelaisuuden vaiheet. Saamelaiskulttuurin ensyklopedia* [The phases of the Sámi. The encyclopaedia of Saami culture]. Helsinki: University of Helsinki. Retrieved July 6, 2011, from http://www-db.helsinki.fi/cgi-bin/thw?${BASE}=saami&${OOHTML}= docu&${TRIPSHOW}=format=artfi&R=1993

Chacón, H., Yanez, F., & Larriva, G. (2010). Ecuadorian Amazonian cultures: Theoretical approaches to the training of researchers. In J.C. Llorente, K. Kantasalmi, & J. De Dios Simon (Eds.), *Approaching indigenous knowledge. Complexities of the research process* (pp. 47–68). Helsinki: University of Helsinki.

Cuban, L. (1993/1984). *How teachers taught. Constancy and change in American classrooms 1880–1990* (2nd ed.). New York, NY: Teachers College Press.

Darnell, F., & Hoëm, A. (1996). *Taken to extremes: Education in the far North.* Oslo: Scandinavian University Press.

Ellsworth, E. (1997). *Teaching positions: Difference, pedagogy and the power of address.* New York, NY: Columbia University.

Finnish Environmental Administration. (2011). *Lapin rakennusperintö* [The construction heritage of Lapland]. Helsinki: Finnish Environmental Administration. Retrieved July 4, 2011, from http://www.ymparisto.fi/default.asp?node=3906&lan=fi#a1

Finnish National Board of Education. (2004). *The national core curriculum for basic education 2004*. Helsinki: Finnish National Board of Education. Retrieved June 16, 2011, from http:// www.oph.fi/english/publications/2009/national_core_curricula_for_basic_education

Fjellström, P. (1985). *Samernas samhälle. I tradition och nutid* [The society of Sámi people. In tradition and today]. Stockholm: Norstedt & Söners Förlag.

Helander, E., & Kailo, K. (1999). *Ei alkua ei loppua. Saamelaisten puheenvuoro* [No beginning no end. The Sámi statement]. Helsinki: LIKE.

Hirvonen, V. (2003/2004). *Sámi culture and the Sámi school. Reflections by Sámi teachers and the realization of the Sámi school. An evaluation study of reform 97.* Karasjok: ČálliidLágádus.

Hirvonen, V., & Balto, A. (2008). Iešmearrideapmi sámi oahppo- ja skuvlensuorggis [Self-government in Sámi schooling]. In J.B. Henriksen (Ed.), *Sámi iešmearrideapmi* [Sámi self-government] (pp. 104–123). Gáldu cála: Álgoálbmotvuoigatvuođaid áigečála.

Hollins, E.R. (2008). Foreword. In H. Kohl (Ed.), *Culture in school learning: Revealing the deep meaning* (pp. xi–xii). New York, NY: Routledge.

hooks, b. (1994). *Teaching to transgress: Education as the practice of freedom.* New York, NY: Routledge.

Hoppers, C.A.O. (2002). Indigenous knowledge and the integrations of knowledge systems. Towards a conceptual and methodological framework. In C.A.O. Hoppers (Ed.), *Indigenous knowledge and the integration of knowledge systems: Towards a philosophy of articulation* (pp. 2–22). Claremont, CA: New Africa Books.

International Labour Organization (ILO). (1996/2011). *Convention no. 169.* Geneva, Switzerland: United Nations. Retrieved from http://www.ilo.org/indigenous/Conventions/no169/lang–en/index.htm

Keskitalo, J.H. (2003). School improvement among indigenous groups of the circumpolar north. Sámi áddejupmi ja sámi skuvla [Sami understanding and Sami education]. In V. Hirvonen (Ed.), *Nordic Sámi educational research conference. Kautokeino November 7th and 9th 2001* (pp. 45–50). Guovdageaidnu: Saami university College.

Keskitalo, J.H. (2009). *Sámi máhttu ja sámi skuvlamáhttu: Teorehtalaš geahčastat. Sámi diečalaš áigečála 1–2* [Sámi knowledge and Sámi school knowledge: Theoretical overview]. Guovdageaidnu: Sámi allaskuvla.

Keskitalo, P. (2010). *Saamelaiskoulun kulttuurisensitiivisyyttä etsimässä kasvatusantropologian keinoin* [Cultural sensitivity in the Sámi School through educational anthropology] (Diečut 1/2010). Guovdageaidnu: Sámi allaskuvla.

Keskitalo, P., & Määttä, K. (2011). *Sámi pedagogihka iešvuođat / Saamelaispedagogiikan perusteet / The Basics of Sámi Pedagogy / Grunderna i samisk pedagogik / Основы саамской педк.* Rovaniemi: Lapland University Press.

Keskitalo, P., Määttä, K., & Uusiautti, S. (2011). Toward the practical framework of Sámi education. *British Journal of Educational Research, 1*(2), 84–106.

Keskitalo, P., & Määttä, K. (in press-a). How do the Sámi culture and school culture converge – or do they. *The Australian Journal of Indigenous Education.*

Keskitalo, P., & Määttä, K. (in press-b). The linguistic special features of the Sámi education. *Indian Journal of Applied Linguistics.*

King, L., & Schiermann, S. (2004). *The challenge of indigenous education: Practice and perspectives.* Paris: UNESCO.

Kuokkanen, R. (2000). Towards an 'indigenous paradigm' from a Sami perspective. *The Canadian Journal of Native Studies, 20*(2), 411–436.

Kuokkanen, R. (2009). *Boaris dego eana. Eamiálbmogiid diehtu, filosofiijat ja dutkan* [Old like the Earth. Knowledge, philosophy and research of indigenous peoples]. Kárášjohka: ČálliidLágádus.

Lassila, J. (2001). *Lapin koulutushistoria – kirkollinen alkuopetus, kansa-, perus- ja oppikoulut, osa 2* [The history of education in Finnish Lapland – elementary education carried out by the Church, primary schools, comprehensive schools and secondary schools, Part 2]. Oulu: University of Oulu.

Lehtola, V.P. (2011). *Elinkeinot* [Livelihoods]. Guovdageaidnu: Gáldu. Retrieved July 4, 2011, from http://www.galdu.org/web/index.php?sladja=25&vuolitsladja=11&vuolitvuolitsladja=4&giella1=spa

Lindgren, A.-R. (2000). *Helsingin saamelaiset ja oma kieli* [The Sámi of Helsinki and own language]. Helsinki: Finnish Literature Society.

Lipka, J., Mohatt, G.V., & the Ciulistet Group (Eds.) (1998). *Transforming the culture of schools. Yup'ik Eskimo examples.* Mahwah, NJ: Lawrence Erlbaum Associates.

Macfarlane, A.H. (2004). *Kia hiwa ra! listen to culture – Maori students' plea to educators.* Wellington: New Zealand Council for Educational Research.

Matriculation Examination Board of Finland. (2002). *Ylioppilastutkinnon juhlavuosi* [The jubilee year of matriculation examination]. Helsinki: Matriculation Examination Board. Retrieved July 12, 2011, from http://www.ylioppilastutkinto.fi/fi/ylioppilastutkinto/150/

Ministry of Education and Culture. (2004). Decree 132/428. Helsinki.

Nordic Sámi Convention. (2005). *Pohjoismainen saamelaissopimus. 13. marraskuuta 2002 nimitetyn suomalais-norjalais-ruotsalais-saamelaisen asiantuntijatyöryhmän 27. lokakuuta 2005 luovuttama luonnos* [Sámi Convention in the Nordic Countries: An outline handed in 27 Oct 2005 by a Finnish-Norwegian-Swedish-Sámi work group established in 13 Nov 2002]. Oslo: Arbeids- og inkluderingsdepartementet.

Pautamo, E. (2010). *Saamenkielisten aineenopettajien koulutuksen nykytila ja kehittämistarpeet* [The present state and development needs of the Sámi-speaking subject teacher education]. Oulu: University of Oulu. Retrieved July 11, 2011, from http://www.oulu.fi/giellagas/tiedostot/AJANKOHTAISTA/Aineenopettajakoulutus%20raportti_2010.pdf

Rasmus, E.-L. (2004). *Saamelaisen identiteetin merkitys Utsjoen nuorille. Kasvatusantropologinen tutkimus saamelaisten maailmankuvasta ja identiteetistä* [The Sámi identity and its meaning for the Sámi youth in Utsjoki. Educational anthropological research about worldview and identity of the Sámi people] (Master's thesis). University of Lapland, Rovaniemi.

Rasmus, M. (2006). *Bággu vuolgit, bággu birget – Sámemánáid ceavzinstrategiijat Suoma álbmotskuvlla ásodagain 1950–1960-loguin* [Force to leave, force to survive – survival strategies of Sámi children in Finnish Elementary School Boarding Houses in 1950's and 1960's] (Master's thesis). University of Oulu, Oulu.

Saamen kielilaki [The Sámi Language Act]. (1086/2003). Retrieved July 12, 2011, from Finlex data base http://www.finlex.fi/fi/laki/alkup/2003/20031086

Sanila-Aikio, T. (2011). *Koltansaamen äidinkielen koe ylioppilaskirjoituksiin* [The matriculation examination of the first language in the Skolt Sámi language]. Kolttauutisia [Skolt News] in 8 Feb 2011. Retrieved July 12, 2011, from http://oddaz.saaminuett.fi/2011/02/08/koltansaamen-aidinkielen-koe-ylioppilaskirjoituksiin/

Schein, E.H. (1992). *Organizational culture and leadership* (2nd ed.). San Francisco, CA: Jossey-Bass.

Singh, M., Kenway, J., & Apple, M.W. (2005). Globalizing education: Perspectives from above and below. In M.W. Apple, J. Kenway, & M. Singh (Eds.), *Globalizing education: Policies, pedagogies, & politics* (pp. 1–29). New York, NY: Peter Lang.

Skutnabb-Kangas, T. (2008). Bilingual education and sign language as the mother tongue of deaf children. In B. Kellett, J. Cynthia, & E. Ochse (Eds.), *English in international deaf communication* (pp. 75–94). Bern: Peter Lang.

Smith, L.T. (1999). *Decolonizing methodologies: Research and indigenous peoples*. London: Zed Books.

Smith, G. (2003). *Kaupapa Maori theory: Theorizing indigenous transformation of education & schooling*. New Zealand: The University of Auckland & Te Whare Wananga o Awanuiarangi. Retrieved March 10, 2011, from http://www.aare.edu.au/03pap/pih03342.pdf

The Constitution of Finland. (731/1999). Finland: Ministry of Justice. Retrieved June 28, 2011, from http://www.finlex.fi/fi/laki/kaannokset/1999/en19990731.pdf

The Constitution of the Russian Federation. (1993). *Adopted at National Voting on December 12, 1993*. Transl. Garant-Service. Retrieved from http://www.constitution.ru/en/10003000-01.htm

The Encyclopaedia of Saami Culture [Saamelaiskulttuurin ensyklopedia] (2003). Helsinki: University of Helsinki. Retrieved July 6, 2011, from http://www.helsinki.fi/~sugl_smi/senc/esittely.htm

The Sámi Parliament. (2008). *The Sámi in Finland*. Inari: The Sámi Parliament.

Turi, J. (1910). *Muittalus samid birra* [A story about the Sámi]. Stockholm: Nordiska bokhandeln AB.

United Nations. (2007). *Permanent forum of indigenous issues. Frequently asked questions declaration on the rights of inigenous peoples*. Retrieved May 30, 2011, from http://www.un.org/esa/socdev/unpfii/documents/FAQsindigenousdeclaration.pdf

Valtioneuvoston selonteot (VNS) [The Council of State Reports]. (2009). *Valtioneuvoston selonteko Suomen ihmisoikeuspolitiikasta* [The Council of State report on Finland's human rights policy]. Retrieved July 11, 2011, from Edilex data base http://www.edilex.fi/virallistieto/mt/uavm20100001

Ventsel, A., & Dudeck, S. (1995). *Do the Khanty need a Khanty curriculum? Indigenous concepts of school education*. Fürstenberg/Havel, Deutschland: Kulturstiftung Sibirien. Siberian Studies. Retrieved January 24, 2011, from http://www.siberian-studies.org/publications/PDF/beventseldudeck.pdf

Vuolab-Lohi, K. (2007). *Pohjoissaamen kielen tilanne sekä kehittämistarpeet* [The situation of the North Sámi language and its development needs]. Retrieved July 12, 2011, from http://www.kotus.fi/files/742/pohjoisSelvitys.pdf

Yosso, T.J. (2006). *Critical race counterstories along the Chicana/Chicano educational pipeline*. New York, NY: Routledge.

Having, loving, and being: children's narrated well-being in Finnish day care centres

Anna-Maija Puroila, Eila Estola and Leena Syrjälä

The aim of this study is to answer the following question: what do children tell about their well-being in Finnish day care centres? The theoretical and methodological framework of this study is based on a narrative approach. The research material was collected by participating in the everyday life of three groups of children and listening to their narratives. The research material, consisting of observations and tape-recorded conversations, is reflected in a model of well-being developed by a Finnish sociologist, Erik Allardt. This model consists of three dimensions: having, loving, and being. With the intention of understanding children's well-being, the meanings of having, loving, and being are explored. Instead of arguing for one objective truth, this study offers diverse narratives, conveying both positive and negative experiences of children's well-being. The most positive experiences deal with inspiring and enabling material environment, responsive adults, good friends, and opportunities for meaningful activities. Darker shades permeate the narratives characterised by unyielding institutional structures, children's separateness from adults, the exclusion from peer relationships, and not being respected as a subject. This study demonstrates both potentials and limitations involved in narrative methodology when exploring young children's experienced well-being.

1. Introduction

Titta [3 years] shows little figures saying: 'Look, I have Cinderella! I bought this with my mum from the market yesterday. And this is Bella and this is the Sleeping Beauty'.

Pete [6 years] says to his mother: 'Last week and today were dull because all the other pre-schoolers were picked up so early, and I didn't have any mates. Those who stayed at the day care centre didn't play with me'.

Pete [6 years] says to me: 'I had a good day at the day care centre yesterday. We had a very pleasant ... sort of ... stall in the corner of the hall. We brought all kinds of things there'.

These excerpts represent the voices of young children in Finnish day care centres. In the first extract, Titta introduces new toys that she has brought from her home to the centre. The second extract addresses a situation in which Pete has been rejected by the other children. The third extract is about a play that has inspired Pete. These excerpts give us glimpses of issues that children view as meaningful at the day care centre. Do these issues have something to do with children's well-being? Many educators, policy-makers, and researchers share the idea that promoting children's well-being is the over-arching goal of education and an indicator of the quality of educational institutions (e.g. Mayr & Ulich, 2009). More difficult questions are as follows: What is the well-being of a child? How do adults know how children experience their well-being?

In the past 10 years, researchers in many disciplines including the social sciences, economics, the medical and nursing sciences, psychology, and education have been interested in children's well-being. Endeavours in defining, measuring, monitoring, and analysing the realms of well-being are numerous. As Camfield, Streuli, and Wood-head (2009) argued, research on children's well-being includes diverse approaches, conceptualisations, and methodologies. The concept of well-being is often linked to other concepts, such as needs, health, economic wealth, social inclusion, happiness, and life satisfaction, or their converses – deprivation, illness, poverty, social exclusion, and dissatisfaction (see Axford, 2009; Camfield et al., 2009; Crivello, Camfield, & Woodhead, 2009). Increasingly, citizenship and children's rights are connected with discussions of well-being (e.g. Ben-Arieh, 2010; Ben-Arieh & Boyer, 2005; Bradshaw, Hoelscher, & Richardson, 2007; Camfield et al., 2009; McAuley, Morgan, & Rose, 2010; Morrow & Mayall, 2009). The conceptual multiplicity of well-being is regarded both as a challenge and as having advantages. On the one hand, the concept of well-being has been characterised as confusing and pervasive (Camfield et al., 2009; McAuley & Rose, 2010; Morrow & Mayall, 2009); on the other hand, researchers have noted that the view of children's well-being has provided a unifying framework for collaboration between scholars in different research areas (McAuley & Rose, 2010; Morrow & Mayall, 2009). Axford (2009) argued that different lenses may even be useful because each sheds a different light on children's well-being.

Since the 1960s, a large body of research has focused on developing indicators of children's well-being (Ben-Arieh, 2010; Fattore, Mason, & Watson, 2007). The interest in indicators grew out of policy demands to create tools for measuring children's con-ditions and the outcomes of programmes aimed at promoting children's lives (Ben-Arieh, 2010). Recently, indicator-based research has been challenged theoretically and methodologically. Fattore et al. (2007, p. 11) argued that the dominant approaches of indicator-based research reflect a positivist model of knowledge, 'a model which assumes the existence of facts about well-being which, when identified and organised into domains, will allow manipulation of causes and effects and guide investment in the future of our society'. This perspective is contrasted with constructivist views, which emphasise children's well-being as a socially constructed, context-specific, and vari-able phenomenon (Camfield et al., 2009; Fattore et al., 2007). From the constructivist point of view, research on children's well-being should take into account the dynamic, contextual, and cultural nature of the phenomenon and especially children's own per-spectives (Fattore et al., 2007; McAuley & Rose, 2010).

Until recently, children themselves have been disregarded in research on their well-being. The younger the children, the less research there is on children's own experiences of well-being. Recent research literature highlights the need to develop appropriate research methodologies that facilitate children's participation in research (Fattore et al., 2007; McAuley & Rose, 2010). Several researchers argue for a strategy of 'asking children directly' about their well-being (e.g. Ben-Arieh, 2010; McAuley et al., 2010).

We approach young children's well-being from a narrative point of view. By employing a narrative approach, we attempt to take a further step in developing research methodologies sensitive to young children's experiences of their well-being. This article is based on our research project 'Children's storied daily lives in day care centres'. We aim to answer the following question: What do children tell about their well-being in Finnish day care centres? We reflect on our empirical material in a classical model of well-being developed by a Finnish sociologist, Allardt (1976). In this framework, well-being is defined as a state in which it is possible for a child to satisfy both material and non-material basic needs (Allardt, 1976; Konu & Rimpelä, 2002). Allardt's (1976) model highlights three dimensions of well-being: *having* (needs related to material resources), *loving* (needs related to social relation-ships), and *being* (the need for respect as a member of society). Although Allardt's model was developed in the 1970s, it has proved to be applicable to contemporary dis-cussions on children's well-being (e.g. Konu & Rimpelä, 2002). Allardt (1976) empha-sised the subjective elements of well-being, arguing that people should have an opportunity to express their own views of their well-being. From this viewpoint, the model seems to offer fertile ground for exploring children's views of their well-being in the context of a day care centre.

2. Opening the doors of Finnish day care centres

In Finland, every child under the compulsory school age (seven years) has a subjective right to municipal day care after the parental leave. The municipalities have an obli-gation to arrange day care for all children whose parents choose to have it. The percen-tage of Finnish children attending municipal day care is 56.7%, with wide variations in the ages of children (Säkkinen & Kuoppala, 2010). The main forms of the services are day care centres, family day care homes, and pre-school classes. The day care centres are staffed by kindergarten teachers, trained nurses, and assistants. Kindergarten tea-chers complete a bachelor's degree in early childhood education (universities) or social sciences (universities of applied sciences). There must be one trained adult for every four children under the age of three years and one trained adult for every seven children over the age of three years. At least one-third of the day care centre staff must be kindergarten teachers (Niikko, 2006; OECD, 2006). The national curricu-lum guidelines (Stakes, 2004) serve as the basis for the implementation and pedagogy of early childhood education. The curriculum guidelines stress care and education as an integrated whole and early childhood education as part of lifelong learning. According to the curriculum guidelines, 'the principal target of ECEC is to promote the child's overall well-being so as to ensure the best possible conditions for growth, learning and development' (Stakes, 2004, p. 15).

We conducted our research among three groups of children: Roses, Violets, and Raindrops (Table 1). All the groups belonged to municipal day care centres located in urban districts in northern Finland.

In terms of pedagogical culture, each group formed an environment of its own. The staff in Violets and Roses applied the primary caregiver approach to their practices. This approach stems from Bowlby's theory, emphasising secure attachment and posi-tive relationships between the child and caregivers (see Ebbeck & Yim, 2009). In Violets, each staff member was responsible for a group of four children. The primary caregiver focused on the daily routines of her 'own' children and communi-cated with their parents. The small groups acted closely with the primary caregiver

Table 1. The groups of children.

	Violets	Roses	Raindrops
Children	12 children	22 children	22 children
	Age: one to three years	Age: three to five years	Age: three to seven years
	5 girls, 7 boys	13 girls, 9 boys	11 girls, 11 boys
	12 full time	22 full time	6 full time, 16 part time
	11 Finnish, 1 other than Finnish	22 Finnish	18 Finnish, 4 other than Finnish
Staff	1 female teacher	2 female teachers	1 female teacher
	2 female nurses	1 female nurse	2 female nurses
	1 female assistant (part time)		1–2 female assistants (full time)
Operating hours	6.30 a.m.–5 p.m.	6.30 a.m.–5 p.m.	6.30 a.m.–5 p.m.
Indoor space	2 rooms	2 rooms	3 rooms
	Corridor	Corridor	Corridor
	Toilet	Toilet	Toilet

throughout the day. In Roses, the staff members had from seven to eight children in their groups. However, the divisions between the small groups were flexible. For the observing researcher, it was not clear which children belonged to a particular small group. Most of the time, the children's activities were organised on a whole-group basis. In the daily schedule, there was a lot of space for the children's free play. In Raindrops, the schedule was highly structured and the emphasis was on adult-directed activities. Each day contained two or three circle times initiated and directed by the adults. The circle times focused on various learning activities and topics, for instance, talking about the calendar and topical matters, nature and the environment, literature, letters, numbers, music, gymnasiums and sports, and arts and crafts.

3. Our point of departure: children's narrated well-being

We approach children's well-being in day care centres from a narrative viewpoint rooted in the constructivist tradition (Sparkes & Smith, 2008; Spector-Mersel, 2010). Along with Sparkes and Smith (2008), we assume that we live in a story-shaped world: stories and narratives constitute social realities, and they have a central place in human existence. Thus, we are not interested in children's well-being as a stable, objective reality that is 'out there', but as a fluid, multifaceted phenomenon constructed through narratives. At the epistemological level, we understand narratives both as a means of knowing and as a way of telling (Bruner, 1990). We share the view that human beings organise and communicate their experiences through narratives (Bruner, 1990; Engel, 2006; Smidt, 2011).

We understand the concept of narrative as a dynamic meeting place where children are active participants and employ many means of expressing, organising, and communicating their experiences (Ahn & Filipenkò, 2007). Our interest is in children's narration as a contextually embedded meaning-making process rather than as the finished product of a well-formed story (Ochs & Caps, 2001). We presume that young children's means of expressing and communicating their experiences are not restricted to their verbal language. In addition to words, children's narratives involve, for example, other linguistic means, emotional expressions, action, body language, play, and art (see Ahn & Filipenko, 2007; Engel, 2006).

The notion of the holistic and multimodal nature of young children's narratives has consequences for our research methodology. Rather than 'asking children directly', we apply a methodology that encourages the exploration of the rich variation of children's expressions of their experiences. Listening to children's narratives requires more than just listening with our ears. Children's multimodal narratives call for living the narratives together with children and listening to the hundreds of languages, symbols, and codes that they use to express their well-being (see Butler-Kisber, 2010; Rinaldi, 2008). In the narration process, telling and listening intertwine, and the narratives become more or less multi-voiced. Although children are active participants, the narratives of our research are not exclusively children's creations. Rather, they are co-constructed in interactions between children and various interlocutors: other children, family members, staff, and the researchers.

After receiving consent from the children, parents, staff members, and the city, we carried out field work over the course of one and a half years. Two of the authors participated in the everyday life of Violets, Roses, and Raindrops. They have a background as kindergarten teachers and also practical experience of working in day care centres. Presumably, our previous experiences influenced our observations as well as our interpretations. When participating in children's everyday life, our purpose was to listen responsively and with ethical sensitivity to the children in order to gain insights into their lived and experienced well-being. Depending on the situation, our role varied between an observing listener and an active interlocutor. We co-constructed a vast amount of research material by means of multiple methods.

This article is based on our observation material and tape-recorded conversations. We transcribed our observation material and reformulated it into multimodal narratives (episodes). Each of the 467 episodes contains at least one event in which the children were involved. The length of the episodes varies from a few minutes to two hours. The episodes deal with diverse occasions, for example, conversational encounters, play situations, circle times, handicraft and drawing situations, transitions from one activity to another, outdoor activities, and meal times. In the tape-recorded conversations, children tell their family members, staff members, or researchers about their life in the day care centres.

The analysis proceeded through three phases (Table 2). In the first phase, we analysed and interpreted our data inductively using the thematic analysis of narratives (Riessman, 2008) in order to identify relevant themes for children's well-being. As a result, we found five preliminary themes: social relationships, learning and capabilities, emotions, activities, and physical growth and development. In the second phase, we reflected on the preliminary themes with Allardt's (1976) model of well-being, consisting of having, loving, and being. We noticed that we can reduce our preliminary themes into the categories of *loving* and *being*. We recognised that we had not paid attention to the perspective of *having* appearing in children's narratives. In the third phase, we reread and reinterpreted our research material with the intention of understanding meanings of having, loving, and being in children's narratives. The findings of this article are based on our field work and the broad material that we have analysed and interpreted. We use a small selection of narratives to illustrate the various meanings of having, loving, and being with regard to children's well-being.

Table 2. Phases of analysis.

Phase 1: thematic analysis	Phase 2: reflecting	Phase 3: interpreting the meanings of having, loving, and being
	HAVING	Material conditions and fulfilling basic needs Potential *vs*. realised having Collective *vs*. individual having Having, not having, dreaming to have Children as consumers Material objects as resources in negotiating social relationships and constructing identity
Social relationships Emotions	LOVING	Child–adult relationship as responsive care: responsiveness, attachment, touch, emotional expressions, sustained interaction, and humour Child–adult relationship reflecting separateness: scarce interaction, avoiding emotional expressions and touch, and adults' practical and controlling role Peer relationships: best friends, negotiating the relationships, including and excluding, social statuses, and conflicts
Physical growth and development Learning and capabilities Activities	BEING	Age-related social order Individual child *vs*. group of children Children's free choice *vs*. institutional practices Children's autonomy *vs*. adults' authority Children's learning *vs*. adults' teaching Being here and now *vs*. becoming in the future

4. Having – the material well-being of children

The perspective of *having* draws attention to the material resources of the day care centres and fulfilment of the basic needs of the children. The material resources consist of physical spaces, equipment, and furnishings as well as the other material goods and impersonal objects of the centres. At first glance, Finnish day care centres seem to offer good material conditions for children's well-being. This is also what international surveys tell us about the well-being of Finnish children (e.g. Bradshaw et al., 2007). When looking at the material environments of the centres, we noticed that they are designed especially for children. The yards are marked out with fences and equipped with swings, sandboxes, and climbing frames. The buildings are quite new. The indoor spaces are warm and clean, albeit sometimes noisy. The furniture for children is of a small size. The shelves are full of children's books, games, toys, and material for drawing and crafts. The children's basic needs are fulfilled. They are offered warm meals twice a day and they have opportunities for rest. They are taught hygiene, such as washing their hands after going to the toilet. They take a xylitol pill after every meal. Altogether, the material environments and the daily practices reflect the aim of promoting children's well-being in terms of health, physical safety, and positive development. However, we were curious to have a closer look at how the relationship between young children and material resources is constructed in the narratives.

Having food, but dislike eating it

It is breakfast time in the group of Roses. Jonas [5][1] says that he has already had breakfast at home.... It is now lunch time. Jonas says that he doesn't like the food. The teacher

EARLY CHILD CARE AND EDUCATION IN FINLAND

cajoles Jonas to eat the food. Jonas eats a little piece of bread but leaves the warm food on the plate.

Having a room for carpentry, but not having permission to use it
Elmeri [6] tells his mother with enthusiasm about a room with carpentry tools in Rain-drops. It appears that Elmeri has not had an opportunity to work in the room. Elmeri even argues that nobody uses the room.

The twig is not a toy
Roses are playing in the yard. Leevi [5], Nuutti [5], and Paavo [4] are developing some kind of fighting play. Leevi has a wooden twig in his hand. It is 'a laser stone'. Leevi gives the twig to Nuutti. Nuutti says, 'Thanks!' An adult notices the twig in Nuutti's hand, grabs it, and throws it away. The adult admonishes, 'Hey, don't hit anyone with that twig!'

Waiting and waiting for swings
For the first time this spring, Raindrops get permission to use the swings and summer toys in the yard. Many children want to play on the swings. Because there are only four swings, they begin to debate who gets to use them and for how long. Liza [6] would like to play on a swing, but she must wait her turn. Finally, Liza's turn comes. A couple of girls are still waiting for their turn. After a while, Anna [5] asks Liza to give her the swing. Liza continues to play. Anna goes to Elina [a staff member] and proposes that it should be her turn to play on a swing. Elina asks Anna to wait a couple of minutes. After a while, Anna again comes to Elina and tells her that it is her turn to play. Elina asks Liza to give the swing to Anna. Liza resists, arguing that other children have been on the swings for a longer time than her. Finally, she gives the swing to Anna.

Introducing new items and wanting more
Roses are coming in from the outside. Sinna [4] asks me to close the inside flaps of her pants.

Sinna: Guess whether these are new or old pants!
Anna-Maija: Well, I think they're new?
Sinna: Yeah. I'm wearing them for the first time. I got these yesterday. And I also got dokmodes.
Anna-Maija: What's a 'dokmode'? Is it a toy?
Sinna: No, it's kind of booklet to colour in.
Reeta [5]: And I've got Shu Shu Pets. I'm going to get a new one because I don't like the pink one. I want a brown one.
Anna-Maija: What will happen to the pink one?
Reeta: I'll put it in the garbage bin.

In many narratives, we noticed the distinction between potential having and realised having. There seems to be some kind of barrier between the child and the use of the material. Sometimes, it is the preference of the child, and sometimes it is the adult's controlling behaviour based on security rules or other institutional practices. Jonas' case is an example of children having individual likes that affect their behaviour. Elmeri's story about the unused space for carpentry and the narrative about children's outdoor play highlight the practices of the staff. The splendid spaces or attractive items do not produce anything 'good' for children if they are allowed only to admire them from afar.

The narratives also include both collective and individual forms of having. The perspective of collective having is obvious because most of the material objects, such as outdoor equipment, toys, books, games, and materials for drawing and crafts, are equally available to all children. The children do not own the material, but they are expected to share the material resources with others. The episode about waiting for swings is an example of what sharing means from the viewpoint of the child. It means, for example, taking turns, waiting for shorter or longer periods, and adapting to the time limits.

An individual form of having also appears in the narratives. The children are dressed in their own clothes and they bring their own toys to the centre. As with Friedman and Neary's (2008) study, we note that children – even the youngest ones – express awareness of the ownership of these objects. Sometimes, they know better than the adults to whom the pieces of clothing, the hair slides, and the toys belong. There is variation among the groups when the children are allowed to bring their own toys to the centre. In Raindrops, there are specific days for the children's own toys, while in Roses and Violets, the children are allowed to bring their own toys every day. The nature of children's own toys contrasts with that of the toys of the centres: The toys of the centres do not include the most trendy ones, such as the Bratz dolls, Bionicle figures, Bakugan figures, Zhu Zhu Pets, Littlest Pets, or Disney princess figures. We listen to numerous children's stories ranging from the perspectives of having to those of not having and dreaming of having the trendy toys. Children introduce their toys and other related products, such as films, books, and computer games, with enthusiasm. They bring toy magazines from their homes to the centre and flip through them, commenting on which of the toys they feel are the most attractive. These stories reveal that children have a lot of knowledge about the products directed at them. As the narrative about introducing new items shows, some objects that are familiar to the children are unfamiliar to the adult researcher. This perspective is consistent with recent research on consumerism that argues for the need to recognise children as consumers (Ruckenstein, 2010; Woodrow & Press, 2007). According to Ruckenstein (2010, p. 359), consumerism appears among children as descriptions of how 'as soon as they get a toy, they might want another one; in the process some of the old toys are redefined as worthless'. This view comes close to Reeta's accounts of her Zhu Zhu Pets.

The function of possessing material objects extends to children's social relationships, identity construction, and self-expression. For instance, when Titta brings new Disney princess figures to Roses, many girls express their willingness to play with her. It is Titta who has the right to choose those happy ones who can play with her figures. This example shows how possession may signify appreciation and power in group affiliations. Our observations are parallel to those of Dittmar (2008), who argued that people use material objects to express who they are and who they would like to be. Material objects, such as clothes and toys, are signs of children's ages, genders, and social identities. This is how the perspectives of having, loving, and being overlap in children's lives at the day care centres.

5. Loving – the quality of relationships

The day care centres provide children with a highly social growing environment. An individual child is compelled to form relationships with many adults and children. The number of potential relationships grows together with the group size. The perspective of *loving* underlines the quality of social relationships recognised in many recent studies on young children and their well-being (e.g. Ebbeck & Yim, 2009; Mayr & Ulich, 2009; McAuley & Rose, 2010; McAuley et al., 2010). According to Allardt (1976), all human needs are not defined through having or mastering material resources. The need for love, companionship, solidarity, and belonging is defined by how people relate to each other. The perspective of loving turns our attention to the child–adult and child–child interactions through which relationships are constructed.

5.1 *Two different stories about child–adult relationships*

An essential feature of the day care centre context is that children are separated from their home environments and family members (Woodrow & Press, 2007). Children are cared for, educated, and taught by adults who orient them on a professional basis rather than on a private one. In the following excerpts, children give their views on adults:

Carers of Elmeri's dreams
Elmeri [6] and his mother are talking about the day care centre of Elmeri's dreams. The mother asks Elmeri what the carers would be like. Elmeri answers, 'I'd know everyone. There would be Dad, Mum, or my big brother ... so I'd like to know everyone. For example, there could be someone like my godmother'.

Getting to know the adults
Perttu [5] is talking with his father and mother about his day care centre. His parents ask him, what annoying experiences he has had. Perttu says that during the first days he felt bad because he didn't know anyone. Mum asks Perttu if he still misses Mum and Dad when staying at the centre. Perttu answers that he does not miss them anymore 'because [he has] got so used to all the adults'.

These narratives show how important it is for the child to know the adult. We may ask how this crucial issue is realised in the lives of the children. Our research material enables us to retell two different stories about child–adult relationships at the day care centres. The following extracts demonstrate the first story, in which the relationships between the children and the adults can be characterised as responsive care (see Ebbeck & Yim, 2009; Swick, 2007).

Getting individualised attention
In Violets, four children are playing together with their primary caregiver, Merja. Luca [1] and Merja go to the bathroom. On her return, Merja sits down on the hallway rug holding Luca in her lap. Iida [1] throws herself on her belly on the floor. Merja realises that Iida feels left out. Merja also takes Iida in her arms. Merja puts the two children in her lap, comforts Iida, and plays with her fingers. Iida calms down.

Joint playing
Merja [adult] is sitting on the floor with her 'own' children in Violets. Piia [1] lies under the blanket. Others sing: 'Nobody knows that I have a small baby (cat, dog, etc.)'. While singing, the other children and Merja stroke Piia under the blanket. At the end of the song, the blanket is removed. After Piia, it is Merja's turn to be under the blanket. Piia and Arttu [2] want to join her. The three lie under the blanket. Then Merja suggests another 'baby' game. Arttu wants to be the baby. He lies on a pillow, and Merja begins to feed him from the plate. Piia laughs and goes to eat from Arttu's plate. Piia and Iida stroke baby Arttu. Merja also strokes him and puts the blanket over him. Arttu laughs and kicks the blanket off.

Receiving admiration
The teacher of Raindrops, Sari, sits down by the side of Olli [6], whose hair has been cut very short. Sari asks, 'Who did your lovely hair?' Olli says that his mother cut his hair. Sari asks if she can smooth his hair. Olli nods. Sari smooths his hair and says, 'This is like a teddy bear!'

These excerpts are all about encounters between an adult and an individual child or a small group of children. We noticed that the encounters contain physical contact, the adults' sensitivity to the children's expressions, responsiveness, and humour. The adults are engaged in interactions with the children, and the children receive individualised attention. The following episodes construct a distinctively different story about child–adult relationships:

Free play
After breakfast, there is time for free play in Roses. Children seek different activities: drawing, playing with blocks, and playing with their own toys. Some children hang around with nothing to do. The adults are talking together.

Sitting quietly – or not?
The children at Raindrops are gathered for circle time with their teacher, Sari. Sari plans to read a book to the children. The children are fidgeting and talking together. Sari asks, 'Do you all have good places to sit down?' Some children complain that Veikko [7] and Lauri [6] are teasing them. Sari threatens to exclude Lauri and Veikko from circle time. Antti [6] asks, 'May I leave for a while with Lauri and Veikko?' Sari does not give anyone permission to leave. She begins to read the book. The children are moving restlessly. Sari has to stop reading many times and ask the children to sit quietly.

Being rebuked
Roses are playing outside. Four girls are sitting in the sandbox. The adults stand apart from the children and talk together. Suddenly Kreeta [3] begins to cry. She has sand in her face. Paula [the adult] goes to her, cleans her face, shakes her clothes, and interrogates Alli [4]. Alli looks confused. 'Why did you throw the sand?', Paula asks. Alli answers quietly, 'I was playing'. Paula firmly tells Alli that she is not allowed to play that kind of game and draws Alli's attention to Kreeta's sandy jacket. Alli whispers that the jacket can be washed. Paula repeats that that kind of play is not allowed.

Crying for no reason
The adults ask the children of Roses to go to the toilet before the outdoor activities. After going to the toilet, Mikael [5] puts on his gloves and scarf, and looks for his cap in his locker. He tells the teacher, with a tearful face and cracking voice, that he can't find his cap. The teacher finds the cap at the bottom of Mikael's locker and says that Mikael has not really looked for the cap and that he should not cry for no reason.

In some of these narratives, for instance, in the free play and in the outdoor situations, the separateness of the children and the adults is obvious. The adults stay at a distance from the children and their function is to create opportunities for the children to act, to ensure their physical safety, and to maintain discipline. Child–adult interaction is scarce, and it mostly focuses either on controlling the children (e.g. talking about rules and intervening misbehaviour) or on practical arrangements (e.g. giving directions and organising the group). The adults rarely take children in their arms, and they avoid touching and expressions of emotion. We also noted that the adults do not encourage children to express their emotions. There is little humour and playfulness in the interaction between children and adults. These observations are consistent with studies highlighting the scarceness of child–staff interaction and the domination of the practical and controlling roles of the adult in the early childhood contexts (e.g. Bae, 2009; Jingbo & Elicker, 2005; Kalliala, 2008; Kyrönlampi-Kylmänen, 2007; Pramling Samuelsson & Johansson, 2009).

The two different stories demonstrate variation in the quality of child–adult relationships. On the basis of previous studies, potential reasons for this may be the children's age and the group sizes (e.g. Jingbo & Elicker, 2005). We argue, however, that the differences in the pedagogical cultures may also frame the quality of the child–adult relationships. Of the groups participating in this research, the adults of Violets are the most committed to the ideology of the primary caregiver approach, emphasising the establishment of early relationships, secure attachments, and sustained, positive child–adult interactions (see Ebbeck & Yim, 2009).

5.2 *Peer relationships: friends, negotiations, rejection, and conflicts*

When exploring children's well-being in terms of loving, we cannot bypass children's relationships with peers. Children express that peer relationships form a crucial part of their daily lives. When the children enter the centre, one of their first activities is to make contact with peers. The children use different communicative strategies: they ask direct questions (e.g. 'Can you play with me?'), they make suggestions (e.g. 'Come and draw with me!'), or they indirectly express their willingness to act together (e.g. by moving near and by showing their own toys). Sometimes, they succeed in joining in the other children's activities; sometimes they are rejected.

Waiting for the best friend
In Roses, Ilari [3] and Veikko [3] mostly play together. This morning, Ilari enters the day care centre before Veikko. Ilari complains that he has no friends. The adult says that Veikko will come soon. Ilari comes to me and introduces a small toy figure, 'When Veikko comes to the day care centre, I'll show him this. He'll ask if this is mine and I'll say that Olli [big brother] gave me this!'

Negotiating relationships
Nuutti [5]: Paavo, should we leave Pekka when we go outside?
Paavo [4]: But he'll follow us.
Pekka [5]: I'll play outside with Veikko.
Nuutti: See, he won't follow us! But, Pekka, do you want to play inside with us?
Pekka: I can play inside and outside with you.

Being rejected
In Raindrops, we see many situations in which the other children don't want to play and work with Julius [6].

In the photographs project, the staff arranges the children into pairs. Julius and Mikko [5] form a pair. When Mikko hears who his partner is, he goes to the other boys, saying (with disgust), 'Imagine who my partner is – Julius! I don't want to be his partner!'

When the adult asks Julius and Anton [5] to help her, Anton says, 'I can help you but not with Julius'.

The adult asks some boys including Julius to play with cards. Julius is mainly looking at how the others are playing and listening to how they talk about the cards. Then, he says in a quiet voice, 'I've got skateboard shoes of my own. I've a skateboard of my own'. Nobody listens, nobody hears, and nobody comments.

Teasing
Timo [5] and Erkka [5] have built a fine, big car using Lego blocks. They have played with it the whole day. Jonas [4] comes and begins to handle the car.

Timo: Jonas, don't touch the car!

Timo and Erkka take the car to another corner of the room. Jonas follows them and begins to touch the car again.

Timo: Don't touch! [in a loud voice] You cannot touch it! Jonas, don't touch!
Erkka [to the teacher]: Jonas is teasing us.

The teacher asks Jonas to build his own car.

The narrative about waiting for the best friend provides an example of an intensive and mutual friendship between two boys. As with previous research, the narratives of our study concern children who develop preferences for certain companions (Dunn, 2004; Hay, Payne, & Chadwick, 2004). Quite often, though not always, the best friends are of the same gender, and the friendships are tight. If the preferred peer is not present, the child misses her or him and may have difficulties in joining the other children's activities.

Some children, however, express more flexibility when choosing friends. For these children, negotiating the relationships becomes an integral aspect of their daily lives. In the conversation between Nuutti, Paavo, and Pekka, it is especially Pekka's position that is being debated about. Is Pekka allowed to join in Nuutti's and Paavo's play and under what conditions? In the negotiations about relationships, the social hierarchies of the groups come up. As the children spend a great deal of their daily lives together, they develop particular social statuses. In each of the three groups, some children are more popular than others. The other children both compete for the favour of the children of high status and resist their domination. There are also children who have difficulties in integrating themselves into peer groups. Julius is an example of a child who often seems to be excluded by his peers. In Raindrops, he is 'an invisible child': the other children do not recognise his absence, nobody misses him, and nobody wants to play or work with him.

There are numerous narratives about conflicts among the children. The reasons for the conflicts are similar to those highlighted in previous studies: the children want to play with the same items; a child enters the territory of another child's play; a child acts or talks in a way that another child does not like; the children disagree about the continuation of their actions (see Rourou, Singer, Bekema, & De Haan, 2006). Sometimes, the source of the conflict is a tongue-lashing or name-calling; sometimes, conflicts develop into fights with hitting and kicking. We noticed that children have different strategies to cope with conflicts. In the last excerpt, Timo attempts to stop Jonas' intrusion by forbidding him, going farther, and changing the tone of his voice. However, the help of an adult is needed to settle the dispute.

Our research demonstrates the joy and the pleasure that children experience when engaging in reciprocal friendships and the upset experienced when being rejected, excluded, or left alone by peers. Based on these observations, we support those researchers arguing for the crucial meaning that peers hold for children's experiences of their lives and well-being (e.g. Dunn, 2004; Hay et al., 2004; Mayr & Ulich, 2009).

6. Being – day care centres as spaces for constructing childhoods

When children enter day care centres, they move from the private arena of their homes to the public arena of the service system. The centres represent spaces for early childhood, organised, regulated, and monitored by the society. As Kjørholt (2008) argued, a day care centre as a space for early childhood does not only mean a concrete, physical space but also means a moral and ideological space, based on societal and cultural assumptions about good childhoods. In Allardt's (1976) conception of well-being, the perspective of *being* refers to the relationship between an individual and society. Allardt emphasised issues such as being respected as a member of society, having political resources, and having opportunities to engage in meaningful activities. Applied to our research, the view of being encourages the examination of the moral and ideological space of childhood constructed in the narratives. What kind of opportunities for participation, influence, and self-realisation do children have? What kind of position is constructed for the children?

Being small or being big?
Roses are having their free play time. Elli [3] wants to join in Janita's [5] and Ella's [5] play. Janita, however, rejects Elli, arguing that 'smalls' are not allowed to come.

> Elli: I'm not a small girl, I'm big!

Enjoying music
Merja [adult] is with her small group in Violets' play room.

> Arttu [2]: Let's listen to music!
> Merja: Oh yes, we have not listened to music, yet. What would you like to listen to?
> Arttu: Let's listen to 'Tuttiritari' (Knight of the Pacifier).

Merja turns the recorder on. Arttu starts running. Merja dances with Piia [1] in her arms. Piia crows with delight. Merja puts Piia down and takes Arttu in her arms. Piia tries to put her feet on Merja's shoes and stretches her hands towards her. Iida [1] and Piia twirl and laugh.

Being skilled in colouring
Raindrops are having their free play time. Salli [3], whose family has recently moved to Finland, is sitting at a table and colouring an image of Hello Kitty. She colours carefully – no colour goes across the border. I am sitting next to her. Salli is not able to speak Finnish, but she shows me the picture, smiling; her eyes are smiling too. I say how lovely the picture is. The colouring proceeds, with Salli making a couple of strokes and then showing me the image, over and over again. She seems to expect more praise. Every time she shows me the picture, I say how skilful her colouring is.

Being familiar with the routines
It is lunch time for Roses. Timo [5] and Erkka [5] look at the notice board, which has a series of pictures representing the daily schedule: breakfast, circle time, free play, outdoor activities, lunch, rest, snack, free play, outdoor activities, and home time. Timo and Erkka begin to debate what they must do after lunch. Erkka argues that they must read books before having a rest. Timo explains, 'After eating, we have to take the pill [xylitol], then we must go to the toilet, then we'll take a book from the shelf, and it's after that that we'll read the books!'

Becoming a schoolchild
Circle time in Raindrops is beginning. Sari [teacher] urges the rest of the children to go to their places. Riia [6] is hiding behind the shelf. Sari asks Riia to come and sit down. Riia is still lying in her hiding place. Sari says, 'Riia! Riia, come here!' The other children look at Riia. Someone says, 'She is not coming'. Sari makes an appeal to Riia saying, 'Riia, do you think you'll whinge like that at school next year? Riia! [in a firm tone] Do you think that you can act like this at school?'

At the societal level, these narratives tell about the ideology of placing children of about the same age together in the same institution. As Kjørholt (2008) showed, this age-related social order restricts the choices of the children: during their time at the centre, they are not able, for instance, to cross the boundaries of the institution, to participate in intergenerational relationships, or to engage in activities with their family members. The children are obliged to adapt themselves in an institutional growing environment characterised by circumstances and practices that are essentially different from those of the home environment. From the children's point of view, this means dividing their lives into two areas, going between the two places and adjusting themselves to the everyday rhythm created by adults and society at the expense of their natural pace (Kyrönlampi-Kylmänen, 2007).

At the community level, the narratives show the day care centres to be spaces in which children's opportunities for participation, influence, and self-realisation are framed by dilemmas and tensions: individual child vs. group of children; children's free choice vs. institutional practices; children's autonomy vs. adults' authority; children's learning vs. adults' teaching; and being here and now vs. becoming in the future. In the middle of the dilemmas and tensions, children construct their daily lives and their identities.

The narratives are peopled by individual children who have names, ages, genders, ethnic and cultural backgrounds, mother tongues, strengths, and interests. Concurrent with being individual persons, the children are part of the groupings of the centres. The children's social identities are constructed on the basis of their belonging to the groups of 'Violets', 'Roses', 'Raindrops', 'boys', 'girls', 'pre-schoolers', 'five-year-olds', 'bigs', or 'smalls'. As we have mentioned earlier, the children may receive individualised attention even within the groups. To some extent, the daily practices are based on the individual needs of the children (e.g. the length of naps and diet). The pedagogy demonstrates respect for the children's individual interests, motivations, and learning needs. The children have opportunities to freely choose their activities, especially in the free play and outdoor situations. They have opportunities for various activities, for instance, playing, doing handicrafts, moving, acting, singing, drawing, reading books, and interacting with peers and adults. Episodes concerned with enjoying music and drawing provide examples of how the children express pleasure in engaging in meaningful activities and joy in their skills. The children seem to enjoy being here and now.

Quite often, however, we observe how the view of an autonomous child is limited and challenged by the group, the institutional procedures, or the adults. The children are expected to adapt to schedules, rules, and fixed group activities. The conversation between Timo and Erkka shows the detailed knowledge that they have of these institutional routines. The children are able to predict the smallest steps in the daily choreography of the centre. The schedule is structured by the meals that are offered to all children at the same time. The children are asked to go to the toilet at the same time. They move to the outdoor play area as a group. As in Riia's case, all children, regardless of their ages, vigour, fatigue, or motivation, are supposed to participate in the circle times supervised by the adults. The children's expressions of their own desires and intentions are not respected. Instead of treating the children as beings, the adults treat them as becomings. The children have limited opportunities to influence the key decisions of their everyday lives and the practices of the centres. It is the adult who knows what the children need for their favourable development and learning. It is the adult who has the power and the right to make decisions on behalf of the children. The dominance of the adult is not impugned.

The two distinctively different views of children's being show that the day care centres have the potential for both promoting and restricting children's citizenship from the viewpoints of respecting their subjectivity and enabling their participation in decision-making. In early childhood education worldwide, there has been discussion about children's citizenship and their rights to be involved in decisions that affect them (Bae, 2009; Kjørholt, 2008; MacNaughton, Hughes, & Smith, 2007; Woodrow &

Press, 2007). Ben-Arieh and Boyer (2005), among others, have stressed the importance of citizenship, participation, and the realisation of children's rights for their well-being.

7. Concluding remarks

In addressing children's narratives in a day care centre context, this article challenges the mainstream research both methodologically and by focusing on the youngest children who have often been excluded from well-being research. What kind of view of young children's well-being is constructed through our study? What kind of potentials and limitations are involved in narrative methodology when exploring young children's experienced well-being?

In a global frame, many aspects of Finnish day care centres represent good conditions for children's well-being. This landscape could be mapped with issues such as universal access to municipal day care, low child–staff ratios, good material conditions, and trained staff. From the narrative viewpoint, the landscape of children's well-being becomes more complex. Instead of arguing for one objective truth, our study offers diverse narratives of children's everyday life in a day care centre context. Without any doubt, the narratives convey both positive and negative experiences of children's well-being. According to our interpretations, the most positive experiences deal with inspiring and enabling material environments, responsive adults, good friends, and opportunities for meaningful activities. Darker shades permeate the narratives characterised by unyielding institutional structures, children's separateness from adults, exclusion from peer relationships, and not being respected as a subject. However, we have to accept that narrative truths are always temporal, located, partial, and incomplete (Riessman, 2008). The narratives co-constructed and reflected in this study are context specific and do not allow us to make direct generalisations about children's well-being beyond the research context. Despite the limitations on generalising findings, our study highlights some themes, relevant to be critically considered in various contexts. Our study leads to scrutiny, for instance, questions connected with consumerism, the quality of interactions, and the implementation of children's rights in day care centres.

Developing child-centred and participatory research methodology to capture children's views is a major question increasingly highlighted in research on children's well-being (e.g. Crivello et al., 2009; Fattore et al., 2007; McAuley & Rose, 2010). Our study demonstrates the narrative approach as one potential framework, sensitive to children's experiences. We suggest that the narrative approach contributes to encountering children in their natural settings, appreciating children's expressions of their experiences, facilitating children's participation, and giving voice to young children in well-being research.

Applying narrative methodology in childhood research, and especially in research with young children, requires, however, further development. In the previous narrative inquiry, emphasis has been on children's verbal narratives, which do not do justice to the holistic and embodied nature of young children's expressions of their experiences. In our research, we have paid attention to the multimodality of young children's narratives. Participation in children's everyday life, long-lasting fieldwork, use of multiple data collection methods, and dialogue between researchers and participants have been significant methodological choices through which we have aimed to deepen our understanding of children's well-being and strengthen the credibility of our interpretations. Throughout the research process, we have attempted to take into account the principles of research ethics, reflexivity, and transparency, which are important when evaluating the truthfulness and scientific quality of narrative inquiry (e.g. Heikkinen, Huttunen, & Syrjälä, 2007; Riessman, 2008).

With the emphasis on the multimodality of children's narratives, our interpretations are based not only on what children say about well-being but also on how they live out their daily lives as narratives. On the one hand, living together with young children is probably one of the few means of gaining insights into their experiences of well-being. On the other hand, we are obliged to confront the challenges of interpreting children's lives in terms of experienced well-being. Regardless of our sincere attempts to do justice to children's experiences, we are inevitably linked to our position as adults. Although Allardt's (1976) model offers us a fruitful basis for detecting the multiplicity in the terrain of children's well-being, we find the phenomenon of well-being elusive. We recognise that there is an obvious need to avoid too simplistic and individualistic interpretations of children's well-being. We have to raise the following question: To what extent is the material repletion good for the child? Are momentary disputes in social relationships fatal for children's well-being? How do we balance an appreciation of children's views and adults' educational responsibility? These questions lead us to profound philosophical problems about childhood and adulthood, individual and society, education and well-being that call for further research.

Acknowledgement

We thank the Academy of Finland research project *Children tell of their well-being – Who listens?* (TelLis, project number 21892) for making this study possible.

Note

1. The child's age is given within the square brackets.

References

Ahn, J., & Filipenko, M. (2007). Narrative, imaginary play, art, and self: Intersecting worlds. *Early Childhood Education Journal, 34,* 279–289.

Allardt, E. (1976). *Hyvinvoinnin ulottuvuuksia* [Dimensions of welfare]. Porvoo: WSOY.

Axford, N. (2009). Child well-being through different lenses: Why concept matters. *Child & Family Social Work, 14,* 372–383.

Bae, B. (2009). Children's right to participate – challenges in everyday interactions. *European Early Childhood Education Research Journal, 17*(3), 391–406.

Ben-Arieh, A. (2010). Developing indicators for child well-being in a changing world. In C. McAuley & W. Rose (Eds.), *Child well-being. Understanding children's lives* (pp. 129–142). London: Jessica Kingsley Publisher.

Ben-Arieh, A., & Boyer, Y. (2005). Citizenship and childhood. The state of affairs in Israel. *Childhood, 12*(1), 33–53.

Bradshaw, J., Hoelscher, P., & Richardson, D. (2007). An index of child well-being in the European Union. *Social Indicators Research, 80*, 133–177.

Bruner, J. (1990). *Acts of meaning*. Cambridge: Harvard University Press.

Butler-Kisber, L. (2010). *Qualitative inquiry. Thematic, narrative and arts-informed perspectives*. Los Angeles: Sage Publications.

Camfield, L., Streuli, N., & Woodhead, M. (2009). What's the use of 'well-being' in contexts of child poverty? Approaches to research, monitoring and children's participation. *International Journal of Children's Rights, 17*, 65–109.

Crivello, G., Camfield, L., & Woodhead, M. (2009). How can children tell us about their well-being? Exploring the potential of participatory research approaches within Young Lives. *Social Indicators Research, 90*, 51–72.

Dittmar, H. (2008). To have is to be? Psychological functions of material possession. In H. Dittmar (Ed.), *Consumer culture, identity and well-being. The search for the 'good life' and the 'body perfect'* (pp. 25–48). Hove: Psychology Press.

Dunn, J. (2004). *Children's friendships. The beginnings of intimacy*. Malden, MA: Blackwell Publishing.

Ebbeck, M., & Yim, H.Y.B. (2009). Rethinking attachment: Fostering positive relationships between infants, toddlers and their primary caregivers. *Early Child Development and Care, 179*(7), 899–909.

Engel, S. (2006). Narrative analysis of children's experience. In S. Greene & D. Hogan (Eds.), *Researching children's experience. Approaches and methods* (pp. 199–216). London: Sage Publications.

Fattore, T., Mason, J., & Watson, E. (2007). Children's conceptualisation(s) of their well-being. *Social Indicator Research, 80*, 5–29.

Friedman, O., & Neary, K.R. (2008). Determining who owns what: Do children infer ownership from first possession? *Cognition, 107*(3), 829–849.

Hay, D.F., Payne, A., & Chadwick, A. (2004). Peer relations in childhood. *Journal of Child Psychology and Psychiatry, 45*(1), 84–108.

Heikkinen, H.L.T., Huttunen, R., & Syrjälä, L. (2007). Action research as narrative: Five principles of validation. *Educational Action Research, 15*(1), 5–19.

Jingbo, L., & Elicker, J. (2005). Teacher-child interaction in Chinese kindergartens: An observational analysis. *International Journal of Early Years Education, 13*(2), 129–143.

Kalliala, M. (2008). *Kato mua! Kohtaako aikuinen lapsen päiväkodissa?* [Look at me! Does the adult encounter the child at a day care center?]. Helsinki: Gaudeamus.

Kjørholt, A.T. (2008). The competent child and 'the right to be oneself': Reflections on children as fellow citizens in an early childhood centre. In A. Clark, A.T. Kjørholt, & P. Moss (Eds.), *Beyond listening. Children's perspectives on early childhood services* (pp. 151–174). Bristol: Polity Press.

Konu, A., & Rimpelä, M. (2002). Well-being in schools: A conceptual model. *Health Promotion International, 17*(1), 79–87.

Kyrönlampi-Kylmänen, T. (2007). *Arki lapsen kokemana: Eksistentiaalis-fenomenologinen haastattelututkimus* [Everyday life from the point of view of the child: Insights from existential phenomenological interviews]. Rovaniemi: University of Lapland.

MacNaughton, G., Hughes, P., & Smith, K. (2007). Young children's rights and public policy: Practices and possibilities for citizenship in the early years. *Children & Society, 21*, 458–469.

Mayr, T., & Ulich, M. (2009). Social-emotional well-being and resilience of children in early childhood settings – PERIK: An empirically based observation scale. *Early Years, 29*(1), 45–57.

McAuley, C., Morgan, R., & Rose, W. (2010). Children's views on child well-being. In C. McAuley & W. Rose (Eds.), *Child well-being. Understanding children's lives* (pp. 39–65). London: Jessica Kingsley Publishers.

McAuley, C., & Rose, W. (2010). Child well-being: Current issues and future directions. In C. McAuley & W. Rose (Eds.), *Child well-being. Understanding children's lives* (pp. 207–240). London: Jessica Kingsley Publishers.

Morrow, V., & Mayall, B. (2009). What is wrong with children's well-being in the UK? Questions of meaning and measurement. *Journal of Social Welfare & Family Law, 31*(3), 217–229.

Niikko, A. (2006). Finnish daycare: Caring, education, and instruction. In J. Einarsdóttir & J.T. Wagner (Eds.), *Nordic childhoods and early education. Philosophy, research, policy, and practice in Denmark, Finland, Iceland, Norway, and Sweden* (pp. 133–158). Greenwich, CT: Information Age Publishing.

Ochs, E., & Caps, L. (2001). *Living narratives.* Cambridge: Harvard University Press.

Organisation for Economic Co-operation and Development (OECD). (2006). *Starting Strong II: Early childhood and care.* Retrieved May 13, 2011, from http://www.oecd.org/dataoecd/16/2/37423404.pdf

Pramling Samuelsson, I., & Johansson, E. (2009). Why do children involve teacher in their play and learning? *European Early Childhood Education Research Journal, 17*(1), 77–94.

Riessman, C.K. (2008). *Narrative methods for human sciences.* Thousand Oaks, CA: Sage Publications.

Rinaldi, C. (2008). Documentation and assessment: What is the relationship? In A. Clark, A.T. Kjørholt, & P. Moss (Eds.), *Beyond listening. Children's perspectives on early childhood services* (pp. 17–28). Bristol: Polity Press.

Rourou, A., Singer, E., Bekema, N., & De Haan, D. (2006). Cultural perspectives on peer conflicts in multicultural Dutch child care centres. *European Early Childhood Education Research Journal, 14*(2), 35–53.

Ruckenstein, M. (2010). Time scales of consumption: Children, money and transactional orders. *Journal of Consumer Culture, 10*(3), 383–404.

Säkkinen, S., & Kuoppala, T. (2010). *Lasten päivähoito 2009* [Children's day care 2009]. Statistical report 10. Helsinki: National Institute for Health and Welfare.

Smidt, S. (2011). *Introducing Bruner. A guide for practitioners and students in early years education.* London: Routledge.

Sparkes, A.C., & Smith, B. (2008). Narrative constructionist inquiry. In J.A. Holstein & J.F. Gubrium (Eds.), *Handbook of constructionist research* (pp. 295–314). New York: The Guilford Press.

Spector-Mersel, G. (2010). Narrative research Time for a paradigm. *Narrative Inquiry, 20*(1), 204–224.

Stakes. (2004). *National curriculum guidelines in early childhood education and care in Finland.* Helsinki: Stakes. Retrieved May 13, 2011, from http://kasvunkumppanit.thl.fi/thl-client/pdfs/267671cb-0ec0-4039-b97b-7ac6ce6b9c10

Swick, K.J. (2007). Insights on caring for early childhood professionals and families. *Early Childhood Education Journal, 35*(2), 97–102.

Woodrow, C., & Press, F. (2007). (Re)positioning the child in the policy/politics of early childhood. *Educational Philosophy and Theory, 39*(3), 311–325.

Cortisol levels and children's orientation in day care

Jyrki Reunamo, Nina Sajaniemi, Eira Suhonen and Elina Kontu

Children's stress in day care is related to the stressful qualities of the environment and to children's orientations in that environment. The study involved 55 children in five day centres in Finland. Baseline saliva samples for measuring cortisol (stress) levels were collected five times during the day. Children were interviewed to measure their orientation in regard to perceived change. The educators of the groups evaluated the learning environment qualities. The high cortisol levels at the wake-up time were correlated with chaotic, hectic and emotionally restricted learning environment qualities. However, in the afternoon, the correlations between cortisol levels and the learning environment had disappeared and were replaced by children's orientation to change. Children with more accommodative views had lower cortisol levels and children with uncertain views had higher cortisol levels. The children's different orientations seem to impact their stress levels and participate in the production of the learning environment stressful qualities.

All illustrations provided by Tzung Y
All illustrations provided by Tzung Ying Li

Introduction

The purpose of the research was to study how children's stress levels are related to children's views on change (Reunamo, 2007a) and their learning environment in day care. Children's salivary cortisol levels are indicators of stress experienced by children. Stress responses are mediated by two interrelated systems: the locus coeruleus-norepinephrine/sympathetic adrenomedullary) and the hypothalamic–pituitary–adrenocortical (HPA) systems (Gunnar & Quevedo, 2007). HPA axis functioning is an adaptive process, mobilising the organism's resources through up-regulation of the stress hormone, cortisol, to meet challenges when needed and down-regulate cortisol through a negative feedback loop when challenges have been met (Gunnar & Quevedo, 2007). Cortisol secretion follows a typical diurnal pattern with a peak after awakening and a decreasing pattern towards evening (cf. Legendre, 2003). The stress-sensitive neurobiological system is immature and open to being shaped by experience during the early childhood years (Gunnar & Quevedo, 2007).

Cortisol levels as the descriptors of environmental and personal aspects of stress

The stress exhibited in cortisol levels can be related at least with to different types of phenomena. First, elevated stress is often related to unsafe and unhealthy environments. Children exposed to stressful family conditions or low-quality educational environments tend to have higher levels of cortisol (cf. Blair, Granger, & Razza, 2005; Watamura, Coe, Laudenslager, & Robertson, 2010).

Children from high-stress home environments have been reported to be especially vulnerable to the effects of poor day care. These children show overwhelming stress in insensitive day care environments, which increases their risk for social and emotional problems (Cassiba, van IJzendoorn, & D'Odorico, 2000; Constantino & Olesh, 1999), including aggressive behaviour, attention deficit difficulties, poor emphatic skills and depression (Maughan, Collishaw, Goodman, & Picles, 2004). Previous work also suggests that there is a quality-related variability in children's cortisol and child-specific response to stressful day care settings (Sajaniemi et al., 2011).

On the other hand, modulating emotions and behaviours is central in supporting the engagement in day care learning activities that foster positive day care adjustment over time. Psychophysiological reactivity and regulation in response to stress has been postulated as an important and positive aspect of a child's regulatory capacity describing children's competence, particularly in new situations (Miller, Seifer, Stroud, Sheinkopf, & Dickstein, 2006; Lisonbee, Mize, Payne, & Granger, 2008). Problems with regulation capacity, for example, in increased internalising behaviour and social wariness, may result in higher cortisol levels too.

Both stressful environment and competent exertion have been reported to increase cortisol levels. The dual nature of cortisol secretion makes it hard to evaluate the real meaning of higher or lower levels of cortisol. This is among the first studies in which children's own thoughts have been linked to cortisol levels and environmental quality.

Children's orientations as mediators in the experiences of stress

Stress is heavily related on the interpretation of the situation and children's equilibrium processes or coping strategies. Coping is a constructive way of managing social stressors, because it involves conflict resolution (Valiente, Lemery-Chalfant, & Swanson, 2009). Children's capacity of interpreting their own and other people's activity systems gives stress constructive qualities. Unfortunately, coping strategies are usually considered as regulation of children's own equilibrium processes, not as having effect on others (cf. Sontag, Graber, Brooks-Gunn, & Warren, 2008). However, children's ways to interpret different situations may have an effect on the very situations the children look at (Reunamo, 2007b). If children's interpretations impact on the qualities of the stressful situation, they have impact on the qualities of their stress too.

In addition to the Piagetian way of studying the development of children's adaptive views (cf. Gruber & Vonèche, 1995), Reunamo's (2007c) model of children's orientations includes children's agentive views, that is, views in which children see themselves impacting on the environment. The interview instrument based on the model is used to study children's adaptive and agentive views on pressure situations.

In the study of children's orientations (Reunamo, 2007a), children's views were found to have an impact on the environment. Children not only perceive agency, but their perceptions have an agentive property in and of itself. Children with a lot of adaptive and accommodative views were found to impact on the educational environment most. The effects were integrative and harmonising. Even children who tended to have separate (adaptive assimilation) ways of looking at situations had an effect on the environment. Their interaction could be described as loose and undefined. It is interesting that children with more compelling behaviour (agentive assimilation) could realise their goals, but at the same time they left fewer traces of their action in the educational setting. Children orienting towards mutual change also find themselves in a more dynamic educational setting.

These results make Reunamo's orientation model a possible tool to study children's stress, not only to consider children as adapting or coping with the stressful situations, but also as impacting on the stressful situations. Firstly, children interpret situations differently, which affects children's stress experiences. Secondly, children's interpretations may have an effect on the stressful environment. The model could perhaps be used as a tool to study the processes of the socially constructed stressful environment. To not confuse terminology, in this article, children's orientations are used instead of coping strategies or executive functions to describe children' views in relation to the conditions of situational change.

Methods

Participants

The sample of the study consisted of 55 children. There were 30 girls and 25 boys in the sample. The children were between three and seven years of age, the mean age being 4.8 years (SD = 0.68). The children were attending five different groups, each in a different day care centre. The day care centres were municipal day care centres in one town in southern Finland. The families in the day care centre represented the average Finnish demographic qualities. The families consisted mostly of white families with medium income. Four of the children had special needs, but the special needs were not specified at the time of the research. Two children were reported to be physically ill, but the illnesses are not known. The groups were all full-day groups, where the parents usually brought the children to the day care centre approximately at 08:00 in the morning and picked them up after 16:00 in the afternoon. The day care centres were chosen randomly from all of the day care centres in town, which altogether had more than 20 day care centres. Altogether there were 67 children present in the groups, but because of absence or denial of research permission 12 children in the groups did not participate in the research. Thus, the percentage of participation in the sampled groups was 80%.

Measures and procedure

All five randomly picked day care centres volunteered to take part in the research. The parents gave a written agreement for their children to participate in the research. For some reason, the written agreement was not delivered by the parents of two children who were left out of the research.

Baseline cortisol samples

A total of five samples were taken from the children. The samples were collected (1) by parents on waking up; (2) one hour after waking up (by parents or day care staff); (3) at approximately 10:00 by the staff; (4) in the afternoon at 14:00 by the staff and (5) at night before sleeping by the parents. Both parents and staff were trained in the sampling procedure. The groups followed their normal daily schedule in the day of collection, which was in February 2010. Because the children's cortisol levels were skewed to the left with some outliers with higher cortisol levels, all the statistical significances were also tested with normalised data and with non-parametrical (Mann–Whitney) testing.

Only the results of two samples of the five measured during the day are reported in this article. This is done to show the difference as clearly as possible. The tendency of the correlations shifted from environmentally stressful aspects to correlations related with children's views. We decided to omit the description of the whole process in order to clarify the results and save space. It should be acknowledged that the fifth sample right before sleeping at home was not in any clear way related to the other samples. It seems that different aspects of views and environments invoked different reactions in the course of everyday life.

Interview on children's orientations

Reunamo's (2007a) interview tool was applied in studying children's views on change in day care situations. The interviews were done by the teachers of the group and they were trained to use the interview tool. The interview consisted of sixteen situations. The children were asked to describe how they were seeing themselves acting in the in different situations. A picture was used in each question to help the children orientate to the situation in a similar manner. The interviewers wrote down the children's answers. The interview was conducted in the day care centres in separate quiet rooms in similar circumstances. After the interview, the children's answers were categorised into five groups as accommodative, participative, dominant, withdrawn and uncertain orientations. The continuums open–closed and adaptive–agentive determined the categories. If it was not possible to categorise the children's description in any of the four categories, it was categorised as uncertain which most often meant that the child did not know what to do. The classification was done by two researchers who categorised all the children's views question by question (not child by child) to ensure a unified classification. The classifiers did not use any information about the children's identity, neither did they use any information about the children's qualities (e.g. age or gender), background, group or the learning environment they were attending. The classification was done based solely on the children's descriptions. The learning environment evaluations and the interview classifications were made totally independently from each other. During the analysing stage, it was found that children often had different orientations for children than for adults. Different summary variables were added up for situations with children and situations with adults. The interviews were done in February 2010. The complete interview instrument can be retrieved from http://www.helsinki.fi/~reunamo/apu/interview_instrument_with_pictures.pdf.

Learning environment evaluations

The learning environment was evaluated by using a 57-item survey. The survey was based on Reunamo's (2005) mapping of the day care centres of the city of Helsinki. The evaluated aspects centred on the learning environment aspects of harmony, chaos, objectives and possibilities. The items of evaluation included the pedagogical preferences, the atmosphere of the group, the curriculum emphasis and the practice of everyday proceedings. The range of the Likert scale was from one (does not describe) to five (describes very well). Each team (three educators) discussed the items together and filled out one shared evaluation. Based on a factor analysis of a larger sample (project web-pages at https://sites.google.com/site/agentiveperception/ project-definition), four summary variables were formed, describing the harmonious, chaotic, curriculum and participative qualities of the learning environment. The learning environment evaluations were done in February–March 2010. The learning evaluation instrument can be retrieved from http://www.helsinki.fi/~reunamo/apu/ learning_env_evaluation.pdf.

Results

The baseline cortisol samples followed a typical diurnal pattern which is described in Figure 1.

The expected peak of cortisol secretion was after the wake-up. After that, the cortisol values decreased throughout the day, with the lowest values being in the evening. The gender and age differences were not significant. The largest differences were found at the wake-up time when the cortisol values ranged from 4.62 nmol/l to an outlier exceeding up to 240 nmol/l. In the evening, the values ranged from 0.38 nmol/l up to one outlier reaching 47 nmol/l.

The distribution of children's answers concerning the interview can be seen in Figure 2. The five categories describe children's openness and orientation in the potentially stressful situation.

Most often the children had participative orientation (in 39% of the cases), which means that the children considered the situation openly and saw themselves as impacting on the situation. In accommodative views (30% of the cases), the children looked at

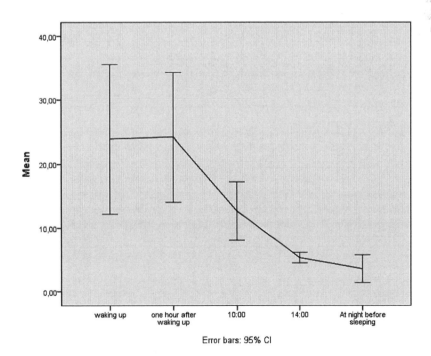

Error bars: 95% CI

Figure 1. The mean cortisol levels of the day care children (with 95% confidence intervals).

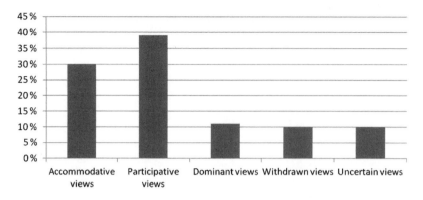

Figure 2.   Children different views on change in day care situations.

the situation openly but adapted their own views. In dominant views (11% of the cases), the children applied their own closed views and overruled the given conditions. Children with withdrawn orientation described a different condition from the given condition, but did not try to change the given condition. Examples of the children's answers are given in the second section of the results. The differences between groups in learning environment qualities are presented in Figure 3.

As can be seen in Figure 3, the groups differ mostly in the harmonic and chaotic qualities of the learning environment. Two groups come forward as harmonic and the same groups come forward as not chaotic groups. However, the differences of the groups cannot be confirmed by statistical significances, because there are only five groups in the stratified sample.

The qualities of the learning environment affecting children's cortisol levels

Altogether 57 items of the learning environment qualities were measured. In Table 1, all the 12 learning environment qualities that had statistically significant ($p < 0.05$)

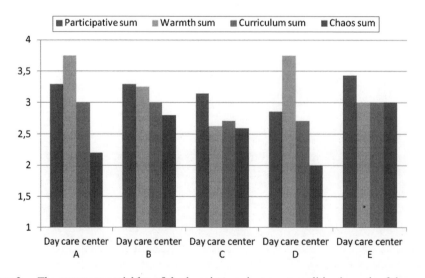

Figure 3.   The summary variables of the learning environment qualities in each of the groups.

Table 1. The statistically significant correlations between learning environment qualities and children's cortisol levels at 07:00 and 14:00 hours.

Correlations	Cortisol level right after waking up at home (07:00)			Cortisol level at 14:00 in the day care centre		
	Correlation coefficient	Sig. (two-tailed)	N	Correlation coefficient	Sig. (two-tailed)	N
Cortisol level at 14:00 hours in the day care centre	0.156	0.251	56	1		58
The educators of the group have been perpetually short of time and short of resources	**0.400**	0.004	49	0.045	0.759	50
The educators have at least once a week a planning and evaluation meeting	**−0.345**	0.015	49	−0.117	0.418	50
The whole group is having a meeting every day	**−0.307**	0.032	49	−0.189	0.188	50
The conditions, the environment and the tools are versatile for physical activities	**−0.283**	0.049	49	0.076	0.601	50
For some reason emotional expression is not so rich or accepted in our group of children	**0.329**	0.021	49	0.2	0.164	50
The controversies of the children are processed and examined together with children	**−0.329**	0.021	49	−0.2	0.164	50
The leadership of the pedagogical work in the day care centre should be strengthened	**−0.351**	0.013	49	0.016	0.911	50
Music (songs, playing, performances and listening) is very important in our group	**−0.319**	0.026	49	0.07	0.63	50
The work in the day care centre is natural, sustaining and harmonic	**−0.369**	0.009	49	−0.099	0.493	50
The work in the day care centre is fragmented, uncontrolled and chaotic	**0.417**	0.003	49	0.032	0.827	50
The summary variable of warm learning environment	**−0.327**	0.022	49	0.042	0.771	50

Note: Correlations in bold have p-values below 0.05.

correlations with the children's cortisol levels either right after waking up or in the afternoon are presented. The children's cortisol levels when they wake up at home are highly correlated with the learning environment qualities of the day care centres. On the other hand, none of the cortisol levels measured in the afternoon correlated statistically significantly with the learning environment qualities.

Certain qualities of the learning environment were increasing children's stress level already when they woke up. The strongest correlation was with the fragmented, uncontrolled and chaotic qualities of the learning environment. If the educators of the group had been perpetually short of time and short of resources, it was a strong indicator of high cortisol levels for the children during waking up. If (for some reason) the emotional expression was not so rich or accepted in the group the children belonged to in the day centre, the children tended to have a higher stress level already early in the morning. It is not hard to understand that a chaotic, hectic and unemotional learning environment stresses children. The striking thing is that these qualities showed so clearly already when the children woke up. The children anticipated the stressful conditions already at home, straight out of their home bed. Because the stress levels were so high at the time the children woke up, the stress was probably showing in their sleep too.

On the other hand, a natural, sustaining and harmonic learning environment decreased children's cortisol level at wake-up time. The leadership of the pedagogical work and educational culture was in better hands in day care centres where children experience lower levels of cortisol early in the morning. The summary variable describing the qualities of a warm learning environment correlated with lower cortisol levels in the first minutes of time children's day. Furthermore, music seemed to be related with a less stressful learning environment. Songs, playing and listening to music had a harmonising effect on children's expectations.

Group meetings seemed to have a harmonious and less stressful effect on the children's early morning experiences. Perhaps the learning environment was more unified or perhaps group meetings produce a more communal atmosphere, but the reasons are speculative. The children experienced less stress early in the morning if their controversies were processed and examined together with them. It is probably easier for the children to feel control over the situations, when they know they can impact and process the difficult situations. It is interesting that good possibilities for physical activities seemed to relieve stress even before children attend the physical activities.

The children's cortisol levels in the afternoon do not relate with any of the evaluated learning environment qualities. A very mild (not statistically significant) positive relation was the higher stress level in the afternoon and less accepted emotional expressions in the group. An equally mild negative connection was found between the cortisol level in the afternoon and children's processing their controversies together with other children. Other correlations are quite randomly located around zero.

Children were experiencing more stress about the learning environment qualities before getting into their stressful day care environment. But when the children spend time in the stressful environment, their stressful traces fade away, at least as far as children's cortisol levels are concerned. There are several possible reasons for this. Firstly, anticipating uncontrolled and chaotic situations might be more stressful than actually experiencing them. Children have time to work on the stressful aspects of the learning environment and perhaps in the afternoon they have already found their place and gained control of their situation. Secondly, afternoon activities are more relaxing in general than activities before lunch. Children have more time to play in the afternoon and the schedule is not as tight as in the morning. The pressures produced by teaching and organised activities are not present in the afternoon. Thirdly, the lacking resources do not affect the group atmosphere in the less demanding activities of the afternoon. Children can orientate more freely in the afternoon. Children's sense of control and meaningfulness can increase.

Table 2.   The correlations between children's orientations and their cortisol levels at 07:00 and 14:00 hours.

Correlations	Cortisol level right after waking up at home (07:00)			Cortisol level at 14:00 in the day care centre		
	Correlation coefficient	Sig. (two-tailed)	N	Correlation coefficient	Sig. (two-tailed)	N
The sum of accommodative schemas with children	−0.174	0.233	49	**−0.462**	0.001	49
The sum of participative schemas with children	−0.094	0.522	49	−0.022	0.88	49
The sum of dominating schemas with children	0.19	0.190	49	0.054	0.715	49
The sum of withdrawn schemas with children	−0.112	0.442	49	0.205	0.157	49
The sum of uncertain schemas with children	0.183	0.209	49	0.173	0.234	49
The sum of accommodative schemas with adults	−0.101	0.491	49	**−0.380**	0.007	49
The sum of participative schemas with adults	−0.065	0.656	49	−0.026	0.861	49
The sum of dominant schemas with adults	0.065	0.657	49	0.230	0.112	49
The sum of withdrawn schemas with adults	−0.124	0.397	49	0.112	0.444	49
The sum of uncertain schemas with adults	0.266	0.064	49	**0.440**	0.002	49

Note: Correlations in bold have p-values below 0.05.

The relations of children's views on change to their cortisol levels

Children's typical orientations were measured with the interview scale. The correlations for the summary variables or each orientation are presented in Table 2.

Accommodative orientation with children

Children with more accommodative orientation with other children tended to have lower cortisol levels than other children in the afternoon (cf. Table 2). To understand the psychological process behind this phenomenon, we need to look more closely at children's views. The accommodative views are open to the environmental conditions and contents of the activities. The children look at the conditions presented, but they do not seek to change them. The children accommodate their views on the situation openly. Altogether 30% of the children's answers were classified as accommodative.

The largest differences found were related with question 'let's think about a situation where you disagree with what the teacher says, what you do?' The picture that was presented for the children describing the situation is shown in Figure 4.

An accommodative orientation was described by 18% ($n = 10$) of the children in the interview for the question presented in Figure 4. The difference in cortisol level was lower among children with accommodative orientation ($M = 3.23$, SD $= 1.24$) than with other children ($M = 5.22$, SD $= 2.41$). The differences were statistically

1 . Let's think that another child has the toy you want.

What do you do?

Figure 4.   An example of an interview question where accommodative schemas concerning other children were related to lower levels of cortisol.

significant, $F(1, 48) = 4.53, p = 0.039$ and $\eta^2 = 0.09$. Because the distributions were somewhat skewed another test with natural logarithms was conducted in comparison, which increased the statistical significance to 0.019. The accommodative answer types are listed below:

- *I see a time when I can play with it.*
- *I let him play.*
- *I wait for my turn.*
- *I let her play.*

The accommodative children adjusted their views to the existing situation. These children did not seek changes. Neither did they concentrate on their self-centred views. The children with accommodative orientation seemed to be able to tolerate the tension of not getting the desired toy. They thought about the other child having the toy, but still they adjusted their own desires and ideas.

The other orientations were not related to stress levels. A participative orientation (*I ask him to give it*) was described by 51% ($n = 28$) of the children. A dominant orientation (*I take it from his hand*) was given by 7% ($n = 4$) of the children, a withdrawn orientation (*I take another toy*) was classified for 15% ($n = 8$) of the children and an uncertain orientation (*I don't know*) was described by 9% ($n = 5$) of the children.

Accommodative orientation with adults

Children who had more accommodative schemas with adults also had lower cortisol levels in the afternoon. An example question in that category is presented next in order to make the dynamics of the situation clearer (cf. Figure 5).

4. Let's think a situation where you disagree with what
the teacher says, what do you do?

Figure 5.   An example of an interview question where accommodative schemas concerning adults were related to lower levels of cortisol.

An accommodative orientation was described by 51% ($n = 28$) of the children in the situation described in Figure 5. As we see, children were much more accommodative in their relations with the adults. Children needed to obey the rules and adapt to teacher's suggestion more than was the case with their peers. This same phenomenon could be seen in all the questions: children tended to accommodate more in the situations with adults. Nevertheless, the differences in the orientations were more similar to those in situations with children. Children who accommodated even more often than others in situations with adults in them, had lower cortisol levels ($M = 4.04$, $SD = 1.42$) than children who gave other types of orientations ($M = 5.88$, $SD = 2.80$). The differences between the groups were statistically significant, $F(1, 48) = 8.58$, $p = 0.005$ and $\eta^2 = 0.154$. Because of the skewness of the cortisol level variable, a natural logarithm was taken of all cortisol levels to compare statistical significance, but the differences remained statistically significant ($p = 0.013$). To get a feel what the accommodative schemas meant in practice, the most usual answer types are listed below:

- *Well I have to do what the teacher says.*
- *Then I agree and do my own thing later.*
- *Then I think likewise.*
- *I listen up.*
- *I say I am sorry.*

Accommodation means that children consider the adults' point of view, but they do not seek to change it. Children who can at the same time be open to the situation and change their own views seem to have less stress experiences. Children disagree with the teacher in the situation, but they are ready to change their views in accordance with the teacher.

The other orientations were not related to stress levels. A participative orientation (*I tell my point of view*) was described by 7% ($n = 4$) of the children. Nine per cent of ($n = 5$) described a dominant orientation (*I say no!*). An answer was classified as withdrawn (*then I go away*) in 7% ($n = 4$) of the cases. Twenty-five per cent ($n = 14$) of the children were uncertain (*I don't know*) about their ideas. The children who did not see themselves accommodating in situations with adults either tried to change the condition given (you disagree with the teacher) by changing the teacher's view or thought about different conditions. Either way, they were not accommodating their views in the situation.

Uncertain orientation with adults

In the afternoon, if children had more uncertain orientations in situations where the other participant was an adult, the children's cortisol level tended to be higher than other children's (cf. Table 2). Altogether 10% of the children's answers were classified as being uncertain. The children said that they did not know what they would do in the situation. The children's answer could also be irrelevant in relation to the situation. For example, when children were confronted with a situation they started to talk about something else, in which case children's relation to the situation could not be evaluated. It is possible that in children's minds the description related in some way to the situation, but if the relation was ambiguous it was classified as uncertain.

The largest differences between uncertain orientations with adults and other children's orientations were related to the question 'teacher doesn't agree with what you are doing, what you do then?' The picture that was presented during interview is in Figure 6.

An uncertain schema was described by 26% ($n = 14$) of the children when the children were asked what to do when the teacher disagrees with them. These children did not know what to do. The cortisol level was higher for the uncertain children ($M = 6.99$, SD $= 2.71$) than for children with not uncertain views ($M = 4.60$, SD $= 2.16$). Not uncertain means that children at least gave some kind of strategy in relation to the situation. The mean differences in the cortisol levels were statistically significant, $F(1, 47) = 6.82$, $p = 0.012$ and $\eta^2 = 0.726$. The observed power ($\eta^2 = 0.726$) is very high. Because the distribution of the cortisol variable is not normally distributed, a natural logarithm was applied for each cortisol level, but the differences remained statistically significant ($p = 0.015$) and the impact remained high ($\eta^2 = 0.694$). The typical uncertain answer types are listed below:

- *I don't understand.*
- *I don't know, I play.*
- *I don't remember.*
- *Nothing comes to mind.*
- *I can't answer.*

The teacher disagrees with the children and children do not give any strategy in relation to the given condition (disagreement). In general, most of the children's orientations were accommodative (I don't do it anymore), in 60% ($n = 33$) of the cases. Most children adapted their views to the situation and thought that the teacher's point of view should be respected. In 7% ($n = 4$) of the cases, the orientations were participative (I ask why she does not agree). These children tried to impact on the situation somehow but still considered the teacher's point of view. Another 7% ($n = 4$) of the

13. Think that if teacher doesn't agree what you do.
What do you do then?

Figure 6. An example of an interview question where uncertain schemas concerning adults were related with higher levels of cortisol.

answers were dominant (I don't agree what she does). These children concentrate on their own point of view and overrule teacher's point of view. There was also 7% ($n = 4$) children, who gave a withdrawing type of schema (I go away). These children do not consider the teacher's point of view; rather, they concentrate on their own ideas. It seems that any strategy relieves stress better than having no strategy at all.

The sum of uncertain orientations with situations concerning children was not statistically significant although there was a mild positive correlation with cortisol levels (cf. Table 1). The reason for not detecting a statistically significant relation could be that children had much more uncertain schemas when they had to confront adults than when they were confronting children. In situations were the other participant was an adult, children gave 17% of uncertain answers and in situations concerning other children only 7% of the answers were uncertain. However, one situation with a statistically significant difference could be detected. To the question 'you are playing with a friend and you would like to change play, but your friend does not, what do you do?' 13% ($n = 7$) children answered in an uncertain way. The picture that was used during the interview to help the child to relate to the situation is shown in Figure 7.

Unfortunately, three of those children were absent in the day when the cortisol sample was taken, but the difference remained statistically significant even with four children in the uncertain group. The mean cortisol level for four children with uncertain strategies was 7.82 (SD = 3.41) and for children with not uncertain values it was 4.68 (SD = 2.13, $F(1, 48) = 7.24$, $p = 0.010$, with a high impact $\eta^2 = 0.750$). To check the impact of the skewed distribution, a natural logarithm was counted for the cortisol levels and the difference remained statistically significant ($p = 0.030$) and the impact high ($\eta^2 = 0.593$). It may be of interest that in general there were 11% of the children absent in the day when the cortisol samples were taken and 57% of the absent children were those who described uncertain views:

9. Let's think that you are playing with a friend and
you would like to change play, but your friend does
not. What do you do?

Figure 7. An example of an interview question where uncertain schemas concerning children were related with higher levels of cortisol.

- *I don't know*
- *Whatever*
- *I think I don't know very well*
- *Well I don't know now*
- *Nothing comes to my mind*

The situation is peculiar. The prerequisite is that children want to change play. Children cannot explicate their own ideas that are different from other children. The children want something different, but they have no idea what to do with their desires. The children face a situation that they want something but do not know how to get it, even though the decision seems not to be very difficult looked at from the outside. A large part of the children (46%, $n = 25$) just plainly said they would change play and do what they want to do. An accommodative answer was given by 27% ($n = 15$) of the children (*then I have to keep on playing*). These children usually wanted to keep on playing with their friend. The third popular option (12%, $n = 8$) was to try to impact on the choices of the other child (e.g. *I persuade my friend to play with me in the new play*).

The openness and the agency of children's orientation in relation to the cortisol levels

In the previous results, children's schemas have been categorised according to four categories: accommodative, participative, dominant and withdrawn. Uncertain schemas have not been possible to categorise in any of the four categories. However, the underlying theory makes it possible to organise the categories in a different way without changing the categories described earlier.

Both in accommodative and participative orientations children took the other's perspective into account and the children were open to suggestions and new clues appearing in the situations. We get the summary variable of *open orientation* by adding accommodative and participative schemas together. In open schemas, children consider the presented condition and either adapt to it or try to interact with it. By adding up the dominant and withdrawn schemas, we get *closed orientations*. In these views, children replaced the presented condition by overruling it or by deviating from it.

We get the *adaptive orientation* by adding up the accommodative and withdrawn schemas together. Children do not seek to change the given condition in adaptive views. They either accommodate their own views to the views of the others or their ideas just deviate from the given condition, but leave the given condition intact. In contradiction to adaptive orientation, both in participative and dominant orientations children saw themselves as having agency on the given condition. By adding *agentive orientations* together in a summary variable, we got the number of children orientating towards environmental change. Children can see themselves confronting the situation and this confrontation carries within it a change in the condition. The other option is that the children just follow their own ideas by overruling the given condition.

By organising children's answers anew in a way that fits in the theoretic model, we get more information about the qualities of the schemas affecting children's level of cortisol. In Table 3, the newly organised summaries and their correlations with the early morning and afternoon cortisol levels are shown.

The sum of open orientations (accommodative or participative) was related with less cortisol levels. In other words, children who did consider the different options of the situations more openly had lower cortisol levels. These children were seeking contact with the situational determinants and either adjusted their own ideas to them or tried to change the determinants that they were confronting. The openness of the schemas means that these children were able to merge their inner schemas with the activities happening in the environment. It means that these children did not perceive a discrepancy between their inner and outer schemas.

The sum of adaptive (accommodative or withdrawn) orientation also related statistically significantly with lower levels of cortisol. This means that children who did not

Table 3. The correlations between children's open *vs.* closed and adaptive *vs.* agentive orientations and their cortisol levels at 07:00 and 14:00 hours.

Correlations	Cortisol level right after waking up at home (07:00)			Cortisol level at 14:00 in the day care centre		
	Correlation coefficient	Sig. (two-tailed)	N	Correlation coefficient	Sig. (two-tailed)	N
The sum of open (accommodative or participative) schemas	−0.161	0.269	49	**−0.383**	0.007	49
The sum of closed (dominant or withdrawn) schemas	0.103	0.483	49	0.245	0.089	49
The sum of adaptive (accommodative or withdrawn) schemas	−0.19	0.192	49	**−0.324**	0.023	49
The sum of agentive (participative or dominant) schemas	0.089	0.541	49	0.088	0.546	49

Note: Correlations in bold have *p*-values below 0.05.

see themselves as changing the situations they were confronted with, did not try to change the course of the situations. Instead, they changed their own schemas or found an alternative schema that did not affect the course of action. The children's tendency to adjust their ideas in different situations or their tendency to find alternative ideas was related with decreased cortisol levels. The children did not perceive any discrepancy between the inner and outer schemas, because they could adjust their own schemas.

Discussion

There are two main results and a major tendency among the research results. Firstly, children felt stress about the chaotic aspects of their learning environment as soon as they woke up in the morning. These children seemed to anticipate the dissonant and hectic everyday routine, which they could not avoid. It seems that the higher cortisol levels in the morning are related to the feelings of discomfort and anxiety. The children have just woken up, they have not started to exert the learning environment qualities and they experience stress even though they do not have contact with the stressful environment. Children probably feel stress when they anticipate the stressful conditions. In preschool years the associations between unfavourable sleep patterns and increased HPA system activity may already be observed (Hatzinger et al., 2008, 2010).

Secondly, in the afternoon, the learning environment qualities no longer determine children's experiences of stress; instead children's perception and interpretations about the day care situations impacted on their stress levels. Children with more accommodative and open views in regard to agency were less stressful in the afternoon. The impact of the learning environment qualities became smaller and the impact of children's personal orientation became larger during the course of the day.

The relation of children's views with the experienced stress levels may have at least two reasons. Children with more accommodative and open orientations were feeling less stress perhaps because there was less discrepancy between children's views and the environment. On one hand, the lower cortisol level for open and adaptive views may represent a harmonious and positive wellbeing. On the other hand, the lower cortisol level can be related to less effective emotion regulation and less intensive engagement in the learning activities. In favour of the first alternative speaks the result that higher cortisol levels were associated with uncertain views, not participative and agentive views. The higher cortisol levels are related with confusing views, not with competence and involved processes.

In addition to the adaptive qualities of children's views, their views have agentive qualities too (cf. Reunamo, 2007c), which means that children's ways of looking at situations have an impact on the situations. The results fit well with Reunamo's (2007c) finding that children with more harmonious views produced more harmonic interaction both with other children and with adults. At the same time, children's uncertain views produce weaker and more uncertain relationships with others, which also fit well within the results in this research. It is possible that more harmonious views produce more harmonious environments and less stress.

The groups differed especially in their chaotic and harmonic qualities and that is probably the reason why they come forward in the results. It is possible that different groups would have raised somewhat different sources for stress. Because the educators of the teams evaluated their own team, the results need to be considered with caution; the evaluators know their groups well but the objectivity of the evaluations is questionable. However, it is still important that children' stress levels vary significantly across groups, but the impact of children's orientation soon becomes more important. The interview instrument has been tested with more than 1300 children in Finland and Taiwan and the instrument seems to give reliable and unified results across very different cultures (Reunamo, 2010). Measuring cortisol levels is an objective and easy way to define criterions for children's levels of stress. Children's age and gender were not important factors in the research results and the demographic differences were not significant. However, more research with children in different situations is needed. The research needs to be duplicated in different types of day care, in children's homes and other environments and in different cultures. Children's cortisol level should be measured on several days to increase the reliability of the results. A larger sample with more groups would help to determine the relation between the environment and children's views more closely.

The statistical analysis in the study is inadequate. The list of separate correlations does not allow the studying of intervening variables or the overlap of correlations. A larger sample is needed for a more valid statistical analysis. For example, a hierarchical regression analysis would make it possible to test the variables in a unified model and test the impact of intervening variables.

Theoretically, the results call for new understanding about child development. In addition to the paradigm of studying children's conceptions as adaptations, we need to consider children's views as independent variables that have the capacity to impact on the environment too. By studying these agentive views, we could get a better contact with the meta-cognitive processes children use in relation to their pressures. We could make a shift from the behavioural reactance to stress and concentrate more on cognitive equilibrium processes. We can have a perspective beyond the temperamental factors (Talge, Donzella, & Gunnar, 2008) into cognitive regulation in pressure situations.

Empirically, the interview tool for children's views on agency seems a promising tool for studying children's relation with environmental changes. At the heart of the interview tool is children's orientations towards change. The children's views are not studied in a given environment; rather, children's views are studied in order to see how they affect their own experiences and development. That development has an effect on others' development too. This may help in the study and measurement of psychological processes.

Practically, considering children as the agents of their stress reactions gives educators tools to help children in conducting their own development. When children become aware of the stress processes between environment and their views, they become better equipped to regulate their activity systems. The conclusion of the research is not that children should have as much accommodative and open views as possible to relieve stress. The conclusion is that it is important to study different views concerning change. Children can probably learn to use and understand stress as a tool needing modulation for empowerment.

References

Blair, C., Granger, D., & Razza, R.P. (2005). Cortisol reactivity is positively related to executive function in preschool children attending head start. *Child Development*, *76*(3), 554–567.

Cassiba, R., van Ijzendoorn, M., & D'Odorico, L. (2000). Attachment and play in child care centres: Reliability and validity of the attachment Q-sort for mothers and professional care-givers in Italy. *International Journal of Behavioral Development*, *24*(2), 241–255.

Constantino, J.N., & Olesh, H. (1999). Mental representations of attachment in day care providers. *Infant Mental Health Journal*, *20*(2), 138–147.

Gruber, H., & Vonèche, J.J. (1995). *The essential Piaget*. Northvale: Jason Aronson.

Gunnar, M., & Quevedo, K. (2007). The neurobiology of stress and development. *Annual Review of Psychology*, *58*(1), 145–173.

Hatzinger, M., Brand, S., Perren, S., Stadelmann, S., von Wyl, A., von Klitzing, K., Holsboer-Trachsler, E. (2008). Electroencephalographic sleep profiles and hypothalamic–pituitary–adrenocortical (HPA)-activity in kindergarten children: Early indication of poor sleep quality associated with increased cortisol secretion. *Journal of Psychiatric Research*, *42*(7), 532–543.

Hatzinger, M., Brand, S., Perren, S., Stadelmann, S., von Wyl, A., von Klitzing, K., Holsboer-Trachsler, E. (2010). Sleep actigraphy pattern and behavioral/emotional difficulties in kindergarten children: Association with hypothalamic–pituitary–adrenocortical (HPA) activity. *Journal of Psychiatric Research*, *44*(4), 253–261.

Legendre, A. (2003). Environmental features influencing toddlers' bioemotional reactions in day care centers. *Environment & Behavior*, *35*(4), 523–549.

Lisonbee, J.A., Mize, J., Payne, A.L., & Granger, D.A. (2008). Children's cortisol and the quality of teacher–child relationships in child care. *Child Development*, *79*(6), 1818–1832.

Maughan, M., Collishaw, S., Goodman, R., & Picles, A. (2004). Adolescent mental health problems on the increase. *Journal of Child Psychology and Psychiatry*, *45*(8), 1350–1362.

Miller, A.L., Seifer, R., Stroud, L., Sheinkopf, S.J., & Dickstein, S. (2006). Biobehavioral indices of emotion regulation relate to school attitudes, motivation, and behaviour problems in a low-income preschool sample. *Annals of the New York Academy of Sciences*, *1094*(1), 325–329.

Reunamo, J. (2005, August 31–September 3). *Curriculum: How open and changeable can it be?* Paper presented at the EECERA Conference in Dublin. Retrieved from http://www.helsinki.fi/~reunamo/article/eecera05.pdf

Reunamo, J. (2007a). Adaptation and agency in early childhood education. *European Early Childhood Education Research Journal*, *15*(3), 365–377.

Reunamo, J. (2007b). The agentive role of children's views in sustainable education. *Journal of Teacher Education for Sustainability*, *8*, 68–79.

Reunamo, J. (2007c). Children's agency: Imperative in education for sustainable development. In A. Pipere (Ed.), *Education and sustainable development: First steps towards changes* (Vol. 2, pp. 20–37). Daugavpils: Daugavpils University Academic Press Saule.

Reunamo, J. (2010, November 19–20). Children's agentive perception uncovered. In R. Wu (Ed.), *International conference on cross-cultural comparison of educational setting and children's agentive perception* (pp. 9–10). Sanxia: National Academy for Educational Research.

Sajaniemi, N., Suhonen, E., Kontu, E., Rantala, P., Hirvonen, A., Hyttinen, S., & Lindholm, H. (2011). Children's stress and the quality of the learning environment. *European Early Education Research Journal, 19,* 5–22.

Sontag, L.M., Graber, J.A., Brooks-Gunn, J., & Warren, M.P. (2008). Coping with social stress: Implications for psychopathology in young adolescent girls. *Journal of Abnormal Child Psychology, 36*(8), 1159–1174.

Talge, N.M., Donzella, B., & Gunnar, M.R. (2008). Fearful temperament and stress reactivity among preschool-aged children. *Infant & Child Development, 17*(4), 427–445.

Valiente, C., Lemery-Chalfant, K., & Swanson, J. (2009). Children's responses to daily social stressors: Relations with parenting, children's effortful control, and adjustment. *Journal of Child Psychology & Psychiatry, 50*(6), 707–717.

Watamura, S.E., Coe, C.L., Laudenslager, M.L., & Robertson, S.S. (2010). Child care setting affects salivary cortisol and antibody secretion in young children. *Psychoneuroendocrinology, 35*(8), 1156–1166.

Bullying in early educational settings

Laura Kirves and Nina Sajaniemi

The aim of this research was to study the prevalence of bullying in early educational settings in Finnish kindergartens. In addition, the study investigated whether bullying in kindergartens differs from school bullying and what forms bullying takes among under-school-age children. Two kinds of data were collected for the study: data from a survey of day care staff in the City of Vantaa ($n = 770$, involving 6910 children) and data from interviews of children, day care staff and parents ($n = 114$). The results of this study indicate that systematic bullying does occur among under-school-age children. The interviews showed that bullying among children under school-age appears to be a rather similar phenomenon to that of school bullying. According to our study, 12.6% of children (age three to six years) in day care were involved in bullying in one way or another. The most common form of bullying was exclusion from peer relationships. Moreover, according to our results, children in early childhood education talked about bullying as an everyday phenomenon and its content varied only slightly from adults' speech on the topic.

Introduction

There is much research on bullying at school and in the work place, but few studies have been made of under-school-age children. However, those studies that have been carried out indicate that bullying is a severe problem among under-school-age children (Alsaker & Nägele, 2008; Alsaker & Valkanover, 2001; Crick, Casas, & Ku, 1999; Hanish, Kochenderfer-Ladd, Fabes, Martin, & Denning, 2004; Kochenderfer & Ladd, 1996; Monks, Ortega Ruiz, & Torrado Val, 2002; Perren, 2000).

Bullying has been found to be a risk factor in the development of children and adolescents (Eriksson, Lindberg, Flygare, & Daneback, 2002). It is important to recognise the early signs of bullying and to prevent its progression. Bullying can lead to problems in relationships later in life, both for the bully and for the victim. It has been observed that bullied children and adolescents suffer from low self-esteem, depression, anxiety and even self-destructive thoughts (Rigby, 2003). Children who bully other children have either an increased risk for anti-social and criminal behaviour or an increased risk of bullying others as an adult. Especially, children who are aggressive victims (bully-victims) seem to have a particular tendency to be socially excluded later in life (Sourander et al., 2009). Being the victim of a bully at an early age (five to seven years) contributes to maladjustment during the first years of schooling. Prevention and intervention programmes aimed at reducing mental health problems during childhood should target bullying as an important risk factor as early as possible (Arsenault et al., 2006).

Finnish kindergartens

The current early childhood education system in Finland is based on the Act on Children's Day Care (1973). Early education consists of municipal or private kindergartens, family day care, use of a home care subsidy and preschool. In 2010, 67.2% of three- to five–year-old children participated in early education in Finland. The participation rate is clearly lower than the average for OECD countries. Preschool is based on the Finnish Basic Education Act (1998). Every child has the right to free preschool one year before compulsory education. In practice, virtually every child participates in the education system from the age of six (preschool and compulsory school) (Tilastokeskus, 2010).

The Act on Children's Day Care regulates the number of qualified members of staff in kindergarten groups. Children under three years of age are generally educated and cared for in the same group (toddlers' groups), where there must be one qualified member of staff per four children. Children aged three to five are generally placed in the same group, and there must be one qualified member of staff per seven children. The maximum size for groups is not regulated. A common group size for children aged three to five is 21–25. However, a wide variety of mixed groups is also possible, depending on the size of the municipality and kindergarten. Six-year-old children comprise the preschool groups, and the size of the group can vary a lot. However, the minimum size of a preschool group is seven children.

The definition of school bullying

The definition of bullying is mainly based on research into bullying among school-aged children. In school, bullying is seen as a subcategory of aggressive behaviour (Smith & Cowie, 1991). Aggressive behaviour, as such, includes the potential harm of an action and the intentionality of the act. In addition, bullying has features which distinguish it from other aggressive acts. For decades, bullying has been seen as a group phenomenon where a few people take part in the actual violence while many more observers allow the gradual increase of the violent behaviour (Heinemann, 1972). There are many studies that consider bullying a group phenomenon where the group's passive acceptance of negative actions has a significant influence on the continuation of bullying (Pikas, 1987).

The most frequently used definition of bullying was formulated by Norwegian researcher Olweus (1973). According to him, 'A person is being bullied or victimised when he or she is exposed, repeatedly and over time, to negative actions on the part of one or more other persons'. He defined negative actions as behaviours that intentionally inflict, or attempt to inflict, injury or discomfort on other persons. Separate negative actions can be defined as bullying if they are continual and occur over a longer period of time. In contrast, occasional, separate and minor negative actions targeted at a variety of people should not be defined as bullying (Olweus, 1973).

In most definitions, bullying is also seen as an imbalance of power relations between the victim and the bully where the victim has trouble defending himself against the negative actions targeted against him (Salmivalli, 2002). Furthermore, bullying has been seen as a part of the problem in interaction processes where a student is regularly hurt, harmed, and/or discriminated against by one or several students without being able to defend himself or affect the way he is treated (Pörhölä, Karhunen, & Rainivaara, 2006). Some researchers also emphasise the use of power and aggression without highlighting the repetitiveness of the actions (Pepler & Craig, 2009).

Some researchers have warned against too strict or narrow definitions of bullying (Eriksson et al., 2002; Hamarus, 2006). It is important to remember that children's experiences of bullying are different both at an individual level and for different age groups. It is important to take the victim's own personal experience of the situation into account. If the definition of bullying is too narrow, there is a risk that behaviour which is perceived by the victim as offensive and degrading, and which can have far-reaching consequences, remains unnoticed and ignored.

The definition of bullying and young children

Definitions based on bullying in school have been used when studying bullying in kindergarten. In Perren and Alsaker's (2006) study, the frequency of the negative action was used to define bullying: a child was considered a victim or a bully if she or he was victimised or bullied others at least once a week. However, there has been a controversy over the labelling of young children as bullies, using traditional definitions of bullying (Hanish et al., 2004). For example, it might be difficult to differentiate between the early emergence of more serious bullying behaviour and normative developmental trends in the expression of aggressive behaviour during early childhood (Hanish et al., 2004). According to Hanish et al. (2004), bullies among young children are children whose behaviour is more frequently aggressive than others. In addition, young children seem to equate bullying with general aggression and consequently view the victim as someone who, while being the target of aggression, is not necessarily unable to defend him or herself (Monks, Smith, & Swettenham, 2003). Monks et al. (2003) suggest that the term aggressor should be used instead of bully among young children.

Awareness of the negative actions perpetrated against a person has been seen as a prerequisite for any definition of bullying (Tattum & Herbert, 1992). However, Slee and Rigby (1994) argue that the focus should be on how often and how long the behaviour continues rather than on evaluating the purpose behind the action, especially for young children. They claim that if the action reoccurs over a longer period of time, it is not a case of aggression but of bullying (Slee & Rigby, 1994).

Young children focus more on forms of physical aggression in their definitions of bullying, whereas school-aged children also pay attention to relational aggression (Monks et al., 2003).

Young children easily equate bullying with physical aggression and physical aggression often forms a part of six-year-old children's definition of bullying (Smith & Levan, 1995; Vaillancourt et al., 2008).

In our study, we aimed to find out whether children, day care staff and researchers have a similar understanding and conception of bullying and whether they use definitions similar to those described above. In Finland, bullying among young children has not been studied before.

The prevalence of bullying

The prevalence of bullying depends both on the definition and the method of data collection, which can be by self-nomination, peer-nomination, teacher ratings or parent ratings

(Nordhagen, Nielsen, Stigum, & Köhler, 2005; Salmivalli, 2002). In a WHO comparison of 40 countries (Currie et al., 2008), Finland had the 6th lowest rate for bullies and victims of bullying among 11-year-old children. The same study produced various figures for bullying in Finland, including the finding that 11% of boys were the victims of bullying and 2% of girls bullied others. In sum, Finland is doing well compared with many other countries. Iceland and Sweden had the lowest rates for bullying in the Nordic countries while Norway and Denmark had the highest.

In Finland there is a large prevention programme to combat school bullying (the KiVa anti-bullying programme) (Salmivalli, Kärnä, & Poskiparta, 2010) funded by the Ministry of Education and Culture. The studies carried out in this programme reveal that the prevalence of victimisation in Finland is higher than the figure in the WHO study. These studies indicate that 8% of 11-year-olds bully others, while 14% are victims of bullying (Salmivalli, 2010). According to evaluation studies done in the KiVa programme, bullying seems to have been significantly reduced in Finnish schools, especially in the lower grades (Salmivalli, Kärnä, & Poskiparta, 2011). This indicates that prevention directed at young children is effective and should start even before children reach school age.

It has been argued that it is especially difficult to discover the actual prevalence rates of bullying among young children. Kindergarten aged children can easily tell who the bullies of the group are, but they appear to have trouble in recognising who the victim is (Alsaker, 1993; Monks et al., 2003). It has been suggested that preschool teachers are most reliably able to evaluate bullies and victims (Alsaker & Nägele, 2008). Perren (2000) states that observation could be the best method for obtaining reliable information on bullying in kindergarten. According to her study, 11% of the children bully other children, 6% are bullied by others and 10% both bully and are bullied (bully-victims) (Perren, 2000).

Different forms of bullying

Many researchers divide bullying into indirect and direct bullying (Marini, Dane, Bosacki, & YLC-CURA, 2006; Olweus, 1996). Direct bullying is characterised by direct attacks such as kicking, hitting, taking the victim's belongings, threatening and name-calling. Indirect bullying involves spreading gossip, lying, talking behind another's back and the deliberate excluding of someone from the group. Indirect bullying is also known as relational or social aggression, in which bullying is based on sabotaging someone's friendships until eventually the victim is isolated and excluded from the community (Crick et al., 1999). Höistad (2005) divides bullying into physical, psychological and verbal bullying. An example of psychological bullying would be behaviour where the victim is treated as non-existent: bullies turn their back on him; he is not answered when he speaks; or the victim is excluded from the group by some other means. Physical bullying means physical violence, breaking or hiding the victim's belongings, or something similar. Verbal bullying is name-calling, spreading gossip, teasing and mocking.

Bullying among children with special education needs and children with an immigrant background

Several studies (Fredericson, 2010; Gresham & MacMillan, 1997; Nakken & Pijl, 2002) have found that pupils with special education needs are generally less accepted and more often rejected than are their classmates. Low social status in the peer group is associated with risks to children's development and well-being. Furthermore, low social acceptance increases the risk of victimisation, and children with special educational needs typically have a lower status in the peer group than their classmates. Thus, children with special educational needs experience higher levels of bullying than their classmates (Carter & Spencer, 2006). Research into bullying related to special educational needs among under-school-age children has not been carried out before.

There are some studies which have shown that foreign children are at a greater risk of peer rejection in their school classes (Graham & Juvonen, 2001; Quintana et al., 2006). In their study, Strohmeier, Kärnä, and Salmivalli (2011) found that immigrants were more often the target of both peer and self-reported victimisation compared with native youth in Finland. They experienced higher levels of physical, racist, and sexual victimisation than native Finns. Studies in Germany have also shown that students preferred peers of their own nationality for friendship (Popp, 1994). However, there is little empirical support for the view that immigrant status *per se* is a risk factor for victimisation (Graham, Taylor, & Ho, 2009).

A study of kindergarten children in Switzerland showed that immigrant children had a higher risk of low peer acceptance and higher peer victimisation than the native population (von Grünigen, Perren, Nägele, & Alsaker, 2010). An American study by Ladd and Burgess (2001) also found that African-American kindergarten children had a high risk of chronic peer rejection.

In our present study, we aimed to investigate the prevalence of bullying in kindergarten. We also aimed to discover the methods and forms of bullying among young children.

Methods

Participants

The quantitative data were collected using a questionnaire on bullying in early educational settings. The questionnaire was sent to every member of the staff working with children aged three to six in every kindergarten in the City of Vantaa. There were a total of 1316 adults working in these groups, and 1116 of them had the required qualification for Finnish early education. The total number of respondents was 770 (58.5%) in 367 different day care groups.

The study included 6910 children. The study covered 89% of children aged four to six in the kindergartens participating in the study. The exact number of children who had already had their third birthday and were still in the toddlers' groups was not available. That is why the scope of the study is stated as only being children aged four to six. However, the real scope of the study is even higher. In short, it is justifiable to say that the data covered nearly all three- to six-year-old children attending kindergarten in the City of Vantaa.

The qualitative data were collected by interviewing children aged three to six ($n = 61$), parents ($n = 24$) and staff ($n = 29$) in eight day care centres. The day care centres were chosen randomly by sending information about the study to kindergartens in two municipalities in the Helsinki metropolitan area. The first to express their willingness to participate were chosen. In both municipalities, the research permits were applied for from the bureaus responsible for early childhood education, and the study was carried out in co-operation with both of these municipalities.

The children were interviewed on a voluntary basis, and therefore not all the children in all the groups were interviewed; instead, children participated according to their own willingness.

Procedure

The questionnaire

The questionnaire sought to detect the prevalence of bullying in day care groups of three- to six-year-old children. In the questionnaire, bullying was defined according to the definition given by Olweus (1973), with the addition that quarrels between equal children were not counted as bullying. When defining special educational needs and immigrant backgrounds, the same definition was used that the City of Vantaa uses in its day care policy.

The staff reported the figures from the groups in which they were working: number of children in the group, gender, number of children with special needs or immigrant backgrounds and number of qualified adults.

The questionnaire had a separate column evaluated by the staff for each child who either bullied others, was victimised, or both. Furthermore, the forms of bullying and the children's recollection of the background information were collected from these children. The identities of the individual children were not revealed in the questionnaire.

The interviews

The child and parent interviews were carried out with the written consent of the parents. The aim of the interviews was to evaluate and understand children's social world as described by them, and to examine the perceptions of adults living and working with young children. Therefore, it was not seen as necessary to point out any background information (age, gender, socio-economic background, special needs, etc.) on the children or the day care centres in question.

The interview used for the children was modified from an interview frame designed for a research project called 'Social relations of young children' at the University of Turku (Laine & Neitola, 2002). The child interviews were well structured, but there was space for the children to spontaneously tell their stories. In the interviews, the children described those issues which they perceived as bullying (What do you think bullying means? What happens then? What kind of actions are bullying? Have you ever seen it? What happened then?), where bullying occurred and what kind of things made them feel bad or sad in day care. They were also asked about friendship;, for example, who was frequently left without a friend, who was popular and who messed up other children's games.

Pilot interviews for six children in two different kindergartens were conducted before the actual interviews commenced. These children did not participate in the study. To support the interviews, the researchers had pictures intended to help children return to the subject and to lighten the atmosphere with shy and sensitive children. However, the children proved to be highly willing to talk about bullying, and these kinds of problems were extremely rare. It was important to establish a trusting relationship with the child, and all interviews began with a discussion about other subjects, such as favourite foods or activities.

The verbal development of children varies greatly between the ages of three and six and children with special education needs were also interviewed. This was taken into account by approaching bullying from various perspectives, for instance, by asking what made the child feel bad in day care. For example, the question 'Have you been bullied in day care?' was also asked in the form 'Do you ever feel bad or sad here in day care?', and the question 'In which ways have you been bullied?' was changed to 'What kinds of things make you feel bad or sad here in day care?' When conducting interviews with children, it is also important that the interviewer does not lead the child into answering in a certain way, and attention was paid to this matter to the greatest extent possible.

The interviews with the members of staff were conducted as themed interviews where the researcher guided the interviewee towards the subject and let the interviewee describe and speak about the subject as widely as possible. Some of the parents who took part in the interviews already had a bullying-related story in mind, in which case, it was these stories that guided the interviews instead of the researcher's questions.

Data analysis

The quantitative data were analysed as either descriptive data or percentages, and the prevalence of bullying in the various groups was then presented in the results. The between group differences were tested using the χ^2-test. A p-value of less than 0.05 was considered statistically significant.

More than one day care member of staff from each day care group answered the questionnaire. The respondents were classified by group, and the average number of bullies, victims or bully-victims per group was reported.

All the interviews were recorded and transcribed. The Interview data were analysed using content analysis and by categorising the data according to frequency and certain themes. Categorisation was based on recurring themes in the answers and on those individual answers used to explain and describe the nature of the phenomenon among under-school-age children which were comparable with definitions of school bullying. Themes were linked to the elements of the definition of school bullying, such as frequency, intentionality of actions and use of power. Several answers were found in each section, and these findings are highlighted by the examples of the interviews in the results.

The data were compared with the theories that generally explain and describe bullying – the aim was to find out whether the features generally pointed out in the literature on bullying can be found among young children as well.

Results

Prevalence of bullying

The total number of children involved, their gender, immigrant status and children with special education needs are presented in Table 1.

Our results show that 7.1% of day care children bullied other children, while 3.3% were bullied by others and 2.2% were bully-victims. This indicates that a total of 12.6% of the children in the study were directly involved in bullying. In addition, there was an average of 1.3 bullies in every group.

Fifteen per cent of the children included in the study had immigrant status. As Figure 1 also shows, 6.9% of immigrant children were bullies, 5.2% were victims and 2.7% were bully-victims. Thus, the immigrant children did not bully others

Table 1.   The total amount of children by group (number and %).

Total		
Children	6910	
Boys	3462	50.10%
Girls	3440	49.78%
Immigrants	1039	15.03%
Special needs	765	11.07%

Note: Children reported with no gender $n = 8$.

more than the native Finnish children ($p > 0.05$), but they were victimised more often ($p < 0.05$) than the native Finns.

Furthermore, 11.6% of the children in the study had special educational needs; of those 13.5% were bullies ($p < 0.05$), 6.7% were victims ($p < 0.05$) and 7.8% were bully-victims ($p < 0.05$). This is clearly higher than the average for the children with no special needs (Figure 1).

Table 2 reveals the total number of boys and girls who bullied, were the victims of bullying, or both. The combined difference between the number of girls and boys in the study was 0.32% in favour of the girls.

The mean age of children who bullied others, were bullied by others or were bully-victims was 4.9 years 4.8 years, and 5.05 years, respectively. Boys (64.3%) were bullies more often than girls (35.7%). The difference is statistically significant ($p < 0.05$). In addition, boys (62.5%) were more often bully-victims than girls (37.3%, $p < 0.05$).

Figure 2 illustrates the total amount of bullying by age. Bullies were more often boys than girls in every age group. As can be seen, at age six there were more victimised girls than boys. In all age groups there were more boys who were both bullies and victims than girls.

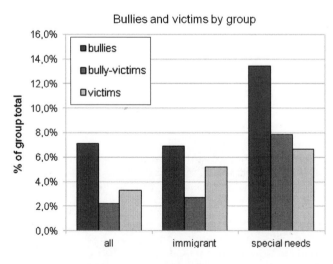

Figure 1.   The amount (%) of bullies, victims and bully-victims by group (all, immigrants and children with special needs).

Table 2.   The total amount of bullies, victims an bully-victims (Incl others = children reported with no gender or age).

	Bullies			Victims		Bully-victims	
	All	Boys	Girls	Boys	Girls	Boys	Girls
Total	811	289	160	107	106	93	56
Incl others	853	309	171	111	109	96	57

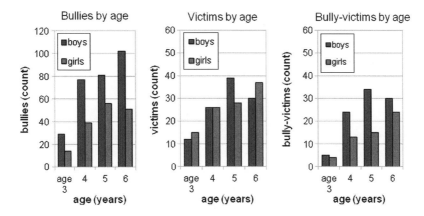

Figure 2.   Bullies, victims and bully-victims by age and gender (the children who were reported without gender or age *n* = 42, not included).

Perspectives on bullying from children, day care staff and parents

The interviews showed that the phenomenon of bullying did occur in kindergarten. Use of the term 'bullying' was commonplace among the children and day care staff. The term described the same kind of phenomenon defined or understood as school bullying, although use of the term among the children varied somewhat. Furthermore, the children did not always recognise that such things as exclusion could be bullying, although they talked about it as a matter that made them feel bad or sad in kindergarten. So it was important to look behind the term when analysing the interviews.

Features of behaviour in keeping with the definition of school bullying were sought from the answers. Those features were intentionality, frequency, and an imbalance of power.

The following examples highlight intentionality:

Interviewer: 'Is here someone who bullies others?'
Boy, aged 5: 'Yes, there is that Niko, he bosses around and intentionally hit me in my head, really intentionally'.
Interviewer: 'If it was an accident?'
Boy, aged 5: 'No, it was intentional'.
Day care teacher: '... And in a sense the other is hurt in a very, very intentional way, that kind of downright plotting and, then this kind of plotting of course occurs in groups as well, it is not only one child who comes up with it, it is decided in a group'.

In the following example, the child describes a situation in which the express purpose is to harm and make the other feel bad:

Interviewer: 'What do you think happens when someone bullies someone?'
Boy, aged 5: 'Does something that the other doesn't like'.

Even young children check whether there is an adult watching before they act. According to the children themselves 'stupid things' happened when there were no adults to witness the occurrence. This supports the argument that even young children are somewhat aware of the fact that they are misbehaving.

The children's answers also included descriptions of frequently occurring actions. In many interviews, the children said that the same person was repeatedly the target of bullying.

Boy, aged 5: 'That the same person is always being tricked'.
Girl, aged 6: 'That the whole group bullies one'.

Elements related to the use of power were also found in the interviews with the children.

Interviewer: 'Well, if someone bullies, what he does to the other?'
Boy, aged 5: 'Well he does something bad'.
Interviewer: 'What that could be?'
Boy, aged 5: 'Threatening and lying'.

In addition, being left without a friend was perceived as a form of threatening, and thus bullying, by the children and the day care staff.

Girl, aged 5: 'They say I cannot play with them cause I'm stupid. I am not stupid'.

In the staff interviews, use of power was used to mean situations related to the children's social relations. The members of staff felt that some of the children were able to use power and manipulate the rest of the group. A typical form of manipulation was blackmail over birthday parties. It was found to be common that children modify their birthday party guest lists according to how well the rest of the group acts as they wish. One day care teacher told the interviewer that a five-year-old boy who had a birthday in May had already started to manipulate the social relations of the boys in the group in January. Children are motivated by a desire to raise their social status in the group, and birthday parties act as a tool to achieve this.

The children's perceptions of bullying only slightly varied from those of the adults. However, there were answers that were difficult to interpret and did not support our overall findings on the phenomenon.

Girl, aged 5: 'Well the boys bullied me outside'
Interviewer: 'How did they do that? What happened?'
Girl, aged 5: 'They showed me a dead bee outside, and it was slimy all over'.

A few children used the term bullying but could not specify the acts that it involved. It was impossible to judge whether the term was used to describe the actual phenomenon or something else, as in the following example:

Interviewer: '... so have you been bullied here in kindergarten?'
Boy, aged 5: 'Yes, many times'.
Interviewer: 'What happened?'

Boy, aged 5: 'I don't remember'
Interviewer: 'Do you remember who bullied you?'
Boy, aged 5: 'No, I don't remember that either'

Furthermore, the staff emphasised the fact that children can also use the term to refer to quite different kinds of actions. They stressed the fact that it is important for adults to assess whether a child is actually talking about bullying or something else. For example, a child might say that other children bully her if they do not play in the way she wants.

The parent's answers differed slightly from those in the interviews with the staff. Highly similar elements of the definition of bullying were found, but the parents were unsure of whether mistreatment by children of this age could be called bullying. They explained the phenomenon as a phase in a child's development or alternatively argued that young children are not supposed to be able to control their aggressive behaviour.

Mother: 'they are more such things that the child does no control that situation, that it comes in the kinds of outbursts that fists swing'

Despite the similarity of their answers to those of the day care staff, the parents said that they had not thought about the definition of bullying before or discussed it in their kindergarten. Most staff members also reported that more information was needed to prevent bullying.

Forms of bullying

According to our survey results, the most common form of bulling was psychological bullying (10.7% of all forms of bulling). The most common method of psychological bullying was exclusion from the peer group. The second most common form of bullying was different kinds of verbal bullying (8.18%), including name-calling, pointing and laughing; physical bullying was less common (7.45%) (Figure 3).

Exclusion and leaving others outside the group were the most common forms of bullying mentioned in the interviews, and they aroused much discussion among both children and adults. The staff viewed excluding others from a game as a way of using power and manipulating social relations within the group.

The children gave accurate answers to questions about who in the group was left out; who was rejected by others and excluded and who was popular; and who messed up or disturbed others' games. Even a three-year-old child recognises what it means to be rejected and isolated by the group. However, the children thought that playing alone was not a problem for the excluded child. In a few groups where there was a child excluded from the group, the children described the fact that the child was prevented from joining the other children's games, but they went on to say that it did not bother the child because he wanted to play alone. From this, it can be concluded that children recognise each other's roles in the group but have more difficulty in understanding the consequences and the fact that group roles are not necessarily voluntarily chosen.

Interviewer: 'Is here someone who never has any friends?'
Pyry, aged 3: 'Well me, it is me'.

Physical bullying	Verbal bullying	Psychological bullying
• Hitting • Kicking • Tripping • Pushing • Being as an obstacle • Tearing clothes • Pinching • Throwing rocks and sand • Messing up with plays • Chasing	• Name-calling • Mocking • Teasing • Pointing and laughing • Commenting on hair, clothes	• Threatening • Manipulating • Blackmailing • Making faces, grinning • Excluding • Changing the rules of a play • Ignoring • Talking behind one's back

Figure 3. The forms and methods of bullying in kindergarten according to the interviews.

Afterwards the day care staff was asked to confirm the information in this example. According to their observations, the boy was lonely and easily rejected by the rest of the group. Another child reported that the boy in question was frequently without a play-mate, but that it was because he did not want to play with others, and thus it did not make him feel bad or a victim.

> Interviewer: 'Do you think that Pyry feels bad because he doesn't have friends?'
> Boy, aged 5: 'He doesn't, I know. He feels good'.
> Interviewer: 'You mean he likes to be alone?'
> Boy, aged 5: 'Yes, he feels good that he doesn't have friends'.

By changing the rules of a game, a child can be seemingly included, but in reality he does not have any real opportunity to take part in the game or influence how it proceeds. This kind of situation may arise when a child repeatedly gets an unsatisfactory role in the game.

> Nurse: 'Then we have that one child who is indeed involved in the play but I have always watched as he has to be a dog, that kind of outdoor dog'.

The children were able to produce answers related to indirect psychological bully-ing, which aims to harm the victim indirectly. In the following example, a six-year-old girl reports that there is such a thing as blackmailing, after which she explains what it means and finally notes that it is bullying.

> Girl, aged 6: 'Then there is a thing called blackmailing, the kind of when somebody black-mails, and that is like when a friend says that I am not your friend if you don't do this and that, and that is bullying'.

In summary, the interviews show that the term 'bullying' is a commonly used term in Finnish early education, although the definition of the term has seldom been discussed. The children's descriptions were highly similar, and their understanding of the phenomenon differed only slightly, despite the fact that the use of the term varied.

The day care staff also placed emphasis on and included in the definition the significance of the child's subjective experience and the varying tolerance children have in regard to different actions.

Discussion

Our study revealed that systematic bullying is a well-recognised and common phenomenon among children who attend institutional day care in Finland. Our results show that 12.6% of day care children aged three to six were directly involved in the phenomenon of bullying. The average number of bullies in each day care group was 1.3. In addition, 2.2% of children involved in bullying were categorised as both bullies and victims in our study. It is noteworthy that many of the children who were bully-victims (39.1%) were children with special education needs.

Interestingly, the children and the adults seemed to agree on what behaviour was judged bullying. From the age of three, children were able to identify bullying, and they accurately knew which kinds of actions were hurtful to others. In addition, they could distinguish bullying from quarrelling.

In light of our results, it is important to emphasise the fact that behaviour patterns related to bullying, and the roles associated with it, already emerge in early childhood. Owing to the lack discussion on bullying, personnel in early childhood education lack sufficient knowledge of bullying as a phenomenon, and thus they may be unable to prevent it. Insufficient preventive practices might jeopardise children's well-being and participation in the group, especially for children with increased developmental risks. Our study revealed that bullying often concerned children with special education needs. Those children can have a double risk of social exclusion, and for them preventive practices are of the utmost importance. In addition, bullying was highlighted among children with an immigrant background in our study. It should be pointed out that they did not bully other children more than did the native Finns – instead, they were more often victimised. This finding is also supported by international studies (von Grünigen et al., 2010).The early onset of bullying in those with ethnic backgrounds is extremely alarming in a globalising, multicultural society, and it needs to be strongly addressed.

Furthermore, our results show that while an equal number of boys and girls are the victims of bullying, boys bully other children more than girls. It might be important to rethink our attitudes towards the behaviour that we expect from boys and girls. It has been argued that boys are allowed to behave more roughly and overtly aggressively than girls (Werner & Grant, 2009). In addition, it is assumed that boys prefer peer group relationships, which involve dominance issues, and girls prefer dyadic relationships (Baron-Cohen, 2010). These attitudes might result in the acceptance of excluding behaviour in the case of girls and competitive, aggressive behaviour in the case of boys. In consequence, negative behaviour associated with bullying might remain unrecognised or even be strengthened.

Our research was the first in Finland to focus on early-age bullying and its prevalence in early educational settings. In contrast, all day care centres and pre-school classes in Sweden are required by law to compile a plan for equal treatment, including intervention against and prevention of bullying (Lag, 2006:67). In Norway, several political parties have signed a manifesto for eradicating bullying, which applies to day care as well (Norwegian Ministry of Education and Research et al., 2010). In Finland, every school is required by law to have an action plan for protecting students from violence, bullying and harassment (Law 629/1998). The law covers pre-primary and further education in comprehensive schools. However, bullying is not mentioned in the legislation on early education (Stakes, 2005). Therefore, it is fundamentally important to create a framework for intervening and developing preventive practices for early education in Finland, and that is exactly what we are aiming to do in the future.

Our study shows that bullying in early childhood education appears to be a similar phenomenon to that in schools, and thus we are justified in using the term among young children as well. The level of bullying shown in our study was approximately the same as that among primary school children in Finland, but it was somewhat lower than in international studies (Perren, 2000). However, the term bullying is not without its problems. By exaggerating the phenomenon, we could actually increase its prevalence and stigmatise individual children. Indeed, it is important not to categorise children at an early age, and so careful consideration should be given to whether it is appropriate to use terms like 'bully' and 'victim' with regard to young children. However, our results clearly indicated that the roles of 'bully' and 'victim' were already visible among children as young as three years old. Therefore, it is important to recognise bullying behaviour at the very beginning and, at the same time, be aware of the harmful effects of stigmatising children. Most importantly, children should be helped to find alternative ways of behaving during challenging moments.

However, it is difficult both to identify the point when occasional negative behaviour turns into bullying, and to understand the various motives behind the behaviour. Defining bullying among young children is by no means trouble-free. In Sweden, the term 'insulting behaviour' is used to refer to bullying among young children, and it is something which should be addressed immediately (Act, 2006:67). This is also a way of ensuring that certain actions which might have far-reaching consequences are not ignored due to narrow definitions. Bullying is also a subjective concept, and children have different tolerances for different actions. It is essential to consider these factors when bullying is defined among young children. It is crucial to guide members of staff in early childhood education towards a common understanding of the nature and a definition of the phenomenon.

Strengths and limitations of the study

Our study provides a comprehensive review of the phenomenon of bullying in Finnish early childhood education. Our quantitative data revealed the incidence of bullying separately for each child. Exact and accurate information was obtained on the children's backgrounds and the forms of bullying. The coverage and the response rate were exceptionally high in our study. The questionnaire reached a very high number of day care staff, and the study covered almost all three- to six-year-old kindergarten children in Vantaa.

The children clarified the phenomenon of bullying and gave credibility to the study. It is important that the subjects of the study – the children themselves – have their voices heard. The similarity between the interview data from the adults and the children confirms that the study gives a real illustration of the social reality shared by both children and the adults in early childhood education. The interviews with the staff also helped in evaluating the reliability of the children's stories and the way they used the concept.

However, our data have a clear limitation. We do not know the number of children in each age group. We have only the number of actual bullies, victims, and bully-victims in each age group. Thus, it is not possible to compare the prevalence of bullies, victims and bully-victims by age.

The nature of the phenomenon itself also sets limitations on the study. Bullying is a subjective concept, and indeed there were notable variations in responses between individual children. Despite the fact that bullying was precisely defined in the questionnaire, some members of staff might have identified a particular child as a bully while others working in the same group did not. It is very difficult, if not impossible, to state the objective truth for a phenomenon which is both hard to define and highly subjective.

Conclusions

In 2009, the City of Vantaa conducted a day care customer satisfaction survey by asking children for their views and opinions on day care and its quality. The study revealed that 21% of day care children were afraid of bullying in day care centres (The City of Vantaa, 2009). This finding is highly alarming and needs to be taken seriously. Our present study shows that there is more fear of bullying than there are actual cases, but fear of being bullied negatively affects the quality of early childhood education.

Our study confirms earlier findings that illustrate the early onset of bullying (Alsaker & Nägele, 2008). However, in Finland it has been commonly believed that young children are incapable of systematic bullying. Consequently, there is a severe lack of research and public debate concerning bullying among under-school-age children.

Even small children can recognise whether they like or dislike the other children in their peer group, and thus the children's social hierarchy begins to develop. As this study revealed, exclusion is a common and serious form of bullying – children get upset and talk about it. It is highly important for the quality of the early education as a whole that the children feel they are accepted members of the group. In addition, bullying has a significant impact on children's learning processes and their well-being in later life. Increasing spending on early education is the most cost-effective way of preventing exclusion and the deepening of social disadvantages (Heymann, Herzman, Barer, & Evans, 2006).

Acknowledgements

This study was supported by Aalto University, Systems Analysis Laboratory. This study forms part of the corresponding author's dissertation *Bullying and its Prevention in Early Educational Settings*.

References

Act on Children's Day Care. (1973/36). Laki lasten päivähoidosta. Ministry of Justice, Finland.

Alsaker, F. (1993). Isolement et maltraitance par les pairs dans les jardins d'enfants: Comment mesurer ces phénomènes et quelles sont leurs conséquences? *Enfance, 47,* 241–260

Alsaker, F., & Nägele, C. (2008). Bullying in kindergarten and prevention. In D. Pepler & W. Craig (Eds.), *Understanding and addressing bullying: An international perspective* (pp. 230–252). Bloomington, IN: Bloomington.

Alsaker, F.D., & Valkanover, S. (2001). Early diagnosis and prevention of victimization in kindergarten. In J. Juvonen & S. Graham (Eds.), *Peer harassment in school: The plight of the vulnerable and victimized.* New York, NY: Guilford Press.

Arsenault, L., Walsh, E., Trzesniewski, K., Newcombe, R., Caspi, A., & Moffitt, T. (2006). Bullying victimization uniquely contributes to adjustment problems in young children: A nationally representative cohort study. *Official Journal of the American Academy of Pediatrics, 118,* 130–138.

Baron-Cohen, S. (2010). The gender delusion: The real science behind sex differences. *Psychologist, 23*(11), 904–905.

Carter, B.B., & Spencer, V.G. (2006). The fear factor: Bullying and students with disabilities. *International Journal of Special Education, 21*(1), 11–23.

Crick, N.R., Casas, J.F., & Ku, H. (1999). Relational and physical forms of peer victimization in pre-school. *Developmental Psychology, 35,* 376–385.

Currie, C., Gabhainn, S.N., Godeau, E., Roberts, C., Smith, R., Currie, D., …, Barnekow, V. (Eds.). (2008). *Inequalities in young people's health: HBSC international report from the 2005/2006 Survey,* Health Policy for Children and Adolescents No. 5, WHO Regional Office for Europe, Copenhagen, Denmark. Retrieved from http://www.euro.who.int/en/what-we-do/health-topics/Life-stages/child-and-adolescent-health/publications2/2011/inequalities-in-young-peoples-health.-hbsc-international-report-from-the-20052006-survey.

Eriksson, B., Lindberg, O., Flygare, E., & Daneback, K. (2002). *Skolan – en arena för mobbning – en forskningsöversikt och diskussion kring mobbning i skolan.* Stockholm: Skolverket.

Finnish Basic Education Act, Perusopetuslaki (628/1998), 29 §. (1998).

Fredericson, N. (2010). Bullying or befriending? Children's responses to classmates with special needs. *British Journal of Special Education, 37*(1), 4–12.

Graham, S., & Juvonen, J. (2001). *Peer harassment in school: The plight of the vulnerable and victimized.* New York, NY: Guilford Press.

Graham, S., Taylor, A., & Ho, A. (2009). Race and ethnicity in peer relations research. In K. Rubin, W.M. Bukowski, & B. Laursen (Eds.), *Handbook of peer interactions, relationships, and groups* (pp. 394–413). New York, NY: Guilford Press.

Gresham, F., & Macmillan, D. (1997). Social confidence and affective characteristics of students with mild disabilities. *Review of Educational Research, 67,* 377–415.

von Grünigen, R., Perren, S., Nägele, C., & Alsaker, F. (2010). Immigrant children's peer acceptance and victimization in kindergarten: The role of local language competence. *British Journal of Developmental Psychology, 28*(3), 679–697.

Hamarus, P. (2006). *Koulukiusaaminen ilmiönä: yläkoulun oppilaiden kokemuksia kiusaamisesta* (Doctoral dissertation). University of Jyväskylä, Jyväskylä.

Hanish, L.D., Kochenderfer-Ladd, B., Fabes, R.A., Martin, C.L., & Denning, D. (2004). Bullying among young children: The influence of peers and teachers. In D.L. Espelage & S. Swearer (Eds.), *Bullying in Amercan schools: A social ecological perspective on prevention and intervention* (pp. 141–160). Mahwah, NJ: Erlbaum Publishers.

Heinemann, P.-P. (1972). *Mobbning. Gruppvåld bland barn och vuxna.* Stockholm: Natur och Kultur.

Heymann, J., Herzman, C., Barer, M.L., & Evans, R.G. (2006). *Healthier societies: From analysis to action.* Oxford: Oxford University Press.

Höistad, G. (2005). *Mobbning och människovärde. Om förtryck, utanförskap och vad vi kan göra.* Solna: Ekelunds.

Kochenderfer, B., & Ladd, G.W. (1996). Peer victimization: Manifestations and relations to school adjustment in kindergarten. *Journal of School Psychology, 34,* 267–283.

Ladd, G.W., & Burgess, K.B. (2001). Do relational risks and protective factors moderate the linkages between childhood aggression and early psychological and school adjustment? *Child Development, 72,* 1579–1601

Lag. (2006:67). *Lag om förbud mot diskriminering och annan kränkande behandling av barn och elever §67* [Swedish law prohibiting the discrimination and other insulting behavior of children and students]. Utbildningsdepartment.

Laine, K., & Neitola, M. (Eds.). (2002). *Lasten syrjäytyminen päiväkodin vertaisryhmästä.* Turku: Suomen kasvatustieteellinen seura.

Marini, Z., Dane, A., Bosacki, S., & YLC-CURA. (2006). Direct and indirect bully-victims: Differential psychosocial risk factors associated with adolescents involved in bullying and victimization. *Aggressive Behavior, 32,* 551–569.

Monks, C., Ortega Ruiz, R., & Torrado Val, E. (2002). Unjustified aggression in preschool. *Aggressive Behavior, 28,* 458–476.

Monks, C., Smith, P., & Swettenham, J. (2003). Aggressors, victims, and defenders in preschool: Peer, self-, and teacher reports. *Merrill-Palmer Quarterly, 49,* 453–469.

Nakken, H., & Pijl, S. (2002). Getting along with classmates in regular schools: A review of the effects of integration on the development of social relationships. *International Journal of Inclusive Education, 6*(1), 47–61.

Nordhagen, R., Nielsen, A., Stigum, H., & Köhler, L. (2005). Parental reported bullying among Nordic children: A population based study. *Child: Care, Health & Development, 31*(6), 693–701.

Norwegian Ministry of Education and Research, Norwegian Ministry of Children and Equality, Norwegian Ministry of Health and Care Services, Norwegian Directorate for Education and Training, Union of Education Norway, The Norwegian Parents Committee, The Norwegian Association of Local Regional Authorities & The Directorate for Health and Social Affairs. Manifest mot mobbing 2011–2014. Et forpliktende samarbeit for et godt og inkuderende oppvekst- og læringsmiljø. (2010). Retrieved from http://www.regjeringen.no/upload/KD/Vedlegg/Grunnskole/Manifest_mot_mobbing2011_2014_hefte_web.pdf

Olweus, D. (1973). *Hackkycklingar och översittare. Forskning om skolmobbning.* Göteborg: Almqvist & Wiksell.

Olweus, D. (1996). Bullying at school. Knowledge base and an effective intervention program. *Understanding an Aggressive Behavior in Children, 794,* 265–276.

Pepler, W., & Craig, W. (2009). Responding to bullying and harassment: An issue of rights. In W. Craig, D. Pepler, & J. Cumming (Eds.), *Rise up for respectful relationships: Prevent bullying* (Vol. 2, pp. 1–16). PREVnet Series. Ottawa: National Printers.

Perren, S. (2000). *Kindergarten children involved in bullying: Social behavior, peer relationships, and social status* (Doctoral dissertation). Department of Psychology, University of Berne.

Perren, S., & Alsaker, F. (2006). Social behavior and peer relationships of victims, bully-vicitims, and bullies in kindergarten. *Journal of Child Psychology and Psychiatry, 47,* 45–57.

Pikas, A. (1987). *Så bekämpar vi mobbning i skolan.* Uppsala: AMA Dataservice.

Popp, U. (1994). *Geteilte Zukunft,* [shared future]. Opladen: Leske & Budrich.

Pörhölä, M., Karhunen, S., & Rainivaara, S. (2006). Bullying at school and in the workplace: A challenge for communication research. In C.S. Beck (Ed.), *Communication yearbook 30* (pp. 249–301). Mahwah, NJ: Erlbaum.

Quintana, S.M., Chao, R.K., Cross, W.E., Jr., Hughes, D., Nelson-Le Gall, S., Aboud, F.E., …, Vietze, D.L. (2006). Race, ethnicity, and culture in child development: Contemporary research and future directions. *Child Development, 77,* 1129–1141.

Rigby, K. (2003). Consequenses of bullying in schools. *The Canadian Journal of Psychiatry, 48*(9), 583–590.

Salmivalli, C. (2002). Is there an age decline in victimization by peers at school. *Educational Research, 44*(3), 269–277.

Salmivalli, C. (2010). Bullying and the peer group: A review. *Aggression and Violent Behavior, 15,* 112–120.

Salmivalli, C., Kärnä, A., & Poskiparta, E. (2010). Development, evaluation, and diffusion of a national anti-bullying program, KiVa. In B. Doll, W. Pfohl, & J. Yoon (Eds.), *Handbook of youth prevention science* (pp. 240–254). New York, NY: Routledge.

Salmivalli, C., Kärnä, A., & Poskiparta, E. (2011). Counteracting bullying in Finland: The KiVa program and its effects on different forms of being bullied. *International Journal of Behavioral Development, 35*(5), 405–411.

Slee, P.T., & Rigby, K. (1994). Peer victimisation at schools. *Australian Journal of Early Childhood, 19,* 3–11.

Smith, P.K., & Cowie, H. (1991). *Understanding children's development.* Oxford: Blackwell.

Smith, P.K., & Levan, S. (1995). Perceptions and experiences of bullying in younger pupils. *British Journal of Educational Psychology, 65,* 267–285.

Sourander, A., Ronning, J., Brunstein-Klomek, A., Gyllenberg, D., Kumpulainen, K., Niemelä, S., ..., Almqvist, F. (2009). Childhood bullying behavior and later psychiatric hospital and psychopharmacologic treatment: Findings from the Finnish 1981 birth cohort study. *Arch Gen Psychiatry, 66*(9), 1005–1012.

Stakes. (2005). *Varhaiskasvatussuunnitelman perusteet* [National curriculum guidelines on early childhood education and care]. Saarijärvi: Gummerus kirjapaino Oy.

Strohmeier, D., Kärnä, A., & Salmivalli, C. (2011). Intrapersonal and interpersonal risk factors for peer victimization in immigrant youth in Finland. *Developmental Psychology, 47*(1), 248–258.

Tattum, D., & Herbert, G. (1992). *Bullying in schools, a positive response – advice for parents, governors and staff in schools.* Cardiff: Institute of Higher Education.

The City of Vantaa. (2009). *Haastattelututkimus Vantaan päiväkodeissa. 5–6 – vuotiaat päivähoidon laatua arvioimassa* [A survey for children age 5 and 6: Quality of the early education in the City of Vantaa. Education Bureau: City of Vantaa]. Sivistysvirasto: Vantaan kaupunki. Retrieved from http://www.vantaa.fi/instancedata/prime_product_julkaisu/vantaa/embeds/vantaawwwstructure/31791_haastattelututkimus_web.pdf

Tilastokeskus. (2010). *Valtionvarainministeriö* [Statistics Finland]. Retrieved from http://www.stat.fi/

Vaillancourt, T., McDougall, P., Hymel, S., Krygsman A., Miller, J., Stiver, K., & Davis, C. (2008). Bullying: Are researchers and youth talking about the same thing. *International Journal of Behavioral Development, 32,* 486–495.

Werner, N., & Grant, S. (2009). Mothers' cognitions about relational aggression: Assosiations with discipline responses, children's normative beliefs, and peer competence. *Social Development, 18*(1), 77–98.

Young children's well-being in Finnish stepfamilies

Mari Broberg

Changing family relationships as a result of divorce are considered a potential threat to children's well-being. This study investigates the well-being of children under the age of eight years in Finnish stepfamilies from the viewpoint of the mother. The goal of this study is to explore how the structural characteristics of the stepfamily and the functioning of its various relationships are linked to a child's well-being. The survey data used in this research are drawn from a sample of 667 stepfamilies. The results indicate that a child's well-being was best supported by the well-functioning relationships within the stepfamily: there was a distinct connection between a child's problems and negative quality of relationships.

Introduction

Changes in family structures are part of everyday life for many children. These changes affect family life in many ways, including some potential risks to childhood. Yet, despite changing family structures and the more flexible attitude of a family, the significance of the family institution has not diminished. After a divorce, the original family still remains a social unit carrying out its tasks, but the way it carries out these tasks changes. With the stepfamily[1] formation, two family units form a new family system. Nowadays, stepfamilies are formed mainly as a result of divorce, in which case the stepfamily usually includes the child's non-resident (biological) parent. In Finland, about 9% of all families with children are stepfamilies (Official Statistics of Finland, 2010).

Stepfamilies differ from nuclear families in operation, structure, and relationships (Bray & Berger, 1993; Pryor & Rodgers, 2001). Stepfamilies are complex relationship networks in which one has to define belonging to the family, the internal relations of the family, and the related rules and roles (Ganong & Coleman, 2004, p. 193; Hetherington, 1999). Negotiation is an essential part of stepfamily relationships (Morgan, 1996; Silva & Smart, 1999). It is important to define what relationships are significant to an individual instead of concentrating only on the biological ones. The family consists of several subsystems to many of which the same person may belong (Cox & Paley, 1997; Deal, Hagan, Bass, Hetherington, & Clingempeel, 1999; Ganong & Coleman, 2004; Minuchin, 1985). In stepfamilies, the new life situation affects the system throughout the whole family. The stepfamily consists of a relationship network within which each member operates separately, but together the members also form a whole which is something more than the sum of its subsystems. The stepfamily formation can be seen as creating an imbalance in the family system. In order to reach a balance, the relationships and responsibilities have to be redefined within the family. The stepfamily usually extends to at least two households, and this fact sets challenges to the functioning of the relationships thus created. Furthermore, the structure of the family may vary; for example, during the week, there may be two children at home and during the weekend four children. In this complex system, everything has an effect on everything else. Thus, it is impossible to define the family or the well-being of its members without taking into account the whole unit.

This research describes the well-being of Finnish children under the age of eight years in stepfamilies. An important goal of this study is to explore how the structural characteristics of the stepfamily and the functioning of its relationship network are linked to a child's well-being. This research concentrates on mothers and their children in stepfamilies with a stepfather. The mother of the family might also be a stepmother to the father's children living regularly with their own mothers. The mothers were chosen as a target group because they are important persons in stepfamilies, and it is likely that one cannot understand the dynamics of stepfamilies without understanding how mothers function in them (Ganong & Coleman, 2004). This study concerns the mothers' children in the stepfamilies, using survey data based on the mothers' responses.

The impact of stepfamily on children

Historically, the living environment offered by the traditional nuclear family has been seen as the best alternative for a child's development (Amato & Keith, 1991), and changes in the family structure are seen to be linked to a child's well-being (Demo, Aquilino, & Fine, 2005). Children who have experienced their parents' divorce have more problems than children living in a nuclear family (Coleman, Ganong, & Fine, 2000). However, research is beginning to challenge the stereotypical assumptions that prioritise the nuclear family as the best environment in which to raise children. How children cope with the divorce of their parents has been emphasised (Smart, 2003). It has been claimed that nowadays the effects of divorce are less severe because divorce is culturally accepted in many countries (Albertini & Garriga, 2011; Amato & Keith, 1991).

Divorce is a complex and multi-level process which changes the family relationships before and after the parental separation. In addition to the relationships, divorce changes many other aspects of a child's life which affect his or her well-being (Emery & Forehand, 1996; Jakobvitz & Bush, 1996; Pryor & Rodgers, 2001; Smart, Neale, & Wade, 2001). When estimating the risk factors involved in divorce, it should be taken into account that family structure alone does not tell the whole history of the family, not about the relationships and the child-rearing practices which have effects on a child's well-being (Demo & Cox, 2000; McFarlane, Bellissimo, & Norman, 1995). In some cases, children might benefit from their parents' separation (Amato, 2000; Hetherington, 1999, p. 24).

Divorce and the remarriage of a parent can be seen as a kind of disorder of the family which affects the children negatively, at least at some level (Amato, 2000). Stepfamily life may generate conflicts, social and economic stress, and many changes concerning family relationships (Duncan & Brooks-Gunn, 2000; Dunn, 2002; McCulloch,

Wiggins, Joshi, & Darshan, 2000). How children evaluate and cope with divorce is related to how they adjust to stepfamily life (Ganong & Coleman, 2004, p. 42). Adjustment is important when considering the functioning of the stepfamily: its structure, socio-economic status and resources, the degree of cooperation between parents, social support, the quality of its relationships, the stress of parents, and other problems of the family are all connected to the adaptation of children to stepfamily life (Fine & Kurdek, 1992; Hetherington & Stanley-Hagan, 1999; Hetherington, Bridges, & Insabella, 1998).

When estimating the effects of family changes, attention must also be paid to the children's age, the amount of changes, their character, preparation, and timing (Demo et al., 2005). The children's age is significant when considering adaptation to the stepfamily: young children accept the new marriage of their parent better than adolescents (Hetherington & Stanley-Hagan, 1999). Several changes in family relationships, for example, living in several stepfamilies, increase the risk related to the children's well-being (Capaldi & Patterson, 1991; Pryor & Rodgers, 2001). Parental separation may change the internal and external resources of the family and, via these, be reflected in the children's well-being. Thus, it is important to take the functioning of the relationships into consideration instead of the family structure alone.

Previous studies focusing on children's well-being have mainly drawn comparisons between the family types: children living in a stepfamily have been compared with children living in a nuclear family or in a single-parent family. Comparing the children in stepfamilies and those in single-parent families is logical because the children who live in both family types have usually experienced the divorce of their parents (Pryor & Rodgers, 2001). On the other hand, it has been reasonable to compare the children in stepfamilies and those in nuclear families because in both family types there are two adults living with the children (Spruijt & Goede, 1997). However, the stepfamily and the nuclear family differ essentially (Pryor & Rodgers, 2001, p. 171). The studies are often cross-sectional studies in which family types are compared. Extremely few studies have utilised a longitudinal design (Demo et al., 2005, p. 126).

According to the results of previous studies, some problems are linked more to children's well-being in stepfamilies than to children's well-being in nuclear families (Coleman et al., 2000; Jeynes, 2006). In various measures of well-being, children in stepfamilies scored more poorly than children in nuclear families and to the same extent as children in single-parent families. The children in stepfamilies face the same risks as those in single-parent families (Amato & Keith, 1991; Dunn, 2002; Ram & Hou, 2003). In some studies, it has been stated, however, that young people living in a stepfamily have fewer problems than young people living in single-parent families (Spruijt & Goede, 1997). Social, economic, and educational support offered by a stepfather or a stepmother will not necessarily be reflected directly on the children's well-being. However, inside the group of stepfamilies, the well-functioning child–stepparent relationship is linked to fewer problems and stronger self-esteem (White & Gilbreth, 2001). The problems of children living in single-parent families are mainly related to the weaker economic situation of the families. The stepfather or the stepmother brings economic resources to the family, but that does not seem to be reflected directly on the children's well-being (Hawkins & Eggebeen, 1991).

The studies related to children's well-being have concentrated mostly on three areas: academic skills, psychological and emotional well-being, and social skills (Amato & Keith, 1991; Coleman et al., 2000; Demo & Acock, 1996; Ganong & Coleman, 2004, p. 145). According to these results, the differences between family types are minor. The academic skills of children in stepfamilies are slightly weaker; they do not succeed as well in school as the children in nuclear families (Bogenschei-der, 1997; Hetherington, 1992; Thompson, Hanson, & McLanahan, 1994). According to a Finnish study, the children in stepfamilies have more problems at home, but fewer problems at school than the children in single-parent families (Luoma et al., 1999). Be-havioural and emotional problems are also found to be more common among children living in stepfamilies than among children living in nuclear families (Amato & Keith, 1991; Demo & Acock, 1996; Hanson, McLanahan, & Thomson, 1996; Hetherington et al., 1998; O'Connor, Dunn, Jenkins, Pickering, & Rashbash, 2001; Zill, Morrison, & Coiro, 1993). The same phenomenon has been reported in studies which emphasised social skills: children living in stepfamilies more often have problems related to peer relationships (Dunn, Deater-Deckard, Pickering, O'Connor, & Golding, 1998; Hether-ington, 1992; Rodgers, 1994).

Explanation for the effects on children

There is quite a lot of variation in children's adaptation to parental separation and step-family formation. Most of the children do not have major problems and they cope with these changes extremely well (Chase-Lansdale, Cherlin, & Kierman, 1995; Coleman et al., 2000; Emery & Forehand, 1996; Zill et al., 1993), but a very small number of children may have quite serious problems (Amato, 2000; Demo & Cox, 2000). Research concerning the effects of parental remarriage on children has presented differ-ent models to explain the greater risks affecting children living in stepfamilies. In all the studies and explanation models, the starting point is the fact that living with a stepfather or a stepmother is in some way detrimental to the child (Coleman et al., 2000).

The problems of children living in a stepfamily have been explained, for example, by the stress model (Henry & Lovelace, 1995; Hoffmann & Johnson, 1998) or by the fact that the adults concentrate on a new relationship and less time is left for child-rearing (Bogenschneider, 1997; Cartwright & Seymour, 2002; Guttmann & Rosenberg, 2003). Hetherington et al. (1998) constructed a transactional model of the predictors of children's adjustment following divorce and remarriage. According to their model, individual characteristics of parents and children, stressful life experiences, parental distress, social support, marital transitions, family composition, and family processes affect the children's well-being in a stepfamily. These factors are linked and interact in complex ways. Parental distress, for example, will first weaken the functioning of the relationships and then, still weakening, affect the children's well-being. Individual factors can also be presented as their own explanation models, but in this model, all these factors have been connected. Divorce can be seen as a process begun years before the parental separation and continuing long after it (Dunn, 2002; Furstenberg & Tietler, 1994; Ram & Hou, 2003; Sun, 2001).

The significance of the positive quality of family relationships for the well-being of children living in a stepfamily is essential (Maccoby, Buchanan, Mnookin, & Dorn-busch, 1993). The children with a good relationship with both parents are seen to cope best with the divorce (Amato & Gilbreth, 1999; Bauserman, 2002; Harper & Fine, 2006; Pryor & Rodgers, 2001). In addition to relationships inside the stepfamily, the role of the non-resident parent is important when considering a child's well-being. In Finland, the majority of parents who are separated by divorce have joint custody in which they share childcare. Still, the majority of these children reside with the mother, so the non-resident parent is often the father.

Research results concerning how children's well-being is linked to contacts with the non-resident father are partly contradictory. Some studies have shown a weak connection between such a contact and the children's well-being (Amato & Gilbreth, 1999). On the other hand, it has not been shown that there is no connection between these factors (Amato, 1993; King, 1994; Seltzer, 1994). This can be partly explained by the fact that it is the quality of their relationships with their fathers rather than the frequency of contact that is linked to the children's well-being (Amato & Gilbreth, 1999; Pryor and Rodgers, 2001). Regular contact between a child and a non-resident father does not alone guarantee a well-functioning parent–child relationship (Amato & Gilbreth, 1999; Spruijt, Goede, & Valdervalk, 2004). According to Clarke-Steward and Hayward (1996), a good relationship between a child and a non-resident father, regular contacts, and common holidays and social activities were positively connected to the child's well-being. The strong role of the father in child-rearing, and his participation in decision-making concerning the child's life, is shown to support the child's balanced development (Bradshaw, Stimson, Skinner, & Williams, 1999). The father's economic support has been found to be related to the child's well-being (Amato, 2000; Greene & Moore, 2000). In addition to the relationship between a child and a non-resident father, the significance of the functioning cooperation of biological parents should also be taken into account (Amato & Afifi, 2006; Amato & Gilbreth, 1999; Moxnes, 2003).

This study concentrates on young children's well-being in Finnish stepfamilies from the maternal viewpoint. The following questions are addressed: How do the mothers report the quality of stepfamily relationships? Do these assessments correlate with each other and do these assessments differ according to the structural factors of the stepfamily? How do the mothers estimate their children's well-being in the stepfamily and do these assessments differ by family type? Are the structural characteristics of the stepfamily and the mothers' assessments of the quality of the relationships linked to children's well-being?

Data and methods

Participants

Data were randomly chosen from Finnish families with children aged three, six and/ or eight years. A mailed questionnaire with two reminders to non-respondents was used. Sample size was 4200 families (1200 nuclear families, 1500 single-parent families, and 1500 stepfamilies). Completed questionnaires were returned by 2236 parents, giving a response rate of approximately 54%. Almost 900 respondents were nuclear families, approximately 700 were single-parent families and 667 were stepfamilies. The respondents represented rather well the situation of families with children in Finland. The stepfamilies participating in the research structurally represented the Finnish stepfamilies extremely well. A vast majority of the families (90%) had formed around the mother and her children. Almost half of the families (46%) had, in addition, a child of both the spouses, and in about 30% of the families, the father's child spent some time living in the family. The stepfamilies had lived together, on average, for three years. All the data were used in the well-being comparison between family types. The subsample used in the other analysis included mothers whose children lived with them and a stepfather and who had a living non-resident father ($n = 512$).

Variables

The structural characteristics of the stepfamily were measured by asking about the length of time the stepfamily has lived together, if there is a child of both the spouses, and if the father's child visits the stepfamily. The quality of family relationships in stepfamilies was measured by asking for the mothers' assessment of the relationships. The mothers estimated the functioning of the relationships according to the Likert scale alternatives from 1 (very unsatisfied) to 5 (very satisfied). The variable describing the marital relationship was formed by combining three items (Cronbach's $\alpha = 0.64$), the child–stepfather relationship by four items (Cronbach's $\alpha = 0.79$), the relationship between the children by two items (Cronbach's $\alpha = 0.62$), the child–non-resident father relationship by three items (Cronbach's $\alpha = 0.69$), and the relationship between grandparents (stepfather's parents) and the family by two items (Cronbach's $\alpha = 0.84$). The cooperation of the biological parents (child's mother and non-resident father) was measured by three items (Cronbach's $\alpha = 0.86$).

The children's problems were measured by an adapted version of Conners' Parent Rating Scale as reported by the mothers. In their study, Conners, Sitarenios, Parker, and Epstein (1998) divided a child's disturbing behaviour into the following groups: cognitive problems, oppositional, hyperactivity–impulsivity, anxious–shy, perfectionism, social problems, and psychosomatic. In the present research, these groups were divided by factor analysis into three dimensions: psychological problems, social problems, and cognitive problems. The sum variable of psychological problems consisted of eight variables describing oppositional behaviour, shyness, and impulsiveness (Cronbach's $\alpha = 0.79$). Social problems (Cronbach's $\alpha = 0.74$) were related to the peer relationships and feeling inferior. Cognitive problems (Cronbach's $\alpha = 0.75$) were related to concentration and academic achievement. Mothers estimated the problems of their children according to the Likert scale alternatives $(1-5)$.

Statistical analysis

The Pearson coefficient of correlation was used to examine the inter-correlations among mothers' appraisals concerning the quality of relationships in the stepfamilies. The t-test and one-way analysis of variance (ANOVA) were performed to determine the mean score differences in the quality of the relationships between variables indicating the structure of the stepfamily. One-way ANOVA was also used to examine the differences between the family types. To evaluate the association between the two sets of variables, a canonical correlation analysis (Tabachnick & Fidell, 2000) was conducted using the structure of the stepfamily and the quality of the relationships within the stepfamily as predictors of the variables concerning children's well-being.

Results

Stepfamily relationships

In stepfamilies, there are relationships between family members living together and also between family members living apart. In this study, the marital relationship of the parents, the child–stepfather relationship, and the sibling relationships represent the relationships between the family members living together. The relationships between two households are those between a child and a non-resident father, cooperation between the biological parents, and the relationship between the family and grandparents. Table 1 presents the means and standard deviations for mothers' reports of the

Table 1. Descriptive statistics for relationship quality in stepfamilies.

	M	SD
Marital relationship	3.92	0.87
Child–stepfather relationship	4.23	0.85
Relationships between children	3.93	1.21
Cooperation between biological parents	3.07	1.49
Relationship between child and non-resident father	2.45	1.20
Relationship between family and paternal grandparents	3.67	1.54
Relationship between family and parents of the stepfather	4.06	1.22

quality of the relationships. The mothers in stepfamilies estimated the relationships between the family members living together as functioning better than those between two households, with most problems found in the child's relationship with the non-resident father (Friedman test, $\chi^2 = 683.359$, df = 6, $p < 0.001$). There were quite many problems in the cooperation between the parents. The mothers estimated the child–stepfather relationship to be the best functioning relationship in their stepfamily. The mothers reported an almost identical level of quality in the marital relationship of the parents and the child–stepfather relationship. The mothers were also extremely satisfied with the relationships between the children. The mothers estimated the relationship between the family and the stepfathers' parents as functioning better than the relationship with the paternal grandparents.

The correlations were used to examine the association of these relationship measures to each other, as shown in Table 2. The child–stepfather relationship and the marital relationship of the parents were highly correlated ($r = 0.610$). The correlation between the child's relationship to the non-resident father and cooperation between the biological parents were also quite high ($r = 0.658$). The children's relationships with their non-resident fathers were more positive in families where mothers had more supportive co-parenting with their former partner. The assessments of relationships between family members living together were strongly correlated to each other, and

Table 2. Bivariate correlations between stepfamily relationships.

Variable	1	2	3	4	5	6
1. Marital relationship	–					
2. Child–stepfather relationship	0.610**	–				
3. Relationships between children	0.276**	0.214**	–			
4. Relationship between family and parents of the stepfather	0.173**	0.194**	0.036	–		
5. Cooperation between biological parents	0.043	0.014	−0.018	−0.063	–	
6. Relationship between child and non-resident father	0.043	0.014	−0.006	−0.048	0.658**	–
7. Relationship between family and paternal grandparents	0.023	0.031	0.016	−0.016	0.515**	0.473**

**$p < 0.01$.

also the qualities of the relationships between the two households correlated with each other. The relationships within the immediate stepfamily household were not linked to the relationships between the two households. There was almost no correlation ($r = 0.014$) between the child–stepfather relationship and the child–non-resident father relationship. Only the relationship with the stepfather's parents was weakly correlated to the marital relationship of the parents and to the child–stepfather relationship.

The following analysis addresses the issue of whether the relationship quality differs by structural factors of the stepfamily. The birth of a half-sibling was linked statistically significantly to the child–non-resident father relationship quality ($t = -2.094$, df $= 559$, $p = 0.037$). Families with only stepchildren had a better functioning child–non-resident father relationship than the families in which there was, in addition, a child of both spouses. Probably, the child born into a stepfamily strengthens the structure as that happening in a nuclear family. This challenges the relationship between a child and a non-resident father. A father's child living partly in the stepfamily seemed to set challenges, especially to the marital relationship of the parents ($t = 2.126$, df $= 559$, $p = 0.036$). In these families, there were also more problems related to the child–stepfather relationship. Apart from these associations, no other differences in the quality of family relationships existed according to structural factors of the stepfamily.

Problems related to the children's well-being

First, the mothers' estimates of the children's well-being are introduced. The study was limited to cover the stepchildren living with their mother, their stepfather, and their possible stepsisters and stepbrothers. Furthermore, they usually also lived with their non-resident father a part of the time. The children living in stepfamilies had moderately few problems according to the estimates of the mothers. The problems appeared in all the three measured areas relatively evenly: psychological, social, and cognitive problems (Table 3). The most general of the psychological problems was defying the

Table 3.   Children's problems in stepfamilies[a].

	n	%
Psychological problems		
No problems	319	62
Some problems	174	34
Lots of problems	19	4
Social problems		
No problems	295	58
Some problems	201	39
Lots of problems	16	3
Cognitive problems		
No problems	334	65
Some problems	161	32
Lots of problems	17	3

[a]No problems (the average value of the sum variable was under 2.19), some problems (the average value of the sum variable was 2.19–2.99), and lots of problems (the average value of the sum variable was over 3).

adults, while the rarest was depression. Irritating other people was the most general problem in the social area, while difficulties in getting along with other people were the rarest. The most general of the problems related to concentrating was impatience in carrying out tasks, while the rarest was lack of initiative. When examined by groups, there were more social problems than psychological and cognitive problems. In all the areas, about a third of the children had some difficulties. About 3–4% of the children had significant problems.

The children's psychological, social, and cognitive problems were strongly correlated to each other. If the child had problems in one area, he or she probably had problems in the two other measured areas. The correlation between the psychological and the social problems ($r = 0.771$) was even stronger than the correlation between the psychological and the cognitive problems ($r = 0.582$) and the correlation between the social and the cognitive problems ($r = 0.551$).

In the following analysis, the well-being of the children living in stepfamilies is compared with that of the children living in nuclear families or single-parent families. The children's psychological, social, and cognitive problems are given by family type in Table 4. The children living in a stepfamily were, on average, more likely to have psychological and cognitive problems than the children living in a nuclear family. However, the size of these differences was not large, even though it was statistically significant. The children living in a single-parent family had also slightly higher mean scores in these problem areas than the children living in a nuclear family. Social problems did not differ by family type.

Factors associated with the children's well-being in the stepfamily

The central issue in this article is an examination of how the children's well-being is linked to the structure of the stepfamily and to the quality of family relationships. These associations were elaborated in canonical correlation analyses. The first canonical correlation analysis was conducted using the structural characteristics of the stepfamily as predictors of the dimensions of children's problems. Collectively, the model was not statistically significant (Wilks' lambda $F = 1.59$, $p = 0.058$). The correlations remained very low (0.001–0.105). The coefficient of determination of the model was extremely low (5.2%). There was no difference in the outcomes of children from different kinds of stepfamilies. For example, living in a complex stepfamily, in which there were children from both parents' earlier relationships, was not associated with more problems of the children than living in a stepfamily in which all the children were related to the mother. Thus, the structural factors of the stepfamily were not linked

Table 4. Differences in children's problems according to family type, one-way ANOVA.

	Stepfamilies	Nuclear families	Single-parent families	F	df	p
Psychological problems	1.89	1.75	1.82	2.79	2	0.049
Social problems	1.55	1.50	1.50	1.70	2	NS
Cognitive problems	2.07	1.84	1.96	11.36	2	<0.001

NS, not significant.

Table 5. Canonical solution for stepfamily relationships predicting children's problems.

	Function 1	Function 2
The stepfamily relationships		
Marital relationship	0.622	−0.255
Child−stepfather relationship	0.426	0.179
Relationships between children	0.781	−0.184
Child−non-resident father relationship	0.199	0.316
Cooperation between biological parents	0.269	0.639
Relationship between family and parents of the stepfather	0.258	0.204
Relationship between family and paternal grandparents	0.150	0.754
Children's problems		
Psychological problems	−0.977	0.024
Social problems	−0.818	0.101
Cognitive problems	−0.610	−0.753

to the well-being of children under the age of eight years. The duration of living together in the stepfamily, the child born into the stepfamily, and the father's child living apart were not linked to the children's well-being.

The second canonical correlation analysis was conducted using the stepfamily relationships as predictors of children's problems. The model thus formed was statistically significant (Wilks' lambda $F = 3.52, p < 0.001$), explaining approximately 64% of the variance shared between the two variable sets. The analysis yielded two statistically significant canonical functions with squared canonical correlations of 0.353 ($p < 0.001$) and 0.211 ($p = 0.03$) as introduced in Table 5.

The results showed a significant positive association between the quality of relationships and the children's well-being. The prevalence of problems was significantly higher among children who had a negative quality of family relationships. According to the first canonical function, the positive quality of marital relationships between the parents, the child−stepfather relationship, and the relationships between the children were negatively related to children's problems. The association with psychological and social problems was stronger than the connection to cognitive problems. According to the second canonical function, children's cognitive problems were linked to the negative quality of the child−non-resident father relationship, the cooperation between the parents, and the child−paternal grandparent relationships.

Discussion

This study used mothers' reports on their children's relationships in stepfamilies to predict their children's well-being, as also reported by the mothers. The results indicated an association between stepfamily relationship quality and the children's well-being. The problems related to the relationships between stepfamily members living together were associated with the children's psychological and social problems. The stepfather's relationship with the child, the marital relationship of the parents, and sibling relationships contributed to the child outcomes. Difficult relationships with non-resident fathers were associated with high levels of cognitive problems. Thus, the well-functioning relationship network forms an extremely significant part of a child's well-being in the stepfamily context. It is important to highlight the importance of interpersonal relationships within the family prior to parental separation (Fine & Kurdek, 1992; Hetherington & Stanley-Hagan, 1999; Hetherington et al., 1998; Videon, 2002).

According to the results of this study, the relationship between a child and a non-resident father can be seen as a positive resource supporting the child's well-being in the stepfamily. This emerged especially in the area of cognitive development. The support of the non-resident father, for example, in matters related to school, can be considered significant for the child's well-being. The results of previous international studies support these interpretations. Even though earlier studies concerning the connection between a child's well-being and the participation of the non-resident father are partly conflicting, at least weak connections have been reported between them in several studies. Especially parallel with the result of this study is Amato and Gilbreth's (1999) meta-analysis that showed that the child–non-resident father contact was significantly associated with the child's academic outcomes. Furthermore, it has been reported in some studies that the children with regular contacts with their non-resident father had fewer behaviour problems (Amato & Gilbreth, 1999; Dunn et al., 2004; Greene & Moore, 2000).

In this study, the children's well-being was extremely tightly interpreted within the family framework. When the children's well-being is examined from the view point of family resources, the role of the relationship network has been emphasised. In addition to the resources of the family, however, many other factors related to the children's well-being were not considered in this study. For example, children's peer relationships support their well-being (Bierman & Welsh, 1997). This whole network may change fundamentally as a consequence of the migration that takes place with the formulation of the stepfamily. It is also important to take into consideration the advantages of the stepfamily to a child. The most central advantage from a child's point of view is that the new relationships can enrich his or her life and that she or he can be a part of a family again (Mikesell & Garbarino, 1986).

The results presented in this research suggest that the structural characteristics of the stepfamily are not related to the children's well-being and that children's well-being is equal in stepfamilies with different structures. Dunn (2002) found that the more complex structure of the stepfamily is related to a child's problems. This complex structure means that the children of both spouses live in the stepfamily. In this research, the missing connection can be explained by the fact that there were few families in which the father's child lived regularly with the stepfamily. Nor, in this study, was the child born into the stepfamily was linked to the children's well-being. This is probably explained by the fact that earlier studies on this issue have been very conflicting. Hofferth (2006) suggested that the addition of a half-sibling is beneficial to the stepchildren. On the other hand, it has been proposed that the parental involvement with stepchildren decreases when a child of both spouses is born (Stewart, 2005).

The first methodological limitation of this study is the fact that the cross-sectional data employed may give too static a picture of life in stepfamilies. Thus, in the field of stepfamily research, there is a need for longitudinal studies concerning the children's well-being (Ganong & Coleman, 2004, p. 234; Hetherington et al., 1998). The second limitation is that this study made use of a single informant, the mother. It did not, therefore, offer possibilities to compare varying situations, for example, children's problems at home and at day-care or at school. The current research gives a picture of the relationships only from the maternal viewpoint. For example, Kurdek and Fine (1991) concluded that compared with stepfathers, mothers had a more optimistic perspective on stepfamilies, and they reported greater satisfaction with child–stepfather relationships. According to an American study (Ganong & Coleman, 1994), one-third of the stepfathers and stepmothers thought that they had to participate in the step-child's life more than they themselves would actually have wanted to. In the light of these research results, studying the stepfathers' own views would have brought more critical aspects to the results when considering the quality of the relationships.

This study described young children's well-being in Finnish stepfamilies. In the future, it would be important to concentrate on adolescents' well-being. It would also be important to extend the study to concern Finnish children born into stepfamilies, because stepfamily life reflected strongly on them. In earlier studies, it has been found that children born into a stepfamily have more problems related to academic skills (Ginther & Pollak, 2004). Finally, the children themselves have very seldom been asked for their views about living in a stepfamily (Smart et al., 2001), so more studies on these themes from the children's point of view are needed in Finland.

Acknowledgements

This study is part of the research: 'Origins of Exclusion in Early Childhood' funded by the Council for Social Sciences Research, The Academy of Finland.

Note

1. That is, family in which one or more parents have been previously widowed or divorced, possibly including children from two or more sets of biological parents.

References

Albertini, M., & Garriga, A. (2011). The effect of divorce on parent-child contacts. *European Societies, 13*, 257–278.

Amato, P.R. (1993). Children's adjustment to divorce: Theories, hypotheses, and empirical support. *Journal of Marriage and the Family, 55*, 612–624.

Amato, P.R. (2000). The consequences of divorce for adults and children. *Journal of Marriage and the Family, 62*, 1269–1288.

Amato, P.R., & Afifi, T.D. (2006). Feeling caught between parents: Adult children's relations with parents and subjective well-being. *Journal of Marriage and Family, 68*, 222–235.

Amato, P.R., & Gilbreth, J.G. (1999). Nonresident fathers and children's well-being: A meta-analysis. *Journal of Marriage and the Family, 61*, 557–573.

Amato, P.R., & Keith, P. (1991). Parental divorce and the well-being of children: A meta-analysis. *Psychological Bulletin, 110*, 26–46.

Bauserman, R. (2002). Child adjustment in joint-custody versus sole-custody arrangements: A meta-analytic review. *Journal of Family Psychology, 16*, 91–102.

Bierman, K., & Welsh, J. (1997). Social relationships deficits. In E. Mash & J. Terdal (Eds.), *Assessment of childhood disorders* (pp. 328–365). New York, NY: Quilford Press.

Bogenscheider, K. (1997). Parental involvement in adolescent schooling: A proximal process with transcontextual validity. *Journal of Marriage and the Family, 59,* 718–733.

Bradshaw, J., Stimson, C., Skinner, C., & Williams, J. (1999). *Absent fathers?* London: Routledge.

Bray, J.H., & Berger, S.H. (1993). Developmental issues in stepfamilies research project: Family relationships and parent-child interactions. *Journal of Family Psychology, 7,* 76–90.

Capaldi, D.M., & Patterson, G.R. (1991). Relation of parental transitions to boys' adjustment problems. *Developmental Psychology, 27,* 489–504.

Cartwright, C., & Seymour, F. (2002). Young adults' perceptions of parents' responses in step-families: What hurts? What helps? *Journal of Divorce and Remarriage, 37,* 123–141.

Chase-Lansdale, P.L., Cherlin, A.J., & Kiernan, K.E. (1995). The long-term effects of parental divorce on the mental health of young adults: A developmental perspective. *Child Development, 66,* 1614–1634.

Clarke-Steward, K.A., & Hayward, C. (1996). Advantages of father custody and contact for the psychological well-being of school-age children. *Journal of Applied Developmental Psychology, 17,* 239–270.

Coleman, M., Ganong, L., & Fine, M. (2000). Reinvestigating remarriage: Another decade of progress. *Journal of Marriage and the Family, 62,* 1288–1308.

Conners, C.K., Sitarenios, G., Parker, J.D., & Epstein, J.N. (1998). The Revised Conners' Parent Rating Scale (CPRS-R): Factor structure, reliability, and criterion validity. *Journal of Abnormal Child Psychology, 26,* 257–268.

Cox, M.J., & Paley, B. (1997). Families as systems. *Annual Review of Psychology, 48,* 243–267.

Deal, J.E., Hagan, M.S., Bass, B., Hetherington, E.M., & Clingempeel, G. (1999). Marital inter-action in dyadic and triadic contexts: Continuities and discontinuities. *Family Process, 38,* 105–115.

Demo, D.H., & Acock, A.C. (1996). Family structure, family process, and adolescent well-being. *Journal of Research on Adolescence, 6,* 457–488.

Demo, D.H., Aquilino, W.S., & Fine, M.A. (2005). Family composition and family transitions. In V.L. Bengtson, A.C. Acock, K.R. Allen, P. Dilworth-Anderson, & D. Klein (Eds.), *Sourcebook of family theory & research* (pp. 119–142). Thousand Oaks, CA: Sage.

Demo, D.H., & Cox, M.J. (2000). Families with young children: A review of research in the 1990s. *Journal of Marriage & the Family, 62,* 876–896.

Duncan, G.J., & Brooks-Gunn, J. (2000). Family poverty, welfare reform, and child develop-ment. *Child Development, 71,* 188–196.

Dunn, J. (2002). The adjustment of children in stepfamilies: Lessons from community studies. *Child and Adolescent Mental Health, 7,* 154–161.

Dunn, J., Cheng, H., O'Connor, T.G., & Bridges, L. (2004). Children's perspectives on their relationships with the nonresident fathers: Influences, outcomes and implications. *Journal of Child Psychology and Psychiatry, 45,* 553–566.

Dunn, J., Deater-Deckard, K., Pickering, K., O'Connor, T.G., & Golding, J. (1998). Children's adjustment and prosocial behaviour in step-, single-parent, and non-stepfamily settings: Findings from a community study. *Journal of Child Psychology and Psychiatry, 39,* 1083–1095.

Emery, R.E., & Forehand, R. (1996). Parental divorce and children's well-being: A focus on resi-lience. In R. Haggerty, L. Sherrod, N. Garmezy, & M. Rutter (Eds.), *Stress, risk, and resili-ence in children and adolescents* (pp. 64–99). Cambridge: Cambridge University Press.

Fine, M.A., & Kurdek, L.A. (1992). The adjustment of adolescents in stepfather and stepmother families. *Journal of Marriage and the Family, 54,* 725–736.

Furstenberg, F.F., & Tietler, J.O. (1994). Reconsidering the effects of marital disruption: What happens to children of divorce in early adulthood? *Journal of Family Issues, 15,* 173–190.

Ganong, L.H., & Coleman, M. (1994). Adolescent stepchild-stepparent relationships: Changes over time. In K. Pasley & M. Ihinger-Tallman (Eds.), *Stepparenting. Issues in theory, research, and practice* (pp. 87–104). Westport: Praeger.

Ganong, L.H., & Coleman, M. (2004). *Stepfamily relationships: Development, dynamics, and interventions.* New York, NY: Plenum Publishers.

Ginther, D.K., & Pollak, R.A. (2004). Family structure and children's educational outcomes: Blended families, stylized facts, and descriptive regressions. *Demography, 41,* 671–696.

123

Greene, A.D., & Moore, K.A. (2000). Nonresident father involvement and child well-being among young children in families on welfare. *Marriage and Family Review, 29,* 159–180.

Guttmann, J., & Rosenberg, M. (2003). Emotional intimacy and children's adjustment: A comparison between single-parent divorced and intact families. *Educational Psychology, 23,* 457–472.

Hanson, T.L., McLanahan, S.S., & Thomson, E. (1996). Double jeopardy: Parental conflict and stepfamily outcomes for children. *Journal of Marriage and the Family, 58,* 141–155.

Harper, S.E., & Fine, M.A. (2006). The effects of involved nonresidential fathers' distress, parenting behaviors, inter-parental conflict, and the quality of father-child relationships on children's well-being. *Fathering, 4,* 286–311.

Hawkins, A.J., & Eggebeen, D.J. (1991). Are fathers fungible? Patterns of coresident adult men in maritally disrupted families and young children's well-being. *Journal of Marriage and the Family, 53,* 958–972.

Henry, C.S., & Lovelace, S.G. (1995). Family resources and adolescent daily life satisfaction in remarried family households. *Journal of Family Issues, 16,* 765–786.

Hetherington, E.M. (1992). Coping with marital transitions: A family systems perspective. *Monographs of the Society for Research in Child Development, 57,* 1–14.

Hetherington, E.M. (1999). Family functioning and the adjustment of adolescent siblings in diverse types of families. In E. Hetherington, S. Henderson, D. Reiss, & E. Anderson (Eds.), *Adolescent siblings in stepfamilies: Family functioning and adolescent adjustment. Monographs of the society for research in child development* (pp. 1–25). Malden: Blackwell.

Hetherington, E.M., Bridges, M., & Insabella, G.M. (1998). What matters? What does not? Five perspectives on the association between marital transitions and children's adjustment. *American Psychologist, 53,* 167–184.

Hetherington, E.M., & Stanley-Hagan, M. (1999). The adjustment of children with divorced parents: A risk and resiliency perspective. *Journal of Child Psychology and Psychiatry, 40,* 129–140.

Hofferth, S.L. (2006). Residential father family type and child well-being: Investment versus selection. *Demography, 43,* 53–77.

Hoffmann, J.P., & Johnson, R.A. (1998). A national portrait of family structure and adolescent drug use. *Journal of Marriage and the Family, 60,* 633–645.

Jakobvitz, D.B., & Bush, N.F. (1996). Reconstructions of family relationships: Parent-child alliances, personal distress, and self-esteem. *Developmental Psychology, 32,* 732–743.

Jeynes, W.H. (2006). The impact of parental remarriage on children: A meta-analysis. *Marriage and Family Review, 40,* 75–102.

King, V. (1994). Nonresident father involvement and child well-being: Can dads make a difference? *Journal of Family Issues, 15,* 78–96.

Kurdek, L.A., & Fine, M.A. (1991). Cognitive correlates of satisfaction for mothers and stepfathers in stepfather families. *Journal of Marriage and the Family, 53,* 565–572.

Luoma, I., Puura, K., Tamminen, T., Kaukonen, P., Piha, J., Räsänen, E., …, Almqvist, F. (1999). Emotional and behavioural symptoms in 8–9-year-old children in relation to family structure. *European Child & Adolescent Psychiatry, 8,* 29–40.

Maccoby, E.E., Buchanan, C.M., Mnookin, R.H., & Dornbusch, S.M. (1993). Postdivorce roles of mothers and fathers in the lives of their children. *Journal of Family Psychology, 7,* 24–38.

McCulloch, A., Wiggins, R.D., Joshi, H.E., & Darshan, S. (2000). Internalising and externalising children's behaviour problems in Britain and the US: Relationships to family resources. *Children & Society, 14,* 363–383.

McFarlane, A.H., Bellissimo, A., & Norman, G.R. (1995). Family structure, family functioning and adolescent well-being: The transcendent influence of parental style. *Journal of Child Psychology and Psychiatry, 36,* 847–864.

Mikesell, J.W., & Garbarino, J. (1986). Adolescents in stepfamilies. In J. Garbarino, C.J. Schellenbach, & J. Sebes (Eds.), *Troubled youth, troubled families understanding families at risk for adolescent maltreatment* (pp. 235–251). New York, NY: Aldine.

Minuchin, S. (1985). *Families and family therapy.* London: Tavistock.

Morgan, D.H. (1996). *Family connections.* Cambridge: Polity Press.

Moxnes, K. (2003). Risk factors in divorce: Perceptions by the children involved. *Childhood*, *10*, 131–146.

O'Connor, T.G., Dunn, J., Jenkins, J.M., Pickering, K., & Rashbash, J. (2001). Family settings and children's adjustment within and across families. *British Journal of Psychiatry*, *179*, 100–115.

Official Statistics of Finland (OSF). (2010). *Families* [e-publication]. Helsinki: Advisory Board of OSF.

Pryor, J., & Rodgers, B. (2001). *Children in changing families. Life after parental separation*. Oxford: Blackwell Publishers.

Ram, B., & Hou, F. (2003). Changes in family structure and child outcomes: Roles of economic and familial resources. *The Policy Studies Journal*, *31*, 309–330.

Rodgers, B. (1994). Pathways between parental behaviour and adult depression. *Journal of Child Psychology and Psychiatry*, *35*, 1289–1308.

Seltzer, J.A. (1994). Consequences of marital dissolution for children. *Annual Review of Sociology*, *20*, 235–266.

Silva, E., & Smart, C. (1999). The 'new' practices and politics of family life. In E. Silva & C. Smart (Eds.), *The new family?* (pp. 13–30). London: Sage.

Smart, C. (2003). New perspectives on childhood and divorce. *Childhood*, *10*, 123–129.

Smart, C., Neale, B., & Wade, A. (2001). *The changing experience of childhood. Families and divorce*. Cambridge: Polity Press.

Spruijt, A.P., & Goede, M.P. (1997). Transition in family structure and adolescent well-being. *Adolescence*, *32*, 897–912.

Spruijt, A.P., Goede, M., & Valdervalk, I.E. (2004). Frequency of contact with nonresident fathers and adolescent well-being: A longitudinal analysis. *Journal of Divorce and Remarriage*, *40*, 77–90.

Stewart, S.D. (2005). How the birth of the child affects involvement with stepchildren. *Journal of Marriage and the Family*, *67*, 461–473.

Sun, Y. (2001). Family environment and adolescents' well-being before and after parents' marital disruption: A longitudinal analysis. *Journal of Marriage and Family*, *63*, 697–713.

Tabachnick, B.G., & Fidell, L.S. (2000). *Using multivariate statistics*. Boston, MA: Allyn and Bacon.

Thompson, E., Hanson, T.L., & McLanahan, S.S. (1994). Family structure and child well-being: Economic resources vs. parental behaviors. *Social Forces*, *73*, 221–242.

Videon, T. (2002). The effects of parent-adolescent relationships and parental separation on adolescent well-being. *Journal of Marriage and Family*, *64*, 489–503.

White, L., & Gilbreth, J.G. (2001). When children have two fathers: Effects of relationships with stepfathers and noncustodial fathers on adolescent outcomes. *Journal of Marriage and Family*, *63*, 155–168.

Zill, N., Morrison, D.R., & Coiro, M.J. (1993). Long-term effects of parental divorce on parent-child relationships, adjustment, and achievement in young adulthood. *Journal of Family Psychology*, *7*, 91–103.

Care for the other's selfhood: a view on child care and education through Heidegger's analytic of Dasein

Kosti Joensuu

Philosophical analysis concerning selfhood and care is of fundamental importance for child care and education. Martin Heidegger's analytic of Dasein introduces the concepts of self and care within the ontological domain while structuring the holistic understanding of human existence. Because of the ontological emphasis, Heidegger's concepts of self and care have mainly been overridden in relation to the more or less practical questions of child care and education. This article studies Heidegger's analytic of Dasein and its implications for the philosophy of child care and education. The interconnection between the phenomena of care and selfhood and the question of how to pay attention to a child's selfhood are studied in this article. As the outcome of the study, it is proposed that the analytic of Dasein, especially its ideas about selfhood and authentic care, could offer an advantageous ontological perspective for an elaboration of the theory of relational selfhood and reciprocal care.

Introduction

One of the most important problems of the philosophy of education and care is how to pay attention to the unique human being as he or she exists in the world. It is obvious that this problem includes a broad and complex range of questions concerning the idea of man, ethics and goals, purposes and means of education and care. However, the core problem is how do we care for the other's selfhood?

How to pay attention to the self-being[1] of a singular human being that is under the influence of caring and educational interventions? The challenge of care for the other's selfhood interconnects the problem of the idea of man and the problem of selfhood. It is also in relation to a quite commonly shared ideal that the aim of care and education is to support the other's autonomy, individualisation and possibilities of self-being in the world in general. Care for the other's selfhood is of fundamental importance in the thought of education and care as far as it aims to secure what belongs to the core of human existence.

From the phenomenological perspective, educational and caring interventions cover two dimensions: first, they may open up possibilities for one's own-most growth and, second, close or narrow the other's possibilities for creating his or her own-most self-being in the world. Consequently, both education and care taking are phenomena of care as far as their shared main purpose, that is, to avail the offspring to take up a position in the historical–temporal human world. In this article, I consider care as an ontological–existential phenomenon that characterises human existence and its intentionality as a whole. Therefore, care is understood as a constitutional phenomenon of the shared existential world and as a concept that unifies the fundamental structures of education and care taking (e.g. Broström, 2006).

Martin Heidegger's analytic of Dasein or human existence (Being and Time, later referred to as BT) analyses the phenomenon of care and selfhood as interconnected in the ontological and existential dimension while structuring the holistic understanding of human existence in the world. In the analytic of Dasein, selfhood is defined as a 'way of existing' (BT, p. 312) and thematised as the sphere of one's intentional relatedness to the world and existence as a whole that is interestingly characterised as care (Sorge), concern (Besorge) and solicitude (Fürsorge). The analytic of Dasein makes also a distinction between authentic (Eigentlich) and inauthentic (Uneigentlich) care, whereas the former refers to the occasion of disclosing the other's possibilities for self-being and the latter refers to the occasion of closing the other's possibilities to exist as a self.

Because of the ontological emphasis, Heidegger's concepts of care and self have mainly been overridden in the more or less practical questions of child care and education. Heidegger does not write particularly about a child in his analysis of Dasein, but nor does he deny that children could not have the features of Dasein. The aim of the analytic of Dasein is to thematise fundamental existential structures of human existence in the world as such, within which all humane life is supposed to be actualised. The analytic of Dasein offers a perspective on the authentic care for the other's selfhood, which will be studied and discussed in this article.

On method and the theoretical framework

My method and ontological standpoint is phenomenological hermeneutics or phenomenological understanding. Phenomenological hermeneutics[2] endeavours for the understanding through the analysis of experiential phenomena, given within one's own world experience (mineness of existence, e.g. first-person perspective). Due to this, phenomenological hermeneutics tries to avoid abstract and categorical generalisations. Rather, it endeavours to describe the unique and singular lived experience and its structure in *existential generality*, through existentially indicative conceptualisation, as a condition of the existence of meanings and beings as such. In this article, I focus on education and care taking in an existential–ontological generality as a possible basis of educational and caring practice.

I lean on Heidegger's analytic of Dasein as a theoretical framework. Thus, my method of phenomenological understanding includes an interpretation of the analytic of Dasein, concentrating especially to open up an insight into the possibility of authentic care relation as it seems a requisite condition of caring for the other's selfhood. Hermeneutic reading and phenomenological understanding begin with an analysis of the existence of things and phenomena given to us (first personally or experientially). It is always an interpretation that begins with the existential situation in the everyday world where the human being finds himself/herself immersed; rather than bare practice, it has *existence* and the phenomenal world *as its horizon*.

Phenomenological hermeneutics of existence overcomes the theoretical distinction between the human being and the world (subject *vs.* object) and establishes a way of considering the directedness of human existence and the world within which human beings dwell as a whole. This kind of philosophising tries to reach the phenomenon of life through the lived experience (Erfahrung and Erlebnis), not as objectified, stable and from the outside. Regarding the above-mentioned, my study is an applied interpretation of the analytic of Dasein from the perspective of child care and education and the problem of caring for the other's selfhood.

Being-in-the-World and care relation

At first, it seems suitable to consider the crucial existential–ontological[3] standpoint and approach of Heidegger's phenomenological hermeneutics and the notion it produces about the character of the human self. This is important for distinguishing the phenomenological standpoint from the objectifying approaches and notions of self[4] and human being as objects (e.g. Malhotra, 1987).

The question is about the experiential standpoint referred to in the analytic of Dasein as the mineness (jemeinigkeit) of existence (Existenz) or mineness as existence (BT, §9, 4). Differing from the other kinds of beings (animals, things or equipment-like entities), *existence* (Existenz) signifies human beings' unique way of being in the world. Existence signifies the man's way of reaching out of himself or herself and relates back to his or her own Being[5] and existence. Through this existential character of 'reaching out', the human being is not fixed to himself or herself like a rock *is*, but relates to his or her own existence. For example, things and instruments *are* but only a human being *exists* in the sense that he or she has the mode of being-for-itself.

For Heidegger, existence does not signify the all-included collection of beings outside the experience. Rather, existence is an ontological character through which a human being relates himself or herself to the world, time, place, others and back to himself or herself. Finally, existence is a human being's essence: it is an intentional correlate of Dasein[6] as Heidegger calls the unique way of being of a human being. This relatedness of human existence is possible through understanding of Being[7] (Seinverstandnis) which, as an existential–ontological structure, characterises and mediates a human being's relation to his or her own Being and the world. All existential structures of Being-in-the-World are always meaning-relations within which a human being is actualised and through which a human being is a self-relational entity in the first place. Existence as human being's essence signifies the special capacity of humans to know that they *are* as well as knowing *how* they are in various individual ways.

The existential analytic of Dasein forms a theory of human being as Being-in-the-World (In-der-Welt-Sein). For Heidegger, a human being's relatedness to space or Being-in (existential spatiality) must be described in an existential, not in an abstract, categorical manner: man is not in space as herrings in a barrel, but rather through ecstatic meaning-relations. The world is the existential and ontological feature of human intentionality (cf. Bernsen, 1986, pp. 54–56).

The standpoint of Being-in-the-World creates an ontological [and methodological] difference in relation to objectifying research on human subject where the human being is distinguished from his or her Being and considered a more or less rational animal. For Heidegger, human life or existence is experienced and lived through as meanings (Sinn) and needs a non-objectifying method of phenomenological hermeneutics in order to be correctly researched and revealed. To begin research from the experiential position of

Being-in-the-World or existence, the problematic distinction between subject and object will be dispersed.

That distinction emerges in different forms in objectivistic-intellectual human research, for example, in dualities between man and world, body and soul, self and other, adult and child. These dualities obstruct entering into the interconnected phenomena of the self and other as well as selfhood and care. Research into child care and education needs to find an ontological entrance into the essence of the relationship between self and other, man and world or selfhood and care (e.g. Stern, 1985) as they are seen fundamentally intertwined in their co-existence. Phenomenological analysis opens up an existential-phenomenal field of dynamics among a child, an adult and the world: It is the same phenomenal world where children and adults live based on a shared existence.

The analytic of Dasein is generally seen as a response to western objectifying metaphysics, and scientific theories of the human being are based on it (Heidegger, 2000; Marx, 1982). Heidegger sees that objectifying metaphysics and objectifying research provide a problematic basis for understanding human life[8] (cf. Heidegger, 1992). Heidegger states that the human existence in its essential ground is never just an object and cannot 'be objectified at all under any circumstances' and, for that reason, searches for a new ontological beginning for human research:

> In the perspective of Analytic of Da-sein, all conventional, objectifying representations of a capsule-like psyche, subject, person, ego, or consciousness in psychology and psychopathology must be abandoned in favour of an entirely different understanding. This new view of the basic constitution of human existence may be called *Da-sein*, or being-in-the-world. (Heidegger, 2001, p. 4)

Heidegger's view is that it is not possible to define any being, including human being, or its essence in general (universally or absolutely) without first questioning the way or the meaning of its Being. The structures and possibilities of the Being of beings – within which human life is realised as meaningful, and within which psyche, I or persona is constituted as beings (seiendes) – should be prior in the analysis. In other words, an analysis of Being is fundamental in relation to objectifying scientific research. Bernsen concludes Heidegger's intentions as follows: 'The subject-matter of the analysis of Dasein is the specific properties of the kind of entity that has traditionally designated by expressions such as "man", "subject", "life", "psychic individual", or "higher conscious being", or as a combinations of "body" and "mind", "consciousness" or "spirit". [...] Dasein is [...] a contribution to a general theory of man's intentionality or relating of himself to reality, including his relating of himself to himself, [...]' (Bernsen, 1986, pp. 21–23).

When moving into the domain of experientially given existence, we enter to the fundamental sphere (of Being) where the self and others, man and world are existential-ontologically interrelated and to that Heidegger indicates with the terms Being-with (Mittsein) and With-world (Mittwelt) (BT, §26). On this ground of worldly existence, the human being's or Dasein's relation to himself or herself is characterised as care (Sorge). Dasein's relation to his or her own existence is also actualised through care. Care is not to be understood in psychological sense as 'worry' (Besorgnis) or carefreeness (Sorglossigkeit) (BT, p. 237) or as bare emotionality and affectedness. Care is rather the existential–ontological relatedness of human existence as such. It is a deconstructed concept of intentionality: when the classical concept of intentionality is understood as the way consciousness is directed outside itself or as the 'aboutness' of conscious states, care is the directedness and relatedness of human existence (Dasein) as a whole; care is always caring about something. Therefore, care through which a human being reaches out to his or her own Being and 'future' is also the meaning of Being-in-the-World.

Care (Sorge) is phenomenally three-dimensional as it is defined to encompass the fundamental spheres of human existence: as solicitude (Fürsorge), a prior social relatedness to the others; as concern (Besorge), an instrumental involvement with things and equipment totality of the world[9] and as care (Sorge), a fundamental characteristic of human existence that leads us to question the ground, directedness and orientation of our worldly existence as such (BT, p. 237). Solicitude or care for others and concern are general 'intentional' constituents of the human world and existence (BT, p. 308). This means that human relations and a human being's relation to the world are always constituted through care. This three-dimensional structure of care is a constitutive intentional activity of existence and therefore a basis of care-relations within which the shared existential world is always disclosed and within which a human being is always actualised: the constitutive world of care exists where human life takes place and within authentic and inauthentic care-relations.

The central concept of this study is, therefore, *care-relation* or solicitude-relation when emphasising the encounter with the other, for example, in a caring situation. Care-relation is understood in the existential–ontological sense as the intertwined totality of caretaker, cared-for and existential world as they all are interrelated in the situation of care. This definition of care will also serve as an insight into the relational selfhood as the self is fundamentally intertwined with others' selves and the existential world through actualisation of care. In other words, care-relation means the extended understanding of intentionality in the practical dimension through which human beings are involved and immersed with the equipment world, sociality of the others and existence as such. The concept of care-relation is derived from the existentials as initial meaning-relations[10] that are always actualised through care and within which human life is situated. Care-relation is always actualised through concrete and situational human praxis and continuously constitutes the shared existential world. This gives an insight into the character (or way of being) of human selfhood as such and into its relation with the other selves as constituted through solicitude-relation. This means to emphasise that relation to the other is not constituted in bare consciousness but rather within practical social dwelling (or Being-with) through care-relation and towards the horizon of institutional-instrumental world. As 'intentionality', *care-relation* is not to be understood as the relation between two separated entities, but rather as an existential interconnectedness and co-directedness.

The self is interpreted as relational in the first place, and the possibility of selfhood is rather attached with man's own-most (authentic) relatedness – or *Belongingness* – to Being (das Sein) than bare belonging to the world and different social groups (Heidegger, 1969). It is not possible to put the self under objective observation because the self is an experientially given and relational phenomenon. The phenomenon of selfhood is to be given for an experience of co-existing in the world through care-relation. Consequently, the self is to be understood only in an initial ontological relation to other selves and the world on the 'basis' of Being. The self is inextricably related to the actualisation of the care-relations: 'When fully conceived, the care-structure includes the phenomenon of selfhood' (BT, p. 370).

Here, the care-relation is not limited only to a face-to-face encounter which is very well defined by Noddings (2002) as the reciprocal recognition of intentional states between a cared-for and a caregiver. Rather, my analysis tries to keep the whole phenomenon of care-relation together as everyday practical dwelling with others. For the most part, care-relation is not actualised in the face-to-face situation of a genuine encounter. When having everyday human existence as a horizon, daily life, as it surrounds and forms our life situation, becomes the focus. Shared concern about the world and solicitude to others are inextricably bound together by care through which human beings always already constitute the basis for a shared life. In this broad or comprehensive situation, care-relations, for the most part, are actualised tacitly within daily praxis where the 'cared-fors' do not become individually recognised, but are still included and taken care for among other daily matters (influencing the cared-for's selfhood and way of care as a whole). To put this simply and practically but keeping in mind the whole phenomenon of care, the endeavour is to pay attention to the fact how the public and general care orientation of the everyday world affects cared-fors at least as much as face-to-face situations of genuine care; in other words, to notice how the public sphere mediates caregivers face-to-face encounter with cared-for's. According to this standpoint, a child's intentional state is open and directed towards the whole world and existence. To exclude this wholeness of the 'intentional state' of the other would mislead our understanding of the nature of the shared care-relation which includes the cared-fors within their own-most care-relations, caregivers as they belong to the world that is always already taken care of (Besorge) and the world as such that constitutively mediates human being's co-encounter with the existence and phenomena belonging to it (BT, p. 153). The holistic existential–ontological concept of care-relation encompasses the everyday world that affects solicitude-relations and questions human beings and our care institutions as a whole: what it means to consider the care-relation as existence in the horizon proposed by Heidegger.

Encountering the other in care-relation

In the analytic of Dasein, the question of selfhood is approached by questioning the way a human being relates himself or herself to Being by questioning the mode of being through which daily life is actualised (BT, §25, 26). This questioning of Dasein's self is phrased as a question of the 'who' of Dasein. According to Heidegger, an answer that it is always an 'I' (BT, p. 150) gives a formal answer and does not answer to the question in an existential sense. It is not enough to say that it is 'I' or 'me' who is in the world for it leads to conceive of the self as an object and leads to substantial definitions.

Through questioning, Heidegger searches for the existential concept of the self. The question is simple and aimed at one's own existing in the world: 'Who am I as I exist in the world'? First, Heidegger's idea is that it is possible to find a relational understanding of the self and to give an existential meaning to the 'formal I' by approaching the problem from the perspective of everyday existence (BT, p. 150). From the standpoint of a factical or experiential existence, 'I'-saying always indicates and reveals the 'I' as 'I-am-in-a-world' (BT, p. 368).

Dasein is in the world, but the question is who really is in the midst of everyday life? To begin with the everyday experience of existence, it seemingly is not in all cases bare 'I' or 'me' in the question when selfhood is actualised. Beginning with the 'I' also discloses the view to the fundamental relatedness of the self with other selves. One may notice that the experience of 'I' or 'myself' is relatively divided in its existential content: surely, there is something what is 'myself', but presumably there is also something foreign and alien in my own self-experience, for example, in the habits, manners, words and thoughts I am executing. Where are they from? Are they from my own self?

On the existential plane, it is possible to disclose the content of the 'who' – through analysis of a basic way of the being (mode) of human being (BT, §24, 25). The basic modes of existing are *authenticity* (Eigentlichkeit) and *inauthenticity* (Uneigentlichkeit) that are differentiated based on the state (or degree) of the mineness (Jemeingkeit) of self-hood (BT, §9). German 'eigen' refers to 'own', 'mine' and something that is typically characteristic of the Being of an entity. In addition, in the dimension of authenticity and inauthenticity, the answer 'it is always "I" who exists' misleads in its formality because the 'who' of everyday Dasein 'is *not* the "I myself"' in every case (BT, p. 150). This means the existential situation where the 'identity' of the self is under continuous change or even under the threat to lose itself. Experientially approached, we can notice that the relations and actions – or the whole intentionality of care we are actualising in – are not my own-most way to be, or at least it is for the most part determined by the overpower of the publicity or everyday worldliness (Weltlichkeit). Here, Heidegger refers to the power and domination of social conformity of everydayness that he calls the 'they' (das Man,[11] BT, §27). Under the affectedness of the everydayness of the 'they', Dasein also has the character of 'I-hood', but in the modus of self-forgetfulness not as an authentic self (BT, p. 152). In this mode of inauthentic self-forgetfulness, a human being is not aware of the forgetfulness because he or she is satisfied with the formal answer that Dasein is an 'I' (e.g. Theunissen, 1986, p. 173). Rather, a human being self emerges as the 'they' –self (das Man –selbst).

The domination and indifference within which human beings live are the ambience of oblivion of the existentiality of the self and forgetfulness of Being as a surrounding ontological condition. For this reason, the self-relation and relation to the world and others may not necessarily be one's own at all, or the relation remains outer and instrumental. Heidegger refers to this phenomenon of loss of self-, other- and world-relations as forgetfulness of Being with the term 'falling' (Verfallen) (BT, Chapters 4 and 5).

According to the analytic of Dasein, the encounter of the other human being as another Dasein is possible only when one exists in the *authentic* mode of self-being itself. A human being has to find back his or her own authentic self from the fallenness of the everyday worldliness (BT, §54; e.g. Hodge, 1995) in order to encounter the other as another Dasein. In some sense, it is a question of the constitution of the other as a self or Dasein-with (Mitdasein) within one's own world experience: one has to be individualised through the disclosure of one's own finite and groundless existence before able to encounter the other's existence or Being as such (e.g. BT, §60). For Heidegger, that seems to be a fundamental basis where the relation with a human being's own existence is the existential condition of the recognition of the other as another human Dasein. It means the existential experience of the finitude (BT, §53) and limits of a human being's own life that detach him or her from the immersed care-relations towards the equipment totality of the world and the others. This resoluteness (Entschlossenheit) unwinds the determined worldly care-relations and leaves oneself 'alone' to exist on the ground of Being and opens up a horizon towards the other selves *as such* and the shared existential world as a *possibility*. Resoluteness as 'authentic Being-one's-Self' does not mean that human being becomes detached from the world and isolated as 'free-floating "I"', but rather discloses the shared existential situation and the Other in his or her 'own-most potentiality-for-Being' (BT, pp. 344–346).

But where are the other selves to be found in the everyday world? As all inner-worldly beings are disclosed for the experience in practical interaction or concern (BT, p. 161), another human Dasein is encountered through the world in which the other dwells (BT, p. 157). According to the analytic of Dasein, the other is to be found, in the first place, in the practical immersion with the instrumental world at hand and that I share with the other (Being-with). In other words, the other, as well as my own self, is immersed in the world of equipment, instruments, institutions, organisations, factories, workplaces, etc. The other is also immersed in the goals and purposes the equipment totality aim at. Selfhood, my own and others, is to be found in the practice and activity we find ourselves immersed in. The other and his or her selfhood are encountered as he or she is immersed in that equipment totality of the world and emerges as an instrumental part of that environment.

Another human being, in his or her singularity as Dasein, is a part of my Dasein only through the shared existence of being-with (Mitsein) (e.g. BT, p. 156). However, everyday life is also actualised for the most part in the objectifying mode of being-among-one-another where the other remains objectified and as an outsider in relation to my Dasein. It means that the other as experienced is, in a certain sense, my own projection or re-presentation and cannot be separated from practical involvement in the equipmental world ready-to-hand (Zuhandensein) (BT, p. 156; e.g. Theunissen, 1986, p. 179, 181).

Therefore, the other human being is mediated to my experience through the equipment totality of the world (BT, p. 153), so that the Other is constricted to the similar occurrence with equipment; the other human being is determined in the worldly encounter as 'supplier' and 'producer' (BT, p. 153, T183) or as 'care worker', 'nurse', 'teacher' and 'caregiver'. This is what it means to say that the other is mostly encountered environmentally or in its involvement with the equipment totality of the world. The individual human being is encountered environmentally through the existential phenomenal world we are concerned (Besorge) about (BT, p. 163). The other becomes encountered, in the first place, through the world which is always already taken care of and positioned in the socio-legal and political concern.

To encounter the other is, in other words, a matter of care as care ontologically means the interconnecting link between the self, the other and the world. The way the other appears in relation to my experience depends on the mode in which my care is actualised and is directed towards the others, the world and the own-most future. The mode of my own care determines the way I encounter the other. For the most part, care remains inauthentic in fallenness to everydayness and is determined by the past as an un-thoughtfully inherited and sustained historical practice of care-relations. Determined by the past and everydayness, care is actualised in the goals and purposes foreign to one's own-most experience. Therefore, the meaning or aim of care – the future and for-the-shake-of-which (das Worumwillen) of care (cf. BT, §18, 31, 41) – is not disclosed to human existence as a free possibility for the own-most existence. A child, helpless and dependent on the public adult world, is thoroughly penetrated by the ethos of care that is overpowered by the equipment totality of the everyday world.

The existential experience through which (resoluteness) oneself is freed from the instrumental care-relations with the equipmental world and solicitude-relations with the others is a condition of the encounter of the other and his or her selfhood. That disclosedness of the own-most relation to Being and existence frees oneself from the *contingent* world into the possibility of free relation with the future and authentic relation with the others. According to the analytic of Dasein, the existential individua-lisation is the basis or initial condition of the encounter of the other's self and selfhood as the other exists in his or her own care-relations.

The ambiguous self and possibility of authentic care for the other's selfhood

In a complex sense, children, despite existing under the overpower of the everyday world dominated by the 'they' (das Man), also remain in the authentic mode of self-being. This is revealed when children, existing under the power of the ethos of instru-mental care that they depend on, 'always already' show their unique way of relating with and expressing the shared everyday (e.g. 'inter-subjective') features of the world. For example, children alter social habits, gestures and language in a way that gives them and to things themselves new meanings and significance in social contexts. A child's authentic self-being is not at all separated from the relatedness with the public everyday world. This is what Heidegger means when he says: '*Authentic Being-one's-Self* does not rest upon an exceptional condition of the subject, a condition that has been detached from the "they"; *it is rather an existentiell modification of the they – of the "they" as an essential existentiale*' (BT, p. 168). Thrown into the world, a child could not have chosen for himself or herself, a child fights for the shared inter-subjec-tive world in the border of the equipment totality of the everyday world dominated by adults and his or her own – at the beginning, pre-linguistic – meaning-world. A child's self-being is not to be understood as somehow separated from the public social world; rather, it is a child's own-most capability for self-being, to form and emphasise his or her own relations to other things, phenomena and the world, to modify his or her own existence through the own-most care in the world with others.

In a certain sense, a child already exists in an authentic way when his or her relat-edness to Being is not as mediated, through sociality of the 'they', as adults' way of being is. We usually refer to this when wondering about the 'genuineness' of children. From this point of view, it becomes understandable what Heidegger means by consider-ation about – which is, at first glance, quite contradictory one – the idea that the 'they-self, [...] is an existentiell modification of the authentic self' (BT, p. 365). Which is a modification of which when the authentic Being-one's-Self and the 'they-self' are both existentials and each other's [existentiell] modifications at the same time (e.g. Dreyfus, 1991, pp. 240–241)? These dimensions, the inauthentic and the authentic self, are equally original existential–ontological structures of the self. From this point of view, selfhood is actualised within both dimensions: inauthenticity and authenticity. Heidegger seems to think about the ambiguity[12] of selfhood as he, on the one hand, states that the realisation of selfhood is mediated through the public inauthentic world of the 'they' (BT, p. 225; they-self) and, on the other hand, that the own-most (authentic) dimension of the self emerges coincidentally with the former. Even when immersed and lost in the instrumental world and sociality of the 'they', a child holds on to his or hers own-most way of being a self. It is possible to interpret that Heidegger means that the self exists in a continuous tension between conflicting powers of auth-enticity and inauthenticity that constitutes human selfhood in its *ambiguity*. From this basis, the individual personality is temporally constituted.

Considering the ambiguity of selfhood, as one's possibility for authentic and inauthentic ways of being, it is important to pose the question of how to care for the other's selfhood and self-being. Here, it is necessary to distinguish between the two extreme ways of the actualisation of care. A distinction could be made by paying attention (differentiating) to the focus, directedness and character of the solicitude-relationship as it is actualised in both inauthentic and authentic modes: whether solicitude is directed towards the other as one's own projection and an instrumental part of the equipment totality of the world *or* as another co-existing Dasein with the own care-relations and selfhood. In other words, a difference remains between solicitude which is goal-directed and instrumental *and* solicitude which focuses towards the other's self-hood as his or her own-most potentiality for care, freedom and existence in general.

The actualisations of solicitude-relationships seem to have crucial significance for the other's relation to itself, others, world and existence overall. Heidegger states that inauthentic care 'take[s] away "care" from the Other and put[s] itself in his position in concern [...] takes over for the Other that with which he is to concern himself. The Other is thus thrown out of his own position; he steps back so that afterwards, when the matter has been attended to, he can either take it over as something finished and at his disposal (... um nachträglich das Besorgte als fertig Verfügbares zu übernehmen ...), or disburden himself of it completely' (BT, p. 158). In this kind of inauthentic solicitude, which Heidegger calls 'leaping in' (*Einspringen*), the Other becomes dominated and dependent even if the domination remains tacit and hidden to the other. The inauthentic solicitude-relation 'leaps in' and dilutes or even takes away the other's care as it takes care on behalf of the other (BT, p. 158). Heidegger sees that solicitude-relation remains for the most part in inauthenticity and its 'deficient modes' which actualises by being 'without one another, passing one another by, [and] not "mattering" to one another' (BT, p. 158).

However, Heidegger introduces the possibility for authentic care that 'does not so much leap in for the other as *leap ahead* of him (ihm vorausspringt) in his existentiell potentiality-for-Being, [...]' (BT, p. 158). Heidegger calls it authentic care, for it pertains 'to the existence of the Other, [...]' not to a 'what' which the Other is concerned with. This solicitude-relation does not dilute or take away others' care, but rather 'give[s] it back to him authentically for the first time' (BT, p. 158). It 'also helps the Other to become transparent to himself *in* his care and to become *free for* it' (BT, p. 158).

Caregivers have to share the experiential inter-subjective world – to be sensitive to the mind and experiences of the other and not interfere but rather reinforce children's own ability to seize things and live them through in their own experience. Authentic care for the other's selfhood resembles Heidegger's idea of letting be (Gelassenheit) (BT, p. 344), letting the other exist in his own-most relatedness to Being. As already referred, resoluteness towards itself is the necessary condition for the caregiver to find back himself or herself and let the other 'be' in his or hers 'own-most potentiality-for-Being, and to co-disclose this potentiality in the solicitude which leaps forth and liberates' (BT, p. 344). This resoluteness also discloses the shared existential situation for the first time (BT, p. 346).

As care means a human being's relatedness with the others and the world, it is also a basis of selfhood. The possibility of selfhood depends on the actualisation of care as Heidegger states: 'Selfhood is to be discerned existentially only in one's authentic potentiality-for-Being-one's-Self – that is to say, in the authenticity of Dasein's Being *as care*' (BT, p. 369). Therefore, the way care is actualised in solicitude-relations also crucially affects the constitution of the other's selfhood. The inauthentic 'leaping in' solicitude-relation is not distinct from concern that more often is mediated into the solicitude-relation as influencing the simple instrumental and goal-directed orientation towards the other's existence.

When authentic solicitude 'leaps ahead', it actually lets the other exists through own care and is in certain sense affirming the other's freedom (to relate to the existentials and features of everyday world). Affirming the other's freedom to own care, it is possible for the other to become self-aware in the situation. Heidegger also connects the constitution of responsibility to the solicitude-relation as he states that the domination of:

> [t]he 'they' is alongside everywhere [ist überall dabei], but in such a manner that it has always stolen away whenever Dasein presses for decision. Yet, because the 'they' presents every judgment and decision as its own, it deprives the particular Dasein of its *answerability*. (BT, p. 165)

For example, the overflowing discussion concerning socialisation as 'a positive process of a child's development' shows that we are not paying attention to children as ambiguous human selves in a sense that they have own-most care-relations through which they are conscious and understand the shared existential world. Often, it seems that children are only for adults' ready-made world where children's and youngsters' experiences play only a minimal role. The underestimation of children's self-relation is very common even among classical psychology where infants' self-awareness is more and more often denied (Gallagher, 2005; Meltzoff & Moore, 1995; Zahavi, 2006). Temporally existing children assimilate the ethos of the everyday world through the power of language, social manners expected, education, caring, etc., and self-forgetfulness conquers their existence if the adult world does not pay attention to the unique way they relate themselves to the given world, themselves and existence as a whole. This reveals a view on the ontological basis of indoctrination, socialisation, education and caregiving as far as their practices are mainly to serve the instrumental needs, goals and purposes of the equipment totality of the everyday world.

The possibility of authentic care for the other or solitude-relation derives its roots from the existential modes of inauthenticity and authenticity. Authentic care is contrasted with the inauthentic relation of forgetfulness of Being and offers a constitutive possibility to pay attention to the other's possibility to the constitute own-most authentic relation with oneself, others and the shared human world.

Implications for the child care and education

What could the enormous scale of human existence offer to the thought and practice of child care and education? The question concerning a child's possibility for authentic self-being and free relatedness to Being may seem too general, abstract or even empty question when it seems obvious that a child, most of all, needs physical and psychological conditions for growth and well-being.

However, phenomenological analysis reveals the structures and constitution of the lived experience in relation to which it is possible to reflect [and evaluate] everyday practical activities. Moreover, the analytic of Dasein shows how the relation with the existence, world, sociality and human individual itself is always shared with others and co-encountered (e.g. BT, p. 153). Even though the analytic of Dasein lacks the explicit analysis of a bodily face-to-face encounter with the other, it analyses the general structures within the limits of which this encounter takes place and is affected by the world; as we saw, the others (das Man, Dasein-with) are already there when considering the relatedness to Being. This 'co-encountering the world' through care makes existence an ultimate horizon of the evaluation of practical activities and theory that directs that activity.

For the perspective of early child education and care, an essential change in theoretical thought is to begin to understand a child as an existing human Dasein in the world who lives his or her own meaning- and care-relations that constitute his or her own selfhood. Having Dasein as the starting point, the relationship between a child and a caregiver or a teacher as mutuality of Being-with – and as there is no gap between the subject and the object, the caregiver and teacher and the cared-for and student – the interaction is understood as direct and does not need any mechanical explanation. The sphere of caring and teaching is not 'inside' the subject, but in the shared existential world in-between. The concept of Dasein gives us a perspective according to which children are considered equal human beings with adults and that assists to overcome the traditional – the objectifying adult-observer position – suppositions of a child and the young as deficient human beings, undeveloped adults, 'infantility', tabula rasa and so forth. This should not mean overestimation of children (and their potentiality), but rather endeavour to regard them as Being-withers, co-existing in and co-constitutors of the shared existential world (e.g. Merleau-Ponty, 2010, pp. 374–375). In an existential–ontological domain, children's or youngsters' lives are not different or exceptional with regard to the intentionality of care and compared to the existential abysmal incompleteness of an adult life. Or as Merleau-Ponty put it: 'However, the child is not different from the adult in terms of mentality. The difference exists in between what is still confused and polymorphous and what has been defined by culture' (2010, p. 408).

Consequently, care-relation cannot be framed according to strict rules and norms but needs an open and creative attitude that pays attention to the uniqueness of a human child and varying situations of care. Therefore, scientific theories or different recommendations that become outside the experiential situation may distort and obstruct the constitution of authentic solicitude-relation.

Everyday discussions – those of professionals or ordinary parents – reveal that there is no lack of 'worry' about children. However, the attention usually turns into issues such as what and how to feed a child, what the ideal duration of breastfeeding is, how to build an inspiring environment for a child's ideal cognitive development, what the correct time to put a child into day-care is, how to socialise the young, etc. The concern behind these questions focuses on important matters of the material, physical and psychological conditions, but at the same time, they often override the question of a child's existence as such. Heidegger refers to this overtaking with the concept of inauthentic care, for it is concerned about a child only indirectly, instrumentally or through goal-oriented rationalism. Children are offered only egoistic goals and aims outside their own existential situation and are taken care of just like whatever human being (das Man) in the world and interpreted even as 'a standing resource' or instruments for the other more general goals of the equipment totality of society.

To care for a child's selfhood is not a bare everyday concern of his or her daily needs, but merely the affirmation and support of the child's own-most relatedness with his or her own existence. Children, if anyone, thoroughly exist towards the whole existence as their horizon. This reminds caregivers of the situation in which caregiving is most often focused on a child as a being (seiende) and his or her 'basic' needs, while a whole unique universe of experiential existence is disregarded. The concern about the way of our care fulfilling only the necessary and taking care only about the minimum[13] represents this above-mentioned phenomenon.

For a child to exist, it is not only in relation to things and matters available in the present situation, but also about the conscious meaningful life of experience which is also a life of imagined, thought, felt, fantasised and believed objects of transcendental experience. Within that dimension of existence, the own-most relatedness to Being is constituted as well. The problem of caring about a child's selfhood seems to be a real challenge for an adult world where the understanding of Being and existence is mostly constrained with the publicly levelled comprehension of reality, especially when paying attention to the common western worldview determined through natural sciences and modern technology (Heidegger, 1993a). However, as the common care-experience tells, children are naturally ready to share existence and they serve as open doors for adults to enter into the free and liberating play of Being (e.g. Caputo, 1970). Through his philosophy, Heidegger tried to thematise the way Being itself has power over beings. However, from the point of view of the adult world, it seems necessary to dominate and manage Being which may actually be the source of the imbalance and bias of human existence.

The analytic of Dasein offers a perspective on the constant human situation in which inauthentic publicity creates and offers varying practices and recommendations for education and care while forgetting and undermining the own-most life experience based on historical understanding. In a way, Heidegger seems to think that we should lean on the historicity, not so that it would determine our understanding and future practice, but rather that history, when reflected through the own-most life experience, would itself reveal the valuable and mark the path into the authentic existence and care-relation. Inauthentic publicity has a tendency to obstruct our relation with the own-most experience and therefore dilutes the outcomes considered based on shared historical life experience. This confusion is often seen among parents nowadays: the connection to the historical life through those who lived before and their experience is more often cut down in favour of conflicting recommendations offered by scientific theories and different institutions. The situation of care is complex and confused with public 'knowledge', conflicting recommendations, goals, aims and means to achieve them, so that 'it soon become[s] impossible to decide what is disclosed in a genuine understanding, and what is not' (BT, §37, 36, 35, 38).

Conclusions: the way we care for is what we are

The instrumental-institutional world of education and caring mediates our relation to the children. At the same time, the way care-relation is actualised mediates children's relation to the world and their own existence as a whole. Viewed through the analytic of Dasein, especially through the analysis of the inauthentic social conformity (das Man), the practice of care remains under the public instrumental world which is determined by the past, everydayness and understanding of the reality that closes itself in an inauthentic manner. In other words, involving the everyday instrumental world of institutions of care that determine our relation to offspring, the world of the future is already chosen for them. From the parent's or caregiver's situation in the undisclosed world, it is too often referred to the *'only realistic possibility'*, for example, when considering the alternatives of counselling the offspring in their lives or when 'choosing' between parental care or day-care. This reference to 'reality' makes us believe that a future as a free possibility to aim at does not exist. Without the disclosed relatedness to Being and existence, human 'reality' is understood as something where everything is present, already known, stable, past, and thus there is no change for any human being – whether a child, youngster or an adult – to understand and have an 'effect' on the constitution of the world.

The general question of educational philosophy, 'How does one become what he is', is usually interpreted through the question of reaching one's authenticity (Eigentlichkeit) (cf. Thomson, 2004). Often, the question of authenticity is associated with the struggle of a young adult fighting with his or her existential challenge of finding himself or herself. Thomson thematises the outline of Heidegger's 'educational perfectionism' clearly, but pays only a little attention to the constitution of the authentic relation between the self and the other where the ideal of authentic self-being could be opened in the first place. Especially when considering the care-relation on which children depend, it seems necessary to pay attention to the constitutive relation which enables the other to constitute his or her own care-relation, or in other words, to take apart with the shared existential world as an authentic self. It seems that authenticity is not only the 'self-reflective' existential challenge of the human individual – as to experientially encounter the death and anxiousness (angst) which individualises one's own existence (BT, p. 284, 307) – but first of all, a call for the care for the other's existence and selfhood. In the analytic of Dasein, it is the call of care in resolute disclosedness that pushes the caregiver 'into solicitous Being with Others' (BT, p. 344). In the beginning, a human child is dependent on the world and care of adults, and it really includes the possibility of facing another as an existing self through authentic care.

It is not possible to derive practical rules or norms for caring from the ontology of care, for it endeavours only to reveal the constitution of shared world through authentic and inauthentic care. The analytic of Dasein indicates only the possibility of the authentic care-relation that emerges as a call for institutions of care and caregivers to question their own way of caring and their understanding of Being-with-children-in-the-world. How we as caregivers see ourselves connected to our life experiences determines – when immersed in the goals and purpose of the instrumental everyday world – the way we see the others. On the other hand, however, the solicitude for the other as how to take care of the other's existence without interfering the other's own-most potentiality for Being, we get an insight into a certain formal 'principle'. As Heidegger states the inauthentic way of caring may 'leap in and take away "care"' and 'the Other can become one who is dominated and dependent', it becomes clear that if caregiving wants to secure the other's intentional care (authentic selfhood) including autonomy and own-most responsibility, dominating inauthentic care – however it occurs amidst the enormous worry about things and matters – is something unfavourable. Radically speaking, the social area of the constitution of own-most care-relations reveals in itself that domination of the other's existence should be ruled out from caretaking. In the Heideggerian language, it is the display of Being(-with) that the child's selfhood is not to be supported by inauthentic 'leaping-in' care-relation.

The analytic of Dasein is interpreted as a general educational perfectionism that aims to the authentic selfhood, but mainly is overtaken or referred to as not a right starting point for the theory of care (Noddings, 2002, p. 78). This is a pity as the analytic of Dasein includes an insight into the way in which the world penetrates the solicitude relationship transforming the face-to-face encounter. The analytic of Dasein gives a holistic insight into the constitution of the self-other relationship through a practical emphasis on care-relation that is always an educational and caring relation as well. Care-relation considered in the extent of existence does not mean bare 'wandering in the world and finding a home in thinking' (Noddings, 2002, p. 78), when we pay attention to the way in which thinking, dwelling and building belong together in Heidegger's thought (Heidegger, 1993b). It rather seems that the theoretical attitude turns into practical orientation and interaction in the analytic of Dasein (e.g. Theunissen, 1986, p. 182).

For Heidegger, thinking becomes close to practical activity, for example, when the formally indicative concept care puts us into the question: how do I care? What are the goals and aims of my care taking? Without these questions, there is no encounter with the other self and solicitude that would support others' self-being in the world. When we look at the world through the lens of the analytic of Dasein, we have to look through the care-relations we are dwelling in: it pushes us to awake into our own way of caring through which we constitute the shared existential world.

Therefore, the analytic of Dasein may serve as an ontological ground for the theory of care because, first, it elaborates the holistic relational concept of the self and analyses the fundamental structures of the constitution of the existential world through care-relations. The analytic of Dasein and phenomenology overall may also offer advantageous views to the phenomena and theory of mentalisation (Fonagy, Target, Gergely, & Jurist, 2002) as its fundamental concern focuses on the constitution of human beings' relation to themselves and the others' selfhood as an initial condition for well-being.

Merleau-Ponty, in his child psychology, reminds that children are not outside of culture but rather take part in constituting human culture by living cultural life: they get into contact with their peers at an early age and demonstrate interests in the complex phenomena that surround them: 'For example, children acquire a true science of distinguishing and recognizing faces at an age when we would assume they only lead a sensory life' (Merleau-Ponty, 2010, p. 378). What Merleau-Ponty is looking after is that we have to give up talking about and arranging the child's 'nature', 'spiritual age' and rather focus on reconstituting interpersonal dynamics (Merleau-Ponty, 2010, p. 381). Phenomenological studies of face-to-face encounter (Emmanuel Levinas) and embodied subjectivity and interaction (Merleau-Ponty and Edmund Husserl), where the ultimate horizon of existence is not disregarded, offer a non-objectifying and non-metaphysical alternative direction for research on child care and education.

Acknowledgements

I wish to thank Prof. Kaarina Määttä and Dr Satu Uusiautti, the reviewers of the article, and Juho Joensuu for their work, support and assistance that helped me to refine this article. The research has been supported by The Finnish Cultural Foundation, Lapland Regional Fund.

Notes

1. With the concept 'self-being', I refer to the way of one's own existence or being in the world. Therefore, it means the actualisation of selfhood.
2. For Heidegger's concept of phenomenology, see Heidegger (1992, §7). It is important to notice that Heidegger adopts 'tools' from the phenomenological, existential and hermeneutic tradition in his analytic of Dasein.
3. I use the term existential–ontological in a Heideggerian-phenomenological sense. *Existential* refers to the structures of ways of being of a human being; in other words, existentials indicate the shared initial conditions and relations within which human existence is always actualised, a.k.a. Being-in-the-World. *Ontological* refers to structures of Being in general. Therefore, *existential–ontological* refers, in the context of the human situation (Dasein), always to those meaning-relations/-structures that deal with being (seiende) as experienced meaningful (as something rather than nothing) and Being of human beings overall.

4. The phenomenological account of selfhood is not necessarily in full contradiction with the objectivistic insights of selfhood, but within certain limits, it provides a profound ontological basis for more specific theories that focus on the social dimension of selfhood. It is a task of another extensive study to research the connections between the phenomenology of selfhood and more specific psychological theories of selfhood.

5. Heidegger makes an *ontological difference* between beings (Seiendes) and Being (das Sein). The latter signifies the transcendental sphere and kinesthetic nature of man's existence (emerging, for example, through the power of 'consciousness', time or 'living' as Being in significance of a verb). The former signifies all objectified (substantial or thing-like) entities perceived or taken in the theoretical attitude as an object that is not necessarily material. Heidegger uses Being to mean the whole sphere horizon of the meanings of humane life (temporality and spatiality). Human being as Dasein is an ontico-ontological being. As conventional practice in studies on Heidegger, I refer to Being by capitalising the first letter, [B]eing. In addition, the distinction between existential and existentiell refers to the ontological difference; existentials are the pre-structures of human existence in general, while existentiell indicates the domain of daily life where meanings occur in various unique ways.

6. The concept of Dasein means human life and existence in German. In Heidegger's use, the concept of Dasein plays a technical role in overcoming objectifying theoretical attitude by handling the human being as an ontico-ontological being who is determined as self-relational through understanding of his or her own Being (Seinverstandnis). The analytic of Dasein thematises the structures of the Being of a human being. Heidegger uses Dasein as a synonym for Being-in-the-World. I use Dasein as a technical term to emphasise the dimension of Being because there is no good translation for the term Dasein. Heuristically, the 'human situation' is a good translation for Dasein as it 'provided that one at once retains the full temporally distributed particularity of the indexicals, "here, now, mine", that it is meant to convey' (Kisiel, 1995, p. 423).

7. Understanding of Being is fundamentally related to emotional affectedness (Befindlichkeit der Stimmung) and language: these three moments together form the structure of the disclosedness of Being and the existential world.

8. The basic problem of traditional metaphysics, for Heidegger, is the way it has abruptly separated being and Being from each other and even forgot to question Being as an ultimate horizon of all beings and meanings. In western metaphysics, beings are not reached directly in their ambiguous worldly (weltliche) meaning and bodily perception, but rather through objectifying theoretical thought that offers a re-presentation of being (e.g. Heidegger, 2000). For that reason, the understanding of truth and reality has transformed and that what occurs in its own accord is replaced with theoretical representations; it is no longer things and beings revealed to transcendental experience as meaningful that signifies 'what there really is' but rather humane representations of beings and an imagined correspondence between them. Later, Heidegger sees the era of the modern worldview and technology as the fulfilment of western metaphysics that transforms man's relation to the world and Being in general (Heidegger, 1993a).

9. The concept of 'the equipment totality of the world' encompasses the phenomenon of how the whole world is constituted through the instruments that always refer to other things and to other instruments and finally to the goal or aim that the totality in question carries within: for example, the reference between a hammer, nails, plank, house and furniture (BT, §18, Bevandtnis) that form a human being's way of being and finally constitutes the relatedness to existence as such. The 'equipment totality of the world' includes the institutions, organisations and social-legal sphere that support the instrumental organisation and their activity and directedness. Heidegger's idea is that due to his or her concern (besorge, an intentional orientation towards the world), a man is immersed in the equipment totalities of the world in his or her concern and for the most part tacitly affirms the goals and aims that the totality carries with it.

10. By meaning-relation, I refer to a human being's relatedness to his or her own world experiences in (1) grounding pre-reflective (existential pre-structures and mineness of existence [jemeinigkeit]) and (2) more publicly mediated, day-to-day, reflected or interpreted (inauthentic) senses. A human being is always actualised in both dimensions of the

EARLY CHILD CARE AND EDUCATION IN FINLAND

meaning-relation: through existentials on the level of daily life (existentiell). See also notes 3 and 6.

11.　das Man refers to an ontological–existential condition of a human being. In the existential dimension, das Man is often interpreted to mean social conformity and its power over a singular human being in his or her authentic relation with Being (cf. Dreyfus, 1991). The 'they' is related to the concept of everydayness and publicity as Heidegger sees that they are the domain of actualisation of the 'they'. Fallennes (Verfallen) defines the process of forgetting one's own-most self. The structure of das Man is central when considering the way human beings are immersed in the totality of the equipment world and sociality.

12.　Here, I refer the concept of ambiguity to the ontologically relatively divided two-fold structure of the human self and its actualisation in the tension between authenticity and inauthenticity. With the concept of ambiguity, I do not indicate the phenomenon of Zweideutigkeit that is translated by the concept of ambiguity in Being and Time. Whereas zweideutigkeit refers to the certain constituent moment of fallenness, ambiguity is a different phenomenon as I emphasise the actualisation of selfhood in its uniqueness between the tension of authenticity and inauthenticity.

13.　I refer to the general discussion about day-care practice that too often turns out to be only a repository for the children of busy parents and children are not seen as real constitutors of human culture.

References

Bernsen, O.N. (1986). *Heidegger's theory of intentionality* (Hanne Vøhtz, Trans.). Denmark: Odense University Press.

Brostrøm, S. (2006). Care and education: Towards a new paradigm in early childhood education. *Child Youth Care Forum, 35*, 391–409.

Caputo, D.J. (1970). Being, ground and play in Heidegger. *Man and World, 3*(1), 26–48.

Dreyfus, H. (1991). *Being-in-the-world: A commentary on Heidegger's Being and time, division 1*. Cambridge: Massachusetts Institute of Technology.

Fonagy, P., Target, M., Gergely, G., & Jurist, E. (2002). *Affect regulation, mentalization, and development of the self*. New York, NY: Other Publications.

Gallagher, S. (2005). *How the body shapes the mind*. Oxford: Oxford University Press.

Heidegger, M. (1969). *Identity and difference* [Identität und Differenz, 1957] (J. Stambaugh, Trans.). New York, NY: Harper & Row.

Heidegger, M. (1992). *Being and time* [Sein und Zeit, 1927] (J. Macquarrie & E. Robinson, Trans.). Oxford: Blackwell.

Heidegger, M. (1993a). The question concerning technology. In D.F. Krell (Ed.), *Basic writings* (pp. 311–314). London: Routledge.

Heidegger, M. (1993b). Building, dwelling, thinking. In D.F. Krell (Ed.), *Basic writings* (pp. 347–363). London: Routledge.

Heidegger, M. (2000). *Introduction to metaphysics* [Einführung in die Metaphysik, 1953] (G. Fried & R. Polt, Trans.). New Haven, NY: Yale University Press.

Heidegger, M. (2001). *Zollikon seminars: Protocols – conversations – letters* [Zollikoner Seminare, Protokolle – Gespräche – Briefe Herausgegeben von Medard Boss, 1987]. Evanston, IL: Northwestern University Press.

Hodge, J. (1995). *Heidegger and ethics*. London: Routledge.

Kisiel, T.J. (1995). *The genesis of Heidegger's being & time*. Berkeley: University of California Press.

Malhotra, V.A. (1987). A comparison of Mead's 'Self' and Heidegger's 'Dasein': Toward a regrounding of social psychology. *Human Studies, 10,* 357–382.

Marx, W. (1982). *Heidegger and the tradition* [Orig. Heidegger und die Tradition: Eine problemgeschichtliche Einführung in die Grundbestimmungen des Seins, 1961] (T. Kisiel & M. Greene, Trans.). Evanston, IL: Northwestern University Press.

Meltzoff, A.N., & Moore, M.K. (1995). Infants' understanding of people and things: From body imitation to folk psychology. In J.L. Bermúdez, A. Marcel, & N. Eilan (Eds.), *The body and the self* (pp. 43–69). Cambridge: MIT Press.

Merleau-Ponty, M. (2010). *Child psychology and pedagogy – The Sorbonne lectures 1949–1952* [Psychologie et pédagogie de l'enfant: Cours de Sorbonne 1949–1952, 2001]. (T. Welsh, Trans.). Evanston, IL: Northwestern University Press.

Noddings, N. (2002). *Starting at home: Caring and social policy.* Ewing, NJ: University of California Press.

Stern, D.N. (1985). *The interpersonal world of the infant. A view from psychoanalysis and developmental psychology.* New York, NY: Basic Books.

Theunissen, M. (1986). *The other. Studies in the social ontology of Husserl, Heidegger, Sartre, and Buber* [Der Andere: Studien zur Sozialontologie der Gegenwart, 1977] (C. Macann, Trans.). Cambridge: MIT Press.

Thomson, I. (2004). Heidegger's perfectionist philosophy of education in Being and Time. *Continental Philosophy Review, 37,* 439–467.

Zahavi, D. (2006). *Subjectivity and selfhood: Investigating the first-person perspective.* Cambridge: MIT Press.

Accelerating early language development with multi-sensory training

Piia M. Björn, Irma Kakkuri, Pirkko Karvonen and Paavo H.T. Leppänen

This paper reports the outcome of a multi-sensory intervention on infant language skills. A programme titled 'Rhyming Game and Exercise Club', which included kinaesthetic–tactile mother–child rhyming games performed in natural joint attention situations, was intended to accelerate Finnish six- to eight-month-old infants' language development. The participants were 20 infants (10 training group children and 10 control children). Their cognitive skills and both receptive and expressive language skills (Bayley Scales III) were tested three times (pre-, post- and follow-up assessments). The groups differed significantly in receptive language skills at the baseline, in favour of the controls. The results showed that the performance of the training group children in cognition and receptive language increased after the intervention. The training group girls showed more acceleration in receptive language skills than the boys. The results suggested that training consisting of rhyming games and kinaesthetic-tactile stimulation is a useful tool for accelerating early language development and for enriching mother–child interaction.

Introduction

Previous intervention research on early language development has mainly focused on combinations of visual and auditory training (Bahrick & Licklitter, 2000; Pickens & Bahrick, 1995). However, much less is known about combinations of linguistic and tactile interventions aimed at enhancing very small children's language development (for a review, see Lewkowicz, 2000). Furthermore, many of the previous studies using tactile stimulation have focused on premature infants (for a review, see Liaw, 2000).

The aim of the present study was to bring back the culture of children's poems and rhymes in mother–child interaction. Further, these interaction situations were used as a tool in an intervention designed to accelerate early language development. The intervention programme was developed to provide the mothers with concrete and easy, scientifically based ways of interacting with their babies, through joint attention in natural interaction situations and using kinaesthetic–tactile stimulation along with rhyming games. The term 'kinaesthetic–tactile' is used, because the programme included tactile stimulation excercises combined with movements. We were interested in finding out whether the performance of children in the very early stage of their language development (aged six to eight months) would be accelerated by the eight-week intervention programme. We also examined whether children with and without exposure to such rehearsal would differ according to their development in cognitive skills, as well as receptive and expressive language skills.

Early language development and joint attention

Language acquisition starts well before an infant is born. The foetus already reacts to sounds it hears in the uterus (Laakso, Poikkeus, Katajamäki, & Lyytinen, 1999). When the child is born, a preverbal stage begins. The attachment and emotional relationship between the caregiver and the child (i.e. inter-subjectivity; see Trevarthen & Aitken, 2001) is the basis in language development during the postnatal preparatory phase. Babbling, that is the way the baby verbally expresses himself/herself at this stage, already includes all of the basic features of speech – from different sound combinations to controlling the breathing. A babbling baby also perceives all of the prosodic features of speech, such as intonation (Lyytinen, Poikkeus, Leiwo, Ahonen, & Lyytinen, 1996). The preverbal stage lasts until the child utters his/her first word at about one year of age (Lyytinen, Poikkeus, Laakso, Eklund, & Lyytinen, 2001).

According to Bruner (1981), one central basic element in infant language development is the shared (or joint) attention between caregiver and child. When the child reaches approximately six months of age, she/he starts to pay more attention to surrounding objects. As the child explores the world through objects, joint attention with the caregiver also starts to develop (Laakso, Poikkeus, Katajamäki et al., 1999). Eye contact between the caregiver (mother) and the child is crucial in the development of joint attention. The child forms ideas about the mother's way of looking at things and objects and these become a way of exchanging information (Paavola, Kunnari, Moilanen, & Lehtihalmes, 2005). For example, Silvén (2001) observed that the child's ability to follow the mother's direction of attention accounted for the development of receptive language later on.

Bruner (1981) has further suggested that the child is the one showing the willingness to not only to get attention from the caregiver but also to share it. This was the basis for the intervention in our study. Moreover, we used the kinaesthetic stimulation to teach the mothers how to engage their infants' attention during rhyming games. This, in turn, may be also interpreted as one way of enhancing the sensitivity of responsiveness of the mothers towards their children (see Paavola, 2006; Paavola et al., 2005). Laakso, Poikkeus, and Lyytinen (1999) have also found that the quality and nature of mother-infant interaction contributes to early communicative and linguistic skills (see also Bruner, 1983).

Stolt, Haataja, Lapinleimu, and Lehtonen (2008) observed that receptive language developed earlier than expressive language among Finnish nine-month-old infants. Moreover, 26% of these children produced words at this age. No gender differences were found in receptive language; however, in expressive language the girls had significantly larger lexicon size at 1.3 years. Nevertheless, Hohm, Jennen-Steinmetz, Schmidt, and Laucht (2007) have found that girls outperformed boys in both the expressive and receptive language scales (REEL scale) at the age of 10 months.

A study by Kokkinaki and Kugiumutzakis (2000) revealed that, in a natural parent–infant communication situation, parents tended to imitate and support their infants, especially when they produced vowel sounds. In contrast, in our study, no conscious supporting of the infants in the production of sounds was instructed; instead, such support was used to direct their attention to listening to words and sounds produced usually by their mothers and to learn to discriminate the long and short vowel sounds via kinaesthetic–tactile stimulation.

Previous interventions aimed at enriching and enhancing early language skills have been suggested to enhance children's cognitive skills (such as concept formation and memory), which, along with early language skills, also facilitate educational achievements later on (see Taanila, Murray, Jokelainen, Isohanni, & Rantakallio, 2005). Interventions that include coaching of parenting skills, in particular, have been suggested to be effective. Moreover, in comparison to programmes executed solely in home environments, those interventions combining home and centre-based programmes have been suggested to be more effective (see Blok, Fukkink, Gebhardt, & Leseman, 2005). In the present study, the mothers received instructions once a week. This instructional meeting also included a rehearsal of the new programme with the infants.

Sensory stimulation and language skills

As stated before, infants can already discriminate between many different sounds at birth and some speech sounds categorically during the first six months of life, well before the (development of) linguistic communication. However, research indicates that the phonological system, responsible for the speech perception of native speech categories, continues to develop beyond 12 months of age. Infants' general auditory processing skills, which they have at birth, are modified selectively by experience and activities in their language-learning environment. Many important changes related to speech perception and language development also take place in brain development during the first year of life. For example, the brain differentiates between sound frequencies and durations at birth, even during sleep (Leppänen, Eklund, & Lyytinen, 1997; Leppänen, Pihko, Eklund, & Lyytinen, 1999). The connections in the auditory pathway between the thalamus and cortex are nevertheless still immature at approximately 4.5 months (Moore, 2002), and myelination, enabling the fast flow of brain signals, continues in the auditory cortex until the age of approximately four years (Johnson, 1998).

Furthermore, the number of synapses, which are important, for example, in building up speech sound representations, in the auditory brain areas is at its highest somewhat under 12 months of age (Huttenlocher & Dabholkar, 1997). The first year of life is thus an important period in the development of speech perception and is the basis for later language learning.

Early auditory skills are also related to later language development, and impairment in these skills seems to be a risk factor for language-related disorders such as dyslexia and specific language impairment, SLI (see, e.g. Benasich, Thomas, Choudbury, & Leppänen, 2002; Choudhury, Leppänen, Leevers, & Benasich, 2007; Leppänen et al., 1999, 2002; Richardson, Leppänen, Leiwo, & Lyytinen, 2003). Auditory processing impairment/deviancy related to the risk of dyslexia or SLI has involved several features, for example, sound frequency processing (Leppänen et al., 2010), processing of rapidly changing auditory cues (Benasich et al., 2006; Choudhury et al., 2007); vowel and consonant duration perception (Leppänen et al., 1999, 2002; Richardson et al., 2003).

It has also been suggested that an inter-relationship exists between motor and language development (Viholainen, Ahonen, Cantell, Lyytinen, & Lyytinen, 2002).

The period between six and eight months of age, in particular, is essential, as the child begins to move about and interact with the world, simultaneously using increasingly complex verbal utterances (Campos et al., 2000).

Bimodality of stimulus (e.g. visual and tactile), that is, the involvement of at least two sensory channels at the same time in processing given stimuli, has been suggested to facilitate language learning (Kuhl & Meltzoff, 1982; Morrongiello, Fenwick, & Nutley, 1998). According to the intersensory redundancy hypothesis by Bahrick and Licklitter (2000), the use of information presented concurrently and synchronolously via two senses will elicit attention and perception better than presenting the same information in one sense modality only. For example, Flom and Bahrick (2007) found that four- to seven-month-old infants best directed their attention to happy–sad–angry expressions in situations in which bimodal stimuli were used instead of presenting stimuli using only either the visual or auditory channel. This performance pattern also remained stable across the aforementioned ages. Based on the notion of the importance of early auditory/speech perception and efficacy of using two sensory modalities in facilitating perceptual learning, rhythmic speech (rhyme-like) patterns – connected to corresponding motor movements and learning of speech duration differences coupled with kinaesthetic–tactile stimulation – were used in the present study to enrich language skills.

Based on their findings, Bahrick and Licklitter (2000) suggested that the discrimination of rhythmic patterns emerges by the fifth month of life and that the specific time when responsiveness emerges may depend on pattern complexity and whether the stimulation is presented unimodally or bimodally. However, varying rhythms presented at a very fast tempo might not be discriminated by infants even by the age of seven to nine months (Pickens & Bahrick, 1997).

It has been suggested that the importance of tactile discrimination is evident from the very early stages of infancy. For example, intervention studies focusing on infant massage, aimed at premature newborns, have suggested that touching is the best way to support the overall development of these infants (Field, 1995). In tactile interventions, the comfort of touch, gentleness, rhythm, and equilibrium are important. Liaw (2000) has classified three different types of touch: passive touch, active touch, and social touch. In our study, the kinaesthetic–tactile stimuli used were both active and social in nature.

Kinaesthetic–tactile stimulation and speech stimuli with varying vowel durations were combined in our intervention programme. The child's attention was first directed to the targeted elements of language by simultaneously using both auditory and kinaesthetic–tactile stimuli. In addition, our programme included rhyming games with movements that reflected the phrases within the poems (e.g. if the poem included the phrase 'rock the baby', the mother rocked her child). We have attempted to find very simple but effective ways to get the infants' attention during the kinaesthetic–tactile rhyming games and joint attention situations (see also Dunham, Dunham, & Curvin, 1993; Paavola, 2006), in order to accelerate their language development.

Specific aims

Intervention studies such as described in this article are usually aimed to children at risk of problems in language development, for example. However, our main goal was to develop a tool for enriching mother–child interaction and to examine its possible later usability for children identified as having the aforementioned risk for dyslexia, as well. So, this article reports the effects of the intervention to children coming from diverse backgrounds, not differentiating between the possible risk factors.

This study first aimed at investigating the extent to which the six- to eight-month-old training group's (participating in kinaesthetic—tactile and rhyming exercises) cognitive skills and receptive and expressive language skills differed from the control children's skills (between pre-measurement and post-measurement, post-measurement and follow-up measurement or between pre-measurement and the follow-up measurement), after age was controlled for. Secondly, we investigated whether there were any differences between the groups with regard to the aforementioned skills between post-measurement and follow-up measurement, after pre-measurement (baseline) scores were controlled for. Thirdly, we investigated, whether there were any gender differences between measurement timepoints, which were calculated separately for the training group and control group children.

Methods

Participants

The participant families of the present study were recruited in January 2007, in collaboration with maternity clinics in the surrounding area of a medium-sized city in Central Finland. Two types of information letters were given to parents chosen randomly by the maternity clinic personnel. One of the letters provided information about a new Rhyming Game and Exercise Club for six- to eight-month olds and their parents [Finnish: Loruliikuntakerho 6–8 kk ikäisille vauvoille ja vanhemmille], and the other letter about a research project focusing on early language development. This particular age group was chosen for the intervention for two main reasons. First, the Finnish language has a specific feature that has to do with differentiation between short and long vowels. The whole meaning of a word changes according to whether the word includes a short or long vowel combination (e.g. *tuli/tuuli* [fire/wind]. This differentiation is also the core problem with children diagnosed as having dyslexia. Therefore, we included rehearsing this feature of our language into the intervention programme (for more precise information, see the intervention section: *Themes* in this article) with children who do not yet say any words. Secondly, the children in this age group did not yet move around much. This enabled more successful training in the various components of the intervention programme. The research was funded by RAY, Finland's Slot Machine Association. RAY was originally established to raise funds through gaming operations to support Finnish health and welfare organisation. Nowadays, RAY extensively also funds research projects.

The information letter targeted at the training group (the families enrolled for the Rhyming Game and Exercise Club) informed that families willing to enrol for this free-of-charge programme would automatically also participate in a study by the University of Jyväskylä. The letter also described the activities included in the Rhyming Game and Exercise Club; for example, that the programme would require full involvement in both the guided exercises (taking place once a week over an eight-week period) and also in separately guided activities (i.e. rhyming and combined kinaesthetic-tactile exercises), intended to be carried out in the homes with their infant. The families were also told that they would receive information about their child's development. A total of 17 families participated in an information session in which they were told more specifically about the programme. During this session, their formal consents to participate in the study were also gathered.

However, during the project, seven of the families withdrew at some point of the study and, therefore, the final number of participants in the training group was 10 children, aged from 5 months 21 days to 9 months 11 days ($M = 6.40$ months, SD = 0.81). To find out whether there was any common reason for dropping out of the study during the first stage of measurements, various background variables were compared between the families that dropped out and those who stayed in the study. These variables included the child's gender, age at baseline, the number of siblings, mother's year of birth, maternal educational level, and paternal educational level. No group differences were found in t-tests for any of the variables (all $p > 0.05$).

The letter directed at the control group (families only enrolling for the follow-up study without training) informed about our study on early language development. The families were told that they would receive feedback about the development of their child after each stage of measurement. They were also informed that after the study they would receive a collection of rhymes that they could use with their children. The rhymes in this collection were the same as those used in the Rhyming Game and Exercise Club, but without the kinaesthetic–tactile exercises. A separate information session was not arranged for the control group families. The control group infants were matched to the experiment group infants by age and gender. The final number of the control families was 10 with children aged from 5 months 14 days to 9 months 0 days ($M = 6.75$ months, SD = 1.11). The control group data were collected during January 2007–April 2008. One control family interrupted the research and decided not to participate in the follow-up measures.

Demographic information about the participant families ($N = 10$ training group children and 10 controls) is shown in Table 1.

Measurements

Bayley Scales III

The cognition, receptive language, and expressive language subscales were chosen for the purposes of this study. The Bayley Scales of Infant and Toddler Development (Bayley, 2006) is an assessment instrument designed to measure 1–42-month-old children's development. It includes five central areas of development: cognition, language, motor skills, socio-emotional, and adaptive activity. The child gets one point from each correct or expected activity or answer. The starting point of each subtest is defined by the child's age. If the child succeeds in the three first items, she/he also gets the scores from the preceding items. If the child does not succeed in all of the three starting items, the test administrator will search for a new starting point from an earlier age. The test is stopped after the child makes five errors in a row. In this research project, we used the following three subtests.

Cognition

This subtest includes items that assess sensorimotor development, exploration and manipulation, object relatedness, concept formation, memory, and so on. The total number of items in this subtest is 91. The average total sum of items for children in our *age group* at the baseline was 31.20 (SD = 2.35). For example, in this subtest, the child's *reactions to the surrounding environment* (whether or not she/he explores it with his/her gaze) are assessed. Another example is whether she/he *looks at an*

Table 1.   Demographic information.

	Training group (n = 10)		Control group (n = 10)	
	n	%	n	%
Maternal education				
Compulsory school	–	–	–	–
Vocational school	–	–	2	20
Higher education/low	1	10	1	10
Higher education/high	3	30	7	70
University degree	6	60	–	–
Paternal Education				
Compulsory school	–	–	1	10
Vocational school	–	–	4	40
Higher education/low	2	20	1	10
Higher education/high	3	30	3	30
University degree	5	50	1	10
Family type				
Two-parent, married	5	50	6	60
Two-parent, not married	3	30	2	20
Two-parent, new spouse	1	10	1	10
Single parent	1	10	1	10

Note: Higher education/low = first cycle or bachelor's degree in university of applied sciences; higher education/high = second cycle or master's degree in university of applied sciences; university degree = traditional university; either bachelor's or master's degree.

object for 3 s. The reliabilities (Cronbach's α) among Finnish population have been reported to be 0.69 for 8-month-old children and 0.69 for 12-month-old children, respectively (Bayley, 2008).

Language skills

The total number of items in the two subtests is 97.

(a) *Receptive language.* This subtest includes items that assess preverbal behaviour, vocabulary development, such as being able to identify objects and pictures, and vocabulary related to morphological development. In this subtest, the child received one point from *reaction to a rubber duck's sound.* Another example is, whether she/he *reacted to sounds made by the test administrator* by turning his/her head, by facial expressions or other. The raw score *M* for our age group at the baseline was 11.15 (SD = 1.27). The reliabilities for receptive language subscale have been reported to be 0.55 for 12-month-old children (Bayley, 2008). Smaller children's reliabilities have not been calculated.

(b) *Expressive language.* This subtest includes items that assess preverbal communication, such as babbling, gesturing, joint referencing, and turn-taking;

vocabulary development, and morpho-syntactic development. In this subtest, the child received one point for a *social smile*, or making *consonant sounds* (/m/, /p/, /k/, /t/), for example. The raw score *M* for our age group at the baseline was 8.75 (SD = 2.57). The reliabilities for this subscale have been 0.62 for 8-month-old children and 0.72 for 12-month-old children (Bayley, 2008).

Procedure

This study applied a design with a pre-measurement (January 2007), an intervention programme (eight weeks for training group), an immediate post-measurement (March–April 2007), and a follow-up test after six months (October–November 2007). The measurements (pre-measurement, post-measurement, and follow-up measurement) were administered by trained research assistants. The participants were tested at the university facilities. Each testing session started with 10 min free play among the mothers and children.

The mothers (and in some cases the fathers) were with their children during the whole testing session, but they were advised not to take part in the testing situation if not asked to. The families also scheduled the testing times so that their child was at his/her best in terms of overall activity (e.g. they had already taken their nap). Inter-rater reliability was confirmed by having two research assistants present at most of the testing sessions. One of them acted as the 'responsible researcher', while they both filled in the observation form. After the testing session was over, they discussed the case and thus ensured a unified agreement on the child's scores. The parents were given an overall feedback about their child's development after each testing session.

Ethical considerations

Before the actual intervention started, our researcher team had many careful discussions about the possible ethical problems concerning the present study. We had to think about three main questions: first, should we select the participants concerning their background information about risk for familial dyslexia and related disorders, for example? We decided to include all suitable babies (in terms of their age) coming from diverse families because we did not want to test a hypothesis concerning a possible effect on certain types of children but rather to verify to the caregivers that it is useful to include enriched interaction to the everyday life with an infant child. Secondly, we discussed the effect an intervention might have on the regular language development of the infant. The intervention included mother–child interaction exercises done mainly in their home environments. This was considered as a possible way of helping the mothers to learn how to interact with their babies in such a way which might accelerate some specific skills (such as cognition, receptive language, and expressive language, respectively). There would have been more serious problems to think about if the researcher team would have been the one doing the exercises with the children and not by the most important person in their lives. Thirdly, we discussed the amount of information to be given to the families about the research project. As the aim was to get the best results possible, we decided to do everything we could to give information about language development to all participant families (also to the controls). Therefore we, for example, arranged expert lectures about child language development during the research project.

The intervention programme

The 'Rhyming Game and Exercise Club' intervention programme was primarily developed to teach the mothers in the study how to direct their infant's attention during the rhyming games, secondly, to teach the mothers the rhyming games that directed them to implement the kinaesthetic–tactile stimulus during the rhyming, and thirdly, to transfer the rehearsal exercise to the natural home environments as one tool for achieving richer mother–child communication.

The training group received the instruction at the Rhyming Game and Exercise Club once a week, and the training programme then also changed to include new vowels and themes. The main purpose of the weekly instruction was to introduce the mothers to the new vowel–kinaesthetic–tactile stimulation items and rhyming exercises with movements. In addition to the weekly sessions (duration of intense training approximately 20 min each time), the mothers were asked to do the training at home on a daily basis (four times a week in addition to the instructed training session), so that they completed the whole programme once and then trained the vowel discrimination every time that they changed their child's diaper (approximately 10 repeats each time). The parents also filled in a diary of their daily exercises so that we could monitor their activity. The approximate sum frequency reported by the mothers for training the whole programme was 35–44 times during the intervention plus the vowel exercises.

The programme included three main elements in addition to starting and ending poems, which were the same in all of the eight programmes. The first main element of the programme was the *Joint attention* between the mother and the child. Although the infants were not yet walking, the mothers had to train themselves to get their child's attention while they were doing the exercises. The kinaesthetic–tactile activities were crucial to this: when the mothers touched their children, they eventually directed their attention towards the exercises. The joint attention poems (as well as the changing rhymes poems) were chosen from Finnish children's literature, with the criteria of having as much activity in them as possible. Moreover, the vocabulary needed to have elements that we could use in the exercises.

The second element, with the idea of linguistic training, was the *Themes* with vowels and two syllables (a, ä, i, e, o, u, nan and mam). These vowels are the first that emerge in a Finnish infant's speech (see Lyytinen et al., 1996). The syllables used in the exercises were also typical examples of the most common first 'words' with more than one sound. The exercises included two short and one long vowel (e.g. a –a –aa). This feature of categorical variations in the phonemic length in the Finnish language (see Karlsson, 1983; Lehtonen, 1970; Richardson, 1998) was chosen for the intervention programme, as its processing is problematic for children with a language-related difficulty, namely dyslexia (Lyytinen et al., 1996), and as it is important in language learning in terms of distinguishing meaning in many words, for example, in *kato* 'crop failure', *katto* 'roof' and *kaato* 'fall, felling' or *tuli* 'fire' and *tuuli* 'wind'. Phonemic length variation also plays a part in signalling grammatical forms, e.g. *katto* (nominative singular) *vs. katon* (genitive singular). In the programme, when a short vowel was pronounced, the mother stroked (or tapped) the child's arm very briefly, and when a long vowel was pronounced, the touch lasted longer. In this way, the length differences were made clearer using both auditory and kinaesthetic–tactile stimulation.

The third main element of the programme was the *Changing rhymes* that could also be considered as the emotional element of the programme. In each new training programme, there were four new rhymes with movements presented. In some of the rhymes there were, for example, names of body parts, in which case the mothers touched the part of the body (e.g. toes) articulated in the rhyme. This part of the intervention programme guided the mothers towards very warm engagement with their children, as the poems and rhymes we chose contained interesting vocabulary and movements in which the mothers held their babies very close, rocking them, etc.

Analysis steps

To answer the first research aim on differences between training group and control group cognition and receptive and expressive language skills (age controlled for, as the participants' age range had to be taken into account), repeated measures ANCOVAs were calculated. We also used planned contrasts to test specific differences between groups, between pre-measurement and post-measurement, and between post-measurement and follow-up measurement. Additionally, a simple ANCOVA test (controlling for age) was used to calculate performance differences between groups, between pre-measurement and follow-up tests, to find out about the development during the entire period of the research project.

Next, to answer the second research question on performance differences in cognition and receptive and expressive language skills between the two groups in performance between post-measurement *vs.* follow-up measurement, we modified the ANCOVA models by now controlling for the pre-measurement raw scores (as we wanted to even out the possible performance differences before the actual intervention). Again, planned contrasts were used to calculate specific performance differences between groups, between post-measurement and follow-up measurement.

Finally, to answer the third research question on gender differences within the training group and control group performance in cognition and receptive and expressive language skills, we used repeated measures ANOVAs and separately tested gender differences between the measurement timepoints for the training group and controls.

Results

Bayley Scale performance between the training and control groups

First, differences between the groups were calculated with repeated measures ANCOVAs. For mean scores and standard deviations at measurement times within the training and control groups, see Table 2. Also the main results of the repeated measures ANCOVAs are shown.

The results showed that age and measurement time in cognition had an interaction effect. There was also an interaction effect between measurement time and group after age was controlled for. Further inspections of the contrasts showed that the interaction between age and measurement time was statistically significant between post-measurement and follow-up measurement ($F(1) = 4.54, p < 0.05$). Additionally, a group interaction effect emerged between the same period in favour of the training group, although the contrast was not quite statistically significant ($F(1) = 3.71, p = 0.07$). Simple mean difference comparisons confirmed the direction of the difference: training group mean difference was 18.50 (control group mean difference: 16.17), indicating that the training group had better performance in cognition between post-measurement and follow-up measurement.

Table 2. Mean scores and standard deviations at each measurement time within the training ($n = 10$) and control ($n = 10$) groups (ANCOVA results).

	Pre-measurement				Post-measurement				Follow-up measurement			
	TrG		CG		TrG		CG		TrG		CG	
	M	SD	M	SD	M	SD	M	SD	M	SD	M	SD
Subscale (Bayley III)												
Cognition	30.50	2.51	31.90	2.08	32.80	4.42	33.50	2.80	51.30	5.31	49.67	4.61

Main effect: (measurement time) $F = 0.69$; interactions: (measurement time × age) $F = 5.20$**; (measurement time × group) $F = 3.69$*

	Pre-measurement				Post-measurement				Follow-up measurement			
Receptive language	10.40	1.08	11.90	0.99	11.90	1.60	13.10	1.79	21.40	4.60	19.22	5.33

Main effect: (measurement time) $F = 0.78$; interactions: (measurement time × age, covariate) $F = 3.56$*; (measurement time × group) $F = 4.19$*

	Pre-measurement				Post-measurement				Follow-up measurement			
Expressive language	7.70	2.54	9.80	2.25	8.20	2.57	11.60	2.50	16.30	2.79	19.22	3.73

Main effect: (measurement time) $F = 5.65$**; interactions: (measurement time × age, covariate) $F = 1.56$; (measurement time × group) $F = 0.48$

Note: TrG, training group; CG, control group.
*$p < 0.05$. **$p < 0.01$.

Measurement time in receptive language and age, again, had an interaction effect: ($F(2)$ = 3.56, $p < 0.05$). A group interaction effect with measurement time was also found after controlling for age: ($F(1) = 0.51, p < 0.05$). Further inspection of the contrasts suggested that these differences emerged between post-measurement and follow-up measurement. Mean difference comparisons indicated the training group children's development in receptive language to be higher than among the controls (9.50 vs. 6.12). Expressive language and age had no interaction effects, nor were group differences found.

These results suggested that age started to have an effect on cognition skills between post-measurement vs. follow-up measurement (while the children were 8–10 and 14–16 months old). Group differences were found in cognition and receptive language: the training group children showed more development between these two measurements, although age was controlled for suggesting that the training might have accelerated some developmental processes.

Next, group differences between pre-measurements and follow-up measurements were calculated with separate ANCOVAs, in order to find out about the development during the whole time. Age was a statistically significant covariate in cognition ($F(1)$ = 8.33, $p < 0.01$). After age was controlled for, the group difference was still significant: ($F(1) = 5.79, p < 0.05$). In receptive language skills, age was not a statistically significant covariate. However, the two groups differed ($F(1) = 5.17, p < 0.05$). Age was also not a statistically significant covariate in expressive language skills, nor were there any group differences.

These results suggested that in the overall development of cognition and receptive language, age certainly plays a significant role. However, the training group children were better in both the aforementioned skills after age was controlled for.

Differences between groups, controlling for pre-measurement scores

Next, we investigated whether there were any differences between groups in the afore-mentioned skills between post-measurement and follow-up measurement, after the pre-measurement scores were controlled for. To begin with, we investigated the baseline differences between groups in receptive and expressive language skills and cognitive skills. The results showed that the Bayley Scales III raw scores in all the aforemen-tioned subtests were higher in the control group than in the training group at the base-line measurement point. This was a basis for using the pre-measurement scores as a covariate. However, only the difference in receptive language skills was statistically significant between the two groups: ($t(18) = -3.24, p < 0.01$).

The results showed that after controlling for baseline scores, there were no group differences in cognition. In receptive language, there was a nearly statistically significant difference between the groups: ($F(1) = 3.66, p = 0.07$). Baseline scores in expressive language was a statistically significant covariate, but there were no group differences after they were controlled for. When this information is combined with the prior results, these results suggested that especially the training group children's receptive language skills development was accelerated after the intervention period was over.

Gender differences separately for training group and control group children between measurement timepoints

The third aim was to investigate whether there were any gender differences between pre-measurement and post-measurement or between post-measurement and follow-up

Table 3. Means and standard deviations at different measurement timepoints by gender.

	Training group ($n = 10$)*				Control group ($n = 10$)*			
	Girls (6)		Boys (4)		Girls (6)		Boys (4)	
	M	SD	M	SD	M	SD	M	SD
Subscale (Bayley III)/measurement time								
Cognition/pre-meas.	30.83	2.86	30.00	2.16	32.67	1.12	30.75	2.75
Cognition/post-meas.	33.17	5.42	32.25	2.99	34.50	1.87	32.00	3.56
Cognition/follow-up	52.67	5.28	49.25	5.38	49.80	1.92	49.50	7.19
Rec/pre-meas.	10.00	0.63	11.00	1.41	12.00	1.10	11.75	0.96
Rec/post-meas.	11.50	1.52	12.50	1.73	12.67	1.86	13.75	1.71
Rec/follow-up	23.17	2.32	18.75	6.24	21.00	4.30	17.00	6.27
Expr/pre-meas.	7.33	3.08	8.25	1.71	10.00	2.19	9.50	2.65
Expr/post-meas.	7.50	2.74	9.25	2.22	11.83	3.06	11.25	1.71
Expr/follow-up	17.33	2.66	14.75	2.50	20.80	4.44	17.25	1.26

Note: Rec, receptive language; Expr, expressive language.
*All p of t-tests over 0.05.

measurement. See Table 3 for group means and standard deviations by group and by gender. Table 3 shows that there were no statistically significant differences between genders in any of the *exact* measurement times.

The results showed that, in the *training group*, there were no statistically significant differences between girls and boys in cognition measurement times, whereas receptive language measurement timepoint showed an interaction with gender: ($F(2) = 3.99$, $p < 0.05$). Further inspection of the contrasts (measurement time × gender) showed that the difference emerged especially between the post-measurement and follow-up measurement: ($F(1) = 4,40$, $p = 0.07$). A comparison of the mean differences (see Table 3 for means at different measurement times) between the post-measurement and follow-up measurement revealed that this difference was in favour of the girls' (mean difference 11.67, boys' mean difference: 6.25) suggesting that the training might have accelerated particularly the girls' performance in receptive language skills. There was no interaction effect between gender and measurement times in expressive language.

In the *control group*, there was no statistically significant or even nearly statistically significant interaction with gender and measurement times in any of the measures.

Discussion, suggestions for future research and practical implications

The aim of this study was to investigate whether it is possible to accelerate six- to eight-month-old infants' language development by applying a programme developed for enriching mother-child interaction in terms of rhyming games, short and long vowel discrimination exercises, and joint attention. Thus, as our programme focused on directing the child's attention towards the spoken sounds and rhymes produced by the mother, our results were encouraging (see, e.g. Dunham et al., 1993; Paavola, 2006). Also the structure of the intervention programme, in particular, including a large amount of tactility with the child, was in line with the suggestions of Field (1995), for example.

First, we investigated the gains between groups, controlling for age, as there were not enough children born in the same month within the region in which our study was conducted. Luckily, we managed to collect data with age- and gender-matched control group children, evening out the age differences between groups. Between the end measurement and follow-up measurement, our training group showed a statistically significant acceleration in cognition and receptive language skills in comparison with the development of the control group children. Moreover, during the whole period (pre-measurement to follow-up), the training group children's cognitive and receptive language development was higher compared with that of the control group. The results suggested that participation in the Rhyming Games Exercise Club could be used as one tool for the mothers with which to enrich their interaction with their infant children.

Secondly, we investigated whether there were any differences between groups in the aforementioned skills between post-measurement and follow-up measurement, after pre-measurement (baseline) scores were controlled for. The results showed that particularly the training group's receptive language skills developed at a relatively higher rate when compared with the control group.

The third aim of this study was to investigate potential gender differences during the different measurement timepoints separately within the training group and control group, although we could not expect the differences yet to be very large (see Lyytinen et al., 1996). In contrast to the findings of Stolt et al. (2008), who did not find significant gender differences, the girls showed more development in receptive language than in expressive language, when comparing the post-measurement and follow-up measurement. However, Hohm et al. (2007) have found girls to outperform boys in both receptive and expressive language skills.

These results suggest that the intervention programme succeeded in accelerating especially the girls' receptive language development to some extent. This result may be due to two main factors: first, this difference might reflect girls' early interest in language and interaction (for corresponding results regarding the Finnish population, see Ojala, 2006); secondly, the maternal gender-stereotypic behaviour (i.e. the girls are thought to be more interested in language activities than the boys) that possibly emerges at an instinctive level (see Umek, Fekonja, Kranje, & Barjk, 2008), even though the mother also engages her male child while doing the exercises. Thirdly, it could also be argued that the girls' receptive language was developing more rapidly than the boys' over this particular research period. However, as this was not the case among the children in the control group, it could be suggested that the intervention programme had an effect on the training group children's language development and particularly the girls' receptive language development.

Future research suggestions

Next, we present four suggestions for future research based on the experience we obtained during the present study. First, the small size of our research groups limited the analysis possibilities. Overall, one aspect of the assessment and results regarding early language development is that there is usually much variation in scores between subjects (see Hohm et al., 2007). This variation might also explain, to some extent, the disparities between results in different studies. Therefore, studies with more participants are needed and/or a more qualitative approach would be good. Secondly, it was possible that the mothers engaged in the present research project valued the cognitive development of their babies. It would be interesting to get information about parental beliefs on the development of their child in order to find out the possible motives in future research projects. Thirdly, the intervention sessions could have been more carefully and consistently videotaped. We videotaped some of the sessions in order to qualitatively validate the functionality of the exercises. More precise analysis of the exercise situations would facilitate further analysis of the effect of maternal guiding in joint attention situations, mother–child interaction situations and, thus, would enable more reliable analysis in future research projects. Fourthly, the exercises that were completed in the participants' homes could be videotaped, at least partially in studies to come: we now asked for maternal reports about the exercise frequencies (i.e. diaries) in our research project.

Practical implications

Our study adds to the existing body of literature by showing that a multi-sensory approach should be taken into account when developing tools for enriching language development from three perspectives: accelerating early language development, bringing back the culture of rhyming and language games in families, and, especially, enriching mother–child interaction. This kind of programme can also be used as a tool when helping and guiding mothers who have problems with natural and affective interaction with their infants.

Note

We are happy to provide precise details concerning the intervention for researchers that might be interested in replicating our study.

Acknowledgements
We wish to thank professor Anna-Maija Poikkeus for the Bayley Scales training. Dr Saara Salo included some of our data in the Finnish version of Bayley Scales III. The families that so actively participated in our study deserve our upmost gratitude.

References

Bahrick, L.E., & Licklitter, R. (2000). Intersensory redundancy guides attentional selectivity and perceptual learning in infancy. *Developmental Psychology, 36,* 190–201.

Bayley, N. (2006). *Bayley III. Scales of infant and toddler development* (Administration manual, 3rd ed.). San Antonio: PsychCorp.

Bayley, N. (2008). In S. Salo, P. Munck, N. Uusitalo, & R. Korja (Eds.), *Bayley III. Scales of infant and toddler development* (Suomalainen käsikirja, 3rd ed.). Helsinki: Hakapaino Oy [Finnish manual].

Benasich, A.A., Choudhury, N., Friedman, J.T., Realpe-Bonilla, T., Chojnowska, C., & Gou, Z. (2006). The infant as a prelinguistic model for language learning impairments: Predicting from event-related potentials to behavior. *Neuropsychologia, 44,* 396–411.

Benasich, A.A., Thomas, J.J., Choudbury, N., & Leppänen, P.H.T. (2002). The importance of rapid auditory processing abilities to early language development: Evidence from converging methodologies. *Developmental Psychobiology, 40,* 278–292.

Blok, H., Fukkink, R.G., Gebhardt, E.C., & Leseman, P.P.M. (2005). The relevance of delivery mode and other programme characteristics for the effectiveness of early childhood intervention. *International Journal of Behavioral Development, 1,* 35–47.

Bruner, J. (1981). The social context of language acquisition. *Language and Communication, 1,* 155–178.

Bruner, J. (1983). *Childs' talk learning to use language.* New York, NY: W.W. Norton.

Campos, J.J., Anderson, D.I., Barbu-Roth, M.A., Hubbard, E.M., Hertenstein, M.J., & Witherington, D. (2000). Travel broadens the mind. *Infancy, 2,* 149–219.

Choudhury, N., Leppänen, P.H.T., Leevers, H.J., & Benasich, A.A. (2007). Infant information processing and family history of specific language impairment: Converging evidence for RAP deficits from two paradigms. *Developmental Science, 10,* 213–236.

Dunham, P., Dunham, F., & Curvin, A. (1993). Joint attentional states and lexical acquisition at 18 months. *Developmental Psychology, 5,* 827–831.

Field, T. (1995). Massage therapy for infants and children. *Journal of Developmental and Behavioral Pediatrics, 2,* 105–111.

Flom, R., & Bahrick, L.E. (2007). The development of infant discrimination of affect in multimodal and unimodal stimulation: The role of intersensory redundancy. *Developmental Psychology, 43,* 238–252.

Hohm, E., Jennen-Steinmetz, C., Schmidt, M.H., & Laucht, M. (2007). Language development at ten months. Predictive of language outcome and school achievement ten years later? *European Child & Adolescent Psychiatry, 16,* 149–156.

Huttenlocher, P.R., & Dabholkar, A.S. (1997). Regional differences in synaptogenesis in human cerebral cortex. *Journal of Comparative Neurology, 387,* 167–178.

Johnson, M.H. (1998). The neural basis of cognitive development. In W. Damon (Series Ed.) D. Kuhn & R. Siegler (Eds.), *Handbook of child psychology. Cognition, perception, and language* (5th ed., Vol. 2, pp. 1–49). New York, NY: John Wiley & Sons.

Karlsson. (1983). *Suomen kielen äänne ja muotorakenne* [The phonemic and morphological structure of Finnish language]. Helsinki: WSOY.

Kokkinaki, T., & Kugiumutzakis, G. (2000). Basic aspects of vocal imitation in infant-parent interaction during the first 6 months. *Journal of Reproductive and Infant Psychology, 18,* 173–187.

Kuhl, P., & Meltzoff, A. (1982). The bimodal perception of speech in infancy. *Science, 10,* 1138–1141.

Laakso, M.-L., Poikkeus, A.-M., Katajamäki, J., & Lyytinen, P. (1999). Early intentional communication as a predictor of language development in young toddlers. *First Language, 19,* 207–231.

Laakso, M.-L., Poikkeus, A.-M., & Lyytinen, P. (1999). Shared reading interaction in families with and without genetic risk for dyslexia: Implications for toddlers' language development. *Infant and Child Development, 8,* 179–195.

Lehtonen, J. (1970). *Studia Philologica Jyväskyläensia: VI. Aspects of quantity in standard Finnish.* Jyväskylä: University of Jyväskylä.

Leppänen, P.H.T., Eklund, K.M., & Lyytinen, H. (1997). Event-related brain potentials to change in rapidly presented acoustic stimuli in newborns. *Developmental Neuropsychology, 13,* 175–204.

Leppänen, P.H.T., Hämäläinen, J.A., Salminen, H.K., Eklund, K., Guttorm, T.K., Lohvansuu, K., ... Lyytinen, H. (2010). Brain event-related potentials reveal atypical processing of sound frequency in newborns at-risk for familial dyslexia and associations to reading and related skills. *Cortex, 46,* 1362–1376.

Leppänen, P.H.T., Pihko, E., Eklund, K.M., & Lyytinen, H. (1999). Cortical responses of infants with and without a genetic risk for dyslexia: II. Group effects. *NeuroReport, 10,* 969–973.

Leppänen, P.H.T., Richardson, U., Pihko, E., Eklund, K.M., Guttorm, T.K. Aro, M., & Lyytinen, H. (2002). Brain responses to changes in speech sound durations differ between infants with and without familial risk for dyslexia. *Developmental Neuropsychology, 22,* 407–422.

Lewkowicz, D.J. (2000). The development of intersensory temporal perceptions: An epigenetic systems/limitations view. *Psychological Bulletin, 126,* 281–308.

Liaw, J.-J. (2000). Tactile stimulation and preterm infants. *Journal of Perinatal and Neonatal Nursing, 14,* 84–103.

Lyytinen, P., Poikkeus, A.-M., Laakso, M.-L., Eklund, K., & Lyytinen, H. (2001). Language development and symbolic play with and without familial risk for dyslexia. *Journal of Speech, Language and Hearing Research, 44,* 873–885.

Lyytinen, P., Poikkeus, A.-M., Leiwo, M., Ahonen, T., & Lyytinen, H. (1996). Parents as informants of their child's vocal and early language development. *Early Child Development and Care, 126,* 15–25.

Moore, J.K. (2002). Maturation of human auditory cortex: Implications for speech perception. *Annals of Otology, Rhinology, & Laryngology, 189,* 7–10.

Morrongiello, B.A., Fenwick, K., & Nutley, T. (1998). Developmental changes in associations between auditory-visual events. *Infant Behavior and Development, 21,* 613–626.

Ojala, M. (2006). Preschool achievement in Finland and Estonia: Cross-cultural comparison between the cities of Helsinki and Tallinn. *Scandinavian Journal of Educational Research, 51,* 205–221.

Paavola, L. (2006). Maternal sensitive responsiveness, characteristics and relations to early communicative and linguistic development (Doctoral dissertation). *Acta Universitatis Ouluensis. Series B, 73.*

Paavola, L., Kunnari, S., Moilanen, I., & Lehtihalmes, M. (2005). The functions of maternal verbal responses to prelinguistic infants as predictors of early communicative and linguistic development. *First Language, 25,* 17–195.

Pickens, J., & Bahrick, L.E. (1995). Infants' discrimination of bimodal events on the basis of rhythm and tempo. *British Journal of Developmental Psychology, 13,* 223–236.

Pickens, J., & Bahrick, L.E. (1997). Do infants perceive invariant tempo and rhythm in auditory-visual events? *Infant Behavior and Development, 20,* 349–357.

Richardson, U. (1998). *Familial dyslexia and sound duration in the quantity distinctions of Finnish infants and adults* (Doctoral Dissertation, Studia Philologica Jyväskyläensia, University of Jyväskylä, Jyväskylä).

Richardson, U., Leppänen, P.H.T., Leiwo, M., & Lyytinen, H. (2003). Speech perception of infants with high familial risk for dyslexia differ at the age of six months. *Developmental Neuropsychology, 23,* 385–397.

Silvén, M. (2001). Attention in very young infants predicts learning of first words. *Infant Behavior and Development, 24,* 229–237.

Stolt, S., Haataja, L., Lapinleimu, H., & Lehtonen, L. (2008). Early lexical development of Finnish children: A longitudinal study. *First Language, 3,* 259–279.

Taanila, A., Murray, G.K., Jokelainen, J., Isohanni, M., & Rantakallio, P. (2005). Infant developmental milestones: A 31-year follow-up. *Developmental Medicine, 47,* 581–586.

Trevarthen, C., & Aitken, K. (2001). Infant intersubjectivity: Research, theory and clinical applications. *Journal of Child Psychology and Psychiatry, 42,* 3–48.

Umek, L.M., Fekonja, U., Kranje, S., & Barjk, K. (2008). The effect of children's gender and parental education on toddler language development. *European Early Childhood Education Research Journal, 3,* 325–342.

Viholainen, H., Ahonen, T., Cantell, M., Lyytinen, P., & Lyytinen, H. (2002). Development of early motor skills and language in children at risk for familial dyslexia. *Developmental Medicine & Child Neurology, 44,* 761–769.

How were the pupils dressed in a country village in northern Finland in 1909–1939?

Anitta Heikkilä and Kaarina Määttä

In this article, we analyse schoolchildren's clothing at the village school of Rautiosaari in northern Finland between 1909 and 1939. Accordingly, we describe the kind of clothes that schoolgirls and schoolboys used during the target period. Interviews with elderly people were used as sources for the study. The research had a micro-historical approach. The starting point was a group interview with 10 people supplemented by several individual interviews. In addition to interviews, the data included observations of existent relevant environments and historical documents such as photographs, official archive records, magazines and newspapers, local history publications, and other literature. Clothes and schoolchildren as their users create a lively educational discourse covering the chronological continuity in the flow of history which the researchers interpret.

Introduction

The aim of this article is to study pupils' clothing in one little village called Rautiosaari in the Finnish Lapland between 1909 and 1939. At the centre of this dissection are a child as a bearer of clothes and a cloth in a child's life. The aim of this research is to study northern Finnish children's life from the perspective of clothing in their living environment at the beginning of the twentieth century. Children's clothing has not been studied much from this point of view. Especially, the history of children's clothing has interested researchers (e.g. Buck, 1996; Collard, 1973; Huggett, 2006; Martin, 1978; Rose, 1989; Schimpky & Kalman, 1995; Sichel, 1983; Worrell, 1980). Despite the various forms of clothing, earlier research has dissected the contents and meanings of pupils' clothing starting from a child, his/her experiences, adults, dressers, and the actual environment he/she is dressed. Through little details, the examination can proceed from a micro- to a macro-level, from the stitching of an apron to the prevailing historical situation in world politics.

In Finland, every housewife's handbook from 1932 defines the purpose of clothes simply as follows: 'The purpose of clothes is to keep the air layer that is the closest one to body warm, prevent an excessive loss of heat from the body, and protect the body against moisture, wind, dust, and radiant warmth' (Hannula, Gebhard, OllonQvist,

163

Harmaja, & Wiherheimo, 1932, p. 868). In Europe and European culture, children's dressing culture has exemplified not only the history of fashion (Bigelow, 1970; Mansfield, 1953), but also the textiles and materials available (Evans, 1949; Furches & Staley, 1963; Lee, 1953), the wealth of homes (Rensselaer, 1972/1931; Workman, 2009), parents' consuming habits (Horridge & Richards, 1984; Stone & Sternweiss, 1994), and the practicality of clothes from a child's point of view (Inomata & Simizu, 1991) as well as the instrumental value of dressing: with dressing, children seek their own place and define themselves in relation to others (Ford & Drake, 1982; Lapitsky & Smith, 1981; Lennon, 1990; Morganosky & Creekmore, 1981; Perry, Schutz, & Rucker, 1983; Seitz, 2003) as adults do (Kwon & Drayton, 2007; McCullough, Miller, & Ford, 1977).

In Lapland, in the village of Rautiosaari, the northern nature and climate as well as a community consisting of country people formed by Kemijoki River dictated children's possibilities to attend school as it was not common at that time and how they were dressed for school. In this article, we focus on pupils' way of protecting their bodies by clothing and their survival by clothing in the northern climate and with the demands of the weekdays and Sundays and holidays in the countryside of northern Finland at the beginning of the twentieth century.

The obstacles to going to school could be the long and/or rough paths to the school, bad health, difficult situations at home, or the fact that a child did not have clothes or shoes. After framing the law of compulsory education in Finland in 1921, more and more schools were established and school-going was considered as an obligation.

In this research, our aim is not to report about the serious crises, rebellions, revolutionary inventions or even about the trends in clothing. Instead, we dissect pupils' clothing in Rautiosaari between 1909 and 1939 and those everyday ways of surviving that were created at homes at the beginning of the twentieth century in order to clothe the pupils of riverside. We concentrate on a child's everyday life and everyday clothing and show that numerous significant things happen even when nothing seems to happen (cf. Levi, 1992, p. 23).

Our research proved to be topical because in the village of Rautiosaari, there are still people who have personal experiences and stories about the life in last century and their childhood dressing. Their experiential knowledge has affected the birth of this article and the doctoral thesis preceding this article (Heikkilä, 2008). After a couple of decades, these informants will no longer exist. In addition, local historians have collected data about the histories and culture of the villages surrounding the city of Rovaniemi. These data are also used in this article.

The research questions

The main question raised for this research is as follows: how did clothing appear in pupils' lives in a countryside elementary school in Rautiosaari at the beginning of the twentieth century? The more specific questions are as follows:

(1) Based on the extant school photographs, how were the pupils in Rautiosaari dressed between 1909 and 1939?
(2) What was typical of girls' and boys' dressing (parts and materials in it) and how did girls' and boys' ways of dressing differ from each other?

The research has a micro-historical approach. Levi (1992, p. 30), a micro-historian, considered as a salient and positive feature of micro-history the finding of new information through paying attention to small concrete things. On the other hand, Peltonen (1996, p. 10) encapsulated the principle of micro-history as the belief that microscopic contemplation would reveal yet undiscovered phenomena. Ginzburg (1996, pp. 48–49), for his part, introduced a clue method where a new entity of information is concluded by analysing the tracks, symptoms, or other clues of individual cases orientating to the past, present, and future. At its best, micro-history provides a means to criticise the old concepts and theories and to create new conceptions (Peltonen, 1992, p. 9). For instance, a detail in some picture or interview reveals a path to an interesting world where a researcher can reach the significant things that have affected children's everyday life.

Micro-history examines documents such as photographs, interviews and letters, verbal expressions, social structures, cultural factors, and historical dimensions, as well as artistic and creative expressions. A researcher's task is to collect data; analyse, interpret, and determine the significance of the sources; and come up with a synthesis. A researcher finds the clues from perhaps even the most insignificant signals from the past.

The aim and methods

The target period in this micro-historical research is defined between the years 1909 and 1939. It seemed natural to start the research from 1909, the year the school of Rautiosaari was established. Everyday life changed in those homes where children had the opportunity or were allowed to go to school. Children's clothing had to be taken into consideration more carefully than earlier because the concrete path (e.g. a skiing track or footpath) on the way to school in constantly changing weather conditions placed new challenges on clothing. After 1939, the conditions changed totally because the Winter War (Finno-Russo War) began and the northern Finnish children had to be evacuated. The school teachers at Rautiosaari School were assigned military operational tasks and the school facilities served as accommodation for the soldiers. With the change in time, children's clothing was influenced by Sweden, and the new era is significant as a historical period and worth an examination on its own, but this study is delimited to 1939.

Ten pensioners who went to school in the village of Rautiosaari comprised the research subjects. They were interviewed both as a group and personally several times between 1997 and 2006. The oldest of the interviewees was born in 1907 and the youngest in 1929. The interviews were recorded or written down and the participants decided to be identified in the research with their own names. All interviewees had the opportunity to check the written text about the research results. In addition, they gave letters and especially photographs for the researchers' use (see also Heikkilä, 2008). Furthermore, the archival information and scraps from old magazines were utilised in this research. The documents made it easy to remember the past events in the interviews. The interviewees wanted to let the next generations know about their experiences and knowledge.

Furthermore, we used the photographs received from the villagers and interviewees to answer the research questions. Few of the photographs related to the research are located in the province museum of Lapland. The photographs analysed in this article were selected based on their informational value: a picture had to have something to tell the researcher and it can be used for answering the question posed about the clothing and the person who wore it. For example, the school photographs taken in 1911 and 1924 reveal the change in the length and fitting of girls' aprons and dresses. Thus, they tell about children's clothing becoming more inhibited during those periods. The original research included about 60 photographs that illustrate clothing in the village of Rautiosaari. In this article, we illustrate the data with four carefully selected sample photographs. The school photograph taken in 1911 was the oldest one available revealing about the people in Rautiosaari School. Not only does it tell us about the clothes, but it also tells us about the heterogeneous age distribution in the initial years of elementary education as children and youngsters of all ages started schooling (RmlkA. III:I3:IEa,Bc). Another photograph illustrates Finnish children's everyday form of physical activity, skiing, which was also necessary to move from one place to another. Basically, it shows a schoolboy's essential winter-time everyday clothing. The third photograph is that taken in 1924 and functions as the point of comparison with the 1911 school photograph, making it possible to interpret the change in clothing during a decade. Besides clothes, pupils also represented the same age group. In the fourth photograph, the children are dressed in their summer-time Sunday clothes. The children are from the same family and of different ages and genders situated in their home environment.

Only the photographs are evidence from the past and the concrete documents utilised in this research. On the other hand, for many old people, these photographs have been the means to remember as they are connected to personal and common retrospection (cf. Korkiakangas, 1996, p. 24). The crucial cultural and historical contexts of the era under examination in this research are tracked with these photographs. Through these photographs, the researchers were able to relate to the characters, facial expressions, gestures, surroundings, and happenings (Barthes, 1985, p. 32). Barthes (1985, p. 389) called a photograph a mask of its era because it looks for the hidden. According to Koski (1999, p. 25), the moment of their setting can be seen in most photographs. The entity of a picture may emphasise the old, but somewhere within its frames or in its background, a new one may be arising. It can be, for example, a different dressing style, gesture, or impression. The interviewees helped us to interpret the impressions and they also told us about the more concrete things, such as fabrics, dressmakers, surrounding conditions, photographers, and the actual places where the photographs were taken. In the results section, we refer directly to the sample photographs, but their interpretations are also based on the interviews and other sources, such as the magazines of that time and, later on, the regional histories written of Rovaniemi (Ahvenainen, 1970; Enbuske, 1997). As actual contemporary documents of Rautiosaari, only a pair of shoes is available. Clothing was extremely ecological as adults' old clothes were turned into children's clothes that were worn by several children. After that, clothes were used as patch material and weft for rags. Old woollen clothes were spun into balls of rag wool.

The law of elementary education defines the age when one should go to school in the countryside the following way: 'A boy or a girl, who is announced as allowed to go to the lowest grade of upper elementary school, has to be nine years old but not more than twelve...' (Kerkkonen, 1923, p. 75; The Merciful Declaration of Imperial Majesty 7/3 1893, 139§). However, the upper age limit was not valid during the initial years of elementary education because older children also wanted to go to school.

Results

Pupils' clothing in the light of the school photographs

The oldest school photograph of the pupils at Rautiosaari School used in this research was taken in 1911 (Figure 1). It was shot outdoors, at the steps of the new school built in

Figure 1.   A school photograph taken in 1911 (private archive, reproduced with permission).

1909. The photo shooting must have taken place at the time of the spring snow because there are dirty snowdrifts all around and here and there the ground is uncovered by snow.

The children's wide age distribution is clearly visible in this photograph. It is not clear whether some of the girls are pupils or school staff. When school started, 'all who had turned nine' had to go to school (Kerkkonen, 1923, p. 75; Merciful Declaration of Imperial Majesty 7/3, 1893, 139§). The children were at middle school[1] because they went – if they could – to elementary school in the fall before the middle school started and in the spring when it ended. At other times, the children were at their homes learning to read and count. The actual school (comprehensive education and concrete attendance to the school) started that year when children turned nine.

There are no notes in the photograph, but obviously the photographer was a travelling one as they usually were at that time. The same photograph can be found in several home albums in Rautiosaari. The little boys knew how to stand straight in order to be seen in the middle of the girls. Both the children's and adults' expressions are serious and the atmosphere is charged. The girls hold each other's hands to feel togetherness and to show friendship. Half of the pupils are girls and half are boys.

The girls wear long-sleeved dresses and aprons. The colours of the dresses vary so that slightly over half of the girls have dark-coloured dresses. The grey dresses are apparently made of boiji and the checkered dresses of flannel. The dresses have a small upright collar or a neckline that tangles near the neck. The spectrum of colours and patterns in the apron fabric is wide: checks, stripes, flowers, dark, and light. An eye-catching detail is the decoration of aprons with ribbons or embroidery. The model of a dress depended on the available amount of fabric that the local sellers had and the sizes of fabric pieces cut from old clothes. The aprons had wide necklines and the dresses appeared under them as they did below the hems of the aprons. As the girls became older, the model of the dresses and aprons became narrower and the hems became longer. In adolescence, girls dressed in a long skirt and a blouse as did the grown-up women.

On the right-hand side of the photograph, in the second row, there is a boy who is dressed in a schoolboy's typical outfit in the 1910s. He is wearing loden trousers and a dark flannel shirt with buttoning in the front and the essentials such as a leather belt and a sheath that symbolised a big boy's manliness (Heikkilä Mirja, notification 2006). The buttons of the shirt are shining white because the most popular bone and textile buttons were white. In whitish underwear, they did not stick out as they did in the dark winter shirts. The boy, who stands on the upper step, has a collared overcoat that goes with the loden trousers. It has dark buttons referring to the fact that the travelling salesmen had dark buttons that suited outdoor clothes to sell as well.

Figure 2 is a photograph of the pupils of Rautiosaari School wearing dark loden suits. Anyone who looks at this photograph does not have to know the basics of clothing to know what the photograph documenting and to draw an overall picture of it. In this photograph, the meaning is figurative (Uotila, 1995). It means that the one who looks at this photograph forms a concrete impression at first glance: country boys skiing. This impression, thus, tells us about the contemporary countryside environment and the boys' background. A viewer does not think whether the slightly different loden jackets transmit various messages, but he/she sees the basic structure: country boys who were photographed with their skiing equipment.

Skiing was taught at elementary schools since the beginning of the twentieth century as children attended school more commonly. Especially, boys were encouraged to ski. Skiing was defined as an especially Finnish sport that was considered as that developing the national features such as gut ('sisu'), perseverance, and morale among the youth (Tuomaala, 2004, p. 234). The children of Rautiosaari did not ski by the order of the school, but skiing was a common, fast, and fun way of moving from one place to another. Both girls and boys skied to the school if the weather allowed them to. Often, it was the case that skiing was the only way to get to the school because of the night-time snowfall.

In this photograph, the schoolboys pose with their skis (Niemelä, 1997, p. 55). The place where this was shot is a bank by Kemijoki River near the Rautiosaari School. There is a sauna on the beach behind the boys and Kemijoki River flows down

Figure 2.   Rautiosaari boys skiing in the 1930s (private archive, reproduced with permission).

there. The place is located at the Rompa farm sold for the municipality and the school is located behind the photographer. Owning skis was not common at the beginning of the twentieth century and skis were purchased by the school to be used by indigent pupils (Tuomaala, 2004, p. 234). The pupils in Rautiosaari School had skis at home – the kinds they happened to have. It is possible to conclude from the boys' faces how pleased and proud they were when posing with their skiing equipment for the photographer. They are leaning onto the sticks as if they were contemporary skiing heroes. The photograph tells to its interpreter that the boys are the pupils of Rautiosaari School – and the interpretation is confirmed in the interviews by the interviewees who recognised the boys – and at the same time brings out the uniform dressing culture. The schoolboys with their uniform clothing live in the same reality and constitute and tell about their background. Perhaps, it was exactly the photographer's intention to illustrate this when placing the boys in order in front of the camera.

The boys' wooden skis had more or less bent points. Judging by the length of the rattan sticks, not all of them had their own skiing equipment, but children shared skis and sticks at homes or foster homes. The skiing shoes had one-layered bottom with twisted points that held well in the 'mäystin' binding (Group interview, 1997).

The loden trousers and coat with a woollen-knit sweater were common skiing clothes. The same clothes were the boys' winter clothes as well. They wore fur caps (Group interview, 1997). Some of the boys did not wear the cap in the photograph. The reason for this could be the heat generated after skiing hard, respect for photographing, or simply their hurry to be photographed. None of them has gloves; perhaps the reason for leaving them inside is the heat or the hurry to be photographed. The boys' hair was grown into bushy and ruffled shocks during the winter. Judging from the surroundings, the photograph was taken at the time of the spring snow, so the boys must have cut their hair for the summer. Similarly, the shabbiness and dirtiness of the sweater are signs of spring. Usually, woollen clothes were not washed in the winter but in the summer (Halvari Lempi, interview 1997). Also, a skier with a woollen-knit sweater would have a clean sweater in the next fall.

The boys seem to be enjoying being photographed: they seem to find it important to be together in a photograph with their own or borrowed skis. Everyone's attention is focused on how well the skis show and how stylish their positions are. A dirty sweater, cap, and mittens are minor issues. The boys maintain a serious expression as they had been taught to do on being photographed. Only two boys are grinning a little bit, which can partly be put down to the sun. The spring sun is shining down the boys' faces because most of them are screwing up their eyes or looking downwards. It is natural that the photographer has his back towards the sun in order to take a perfect picture.

At the beginning of the twentieth century, the children of Rautiosaari tended to ski exceedingly and loved it. Everyone had skiing equipment at least for getting to the school (Group interview, 1997). The National Board of Education encouraged the pupils to ski and recommended arranging inter-school skiing competitions. Conducting the competition in Ounasvaara starting from 1927 (Enbuske, 1997, p. 220) increased the local children's enthusiasm for skiing. Skiing was significant for children to stay healthy. Their muscles got exercised and lungs got fresh air, which was important for fighting against tuberculosis. The girls skied wearing their dresses and flannel underwear and woollen-knit pants in order to avoid catching a cold (Group interview, 1997). In the photograph, a brisk and content attitude of the boys can be seen. The boys have a common hobby, skiing, that does not cause any worry about clothing problems.

The participants even stated in the group interview that 'we put the available clothes on and off we went' (Group interview, 1997).

The time span between the school picture taken in 1911 (Figure 1) and the picture shown in Figure 3 is 13 years. During this time, a variety of changes took place throughout the world as well as in Finland and Rautiosaari. Finland had become independent, the civil war had also claimed lives in Rovaniemi, and the years of starving had tested the people. On the other hand, the upturn of lumber industry had made people in northern Finland wealthier. The ordinary countrymen in Rautiosaari and sometimes also the schoolboys were able to earn some extra money in the logging sites and from the floating work in Kemijoki River.

This school photograph was taken during a snowless period, probably in the spring. The number of pupils had increased much because of the law of compulsory education passed in 1921. Probably the pupils of the elementary school are also in this photograph because the smaller children in it are clearly younger than the ones in the photograph taken in 1911. The children again have serious expressions, but the atmosphere is no longer that funereal. The signs of a more relaxed style are highlighted by a boy keeping his hand in the pocket and another boy grinning. Again, the place where this photograph was taken is the stairway of the school.

The girls have shorter hems, otherwise their dresses are mostly similar to the dresses seen in the previous school photograph. The models of the aprons seem to be quite inconsistent and the overall shade of the girls' clothes is lighter than those seen in the earlier photograph. The little girls' shoes have one-layered bottom because it is easy for them to walk to the school even in rough terrains. The boys' clothing does not differ from the clothing seen in the photograph taken in 1911.

This photograph shows the values of the Körkkö family as well as the moment of photographing and the atmosphere of dressing up for it (Figure 4). The children in the photograph are those of Körkkö, Hilkka (b. 1919), Helmi (b. 1917), Hannes (b. 1915), and Veikko (b. 1922), who lived in the house of Yliheikkilä.

Figure 3.   A school photograph taken in 1924 (private archive, reproduced with permission).

Figure 4.   Körkkö's children next to a wall at the end of the 1920s (private archive, reproduced with permission).

The surroundings and clothing with all the socks and shirts tell about the chilly weather in the summer and a special photographing situation. In the summer, children wore socks and shoes, and they wore holiday dresses only on holidays and Sundays, on a feast day, or for photographing. After the snow melted, children did not use socks or shoes at home on the weekdays. In this photograph, everyone has stationed himself/ herself outstandingly festively because photographing was not mundane. The photograph has a normal function: to memorialise the flock of children in the house as the travelling photographer happened to be in residence. The photographer might have defined the standing place at the edge of the lawn because the children have placed themselves exactly in a row at the edge of the lawn with the photographing expression on their faces. Veikko holds back his laughter because people were not allowed to laugh while being photographed. At that time, people were supposed to have serious expressions during photographing. Helmi's face shows the tension caused by the holiday clothes and the special situation.

Compared with the clothes seen the photographs used in other studies, their clothes exemplify countryside children's typical clothing because both the girls wore similar light cotton dresses and sports-jacket-like coats. Most probably, the same dressmaker had made the outfits for both the girls at the same time. For example, at that time, it was possible to figure out who the shoemaker was based on the details and technique with which the shoes were made (Heikkilä Mirja, interview, 1998, see Heikkilä, 2008).

Light dresses with short sleeves were usually used in the summer. The coats had but-toning in the front, collar, elasticated waist, and wristbands; in Finnish vernacular, they were called 'lustut'. The wristbands made it possible to add some extra length to the sleeve and held the extra length up. The girls have cotton, well-fitted socks bought from a store. The socks are straight, implying that they are attached with suspenders and buttons to the vest under the dress at that time. In the twentieth century, the small northern Finnish pupils', girls' and boys', underwear consisted of a shirt, under-pants, and a suspender belt (Heikkilä Erkki, letter, 1997). Helmi has the brand-new long leather boots, similar to what the grown-up women had. Shoes of this kind had long laces in the front and relatively high heels. The shoes could be their mothers' or bought readymade waiting for a girl to become a miss. These shoes were a sign of a big girl (Heikkilä Mirja, interview, 2006). Hilkka is wearing cloth-top lace-ups with rubber bottoms.

The difference between big boys' and little boys' clothes is visible. Little Veikko has a typical greyish cotton coat with breast pockets, buttoning in the front, collar, and wristbands and hemlines. The trousers are breeches and stay up usually with fabric braces. The grey socks are attached to the suspender belt with suspenders and buttons. Under Veikko's breeches, he is probably wearing little boys' rear-hatch under-pants. Veikko's leather shoes are most likely to be his big brother's because they are way too big. His big brother has black boots. He is wearing formal clothes for photo-graphing. The worn shape of his cotton suit jacket reveals the history of the jacket. It is made of old jackets in the shape of men's suit jacket with the breast pockets and every-thing (Group interview, 1997). Something had been slipped into the breast pocket. Soon, it would be time to buy a new jacket because this one seems to be too small on the shoulders and the wristbands are closer to the boy's elbows than to his wrists. His pants are ordinary dark cotton pants lifted up with a belt or suspenders. He does not seem to have a sheath belt, so Hannes is still regarded as a little boy. On the other hand, a sheath belt is usually worn with a coat and loden pants. The shirt is a striped shirt with a collar. The boys' hair is cut for the summer: the top of their heads is hairless as people would have their hair cut at that time.

The photograph reveals that Körkkö's children's clothing is mostly in line with the forms of clothing described in the interviews. None of the interviewees mentioned girls' waist-long coats. However, the interviewees specified what the little girls' cloth-top lace-ups with rubber bottoms were as they were previously called just 'summer shoes'. They had separate winter and summer clothes. The clothes were gotten from older siblings, but also new clothes were made by the people themselves or had them made when necessary. They had something to put on – albeit not top quality every time. New garments were appreciated and they were not worn when playing outdoors.

The difference between girls' and boys' clothing

According to the interviews and contemporary magazines, pupils' clothes were made of cotton or wool using a sewing machine or stitched by hands. Cotton fabric was used in the summer clothes and in the indoors clothes in the winters. Socks, mittens, caps, and woollen pants or sweaters were made of woollen thread. Usually, adults' old clothes were used as the material for children's clothes. In what follows, we discuss in more detail the differences between girls' and boys' clothing based on the primary sources used in this article.

A schoolgirl would wear a cotton dress that was light and short-sleeved in the summer and long-sleeved in the winter. The material was thick loden in the winter clothes and it was a thinner plain, checked, striped, or patterned cotton fabric in the summer clothes. Over a dress, the girls would essentially have an apron done up with ribbons or buttons at the back. Still in the 1910s, aprons as well as dresses were close fitting. As children's clothing did not have to follow adults' way of clothing since the World War I after which children's clothing became more free form in nature, the shape of a dress and apron became more loose fitting, and hems became shorter. The girls wore shirt, cotton pants, and a vest with buttoning in the front as underwear. Only a few had an underskirt. The material used was flannel – thin or thick, depending on the season. When necessary, the underwear was made of cotton sacks that, for example, contained wheat flour. The underpants were attached to a shirt with buttons.

Woollen socks were thigh-long in the winter. In the summer, they were long-legged cotton socks that were attached to the suspender belt similar to the woollen socks. In addition, the girls used short-legged woollen socks for their winter boots as extra warmers. From the spring to the fall, as long as possible, children did not use socks on the weekdays. When the temperature was below zero degrees, the girls wore woollen pants and a cardigan with their dresses. They wore several woollen mittens one on the other.

The girls' overcoats were made of adults' used coats. The fabric was turned upside down in order to bring the less worn side of the fabric into view. The coats could be short, waist-long, or a little bit longer. Usually, they had some kind of collar which was sometimes detachable. They were either single- or double-breasted. The winter coats were usually made of wool and summer coats of thickish cotton.

The boys wore a loden suit in the winter. In the spring, it was replaced by a thick cotton coat with buttoning in the front and a collar. Also, the pants were made of thick cotton. The big boys could wear breeches. The little boys still could use knee pants as well. When necessary, they wore long-legged cotton socks underneath the pants attached with suspenders. On top of their undershirt, the boys wore a shirt and its model varied based on the dressmaker. In the summer, the boys had only one shirt. Sometimes, it was made of tricot, especially, for little boys in the home environment. The older boys' shirts were made of flannel or other cotton.

The little boys' underwear was similar to the little girls' underwear. The underpants had a hatch and they were attached to a shirt with buttons. The bigger boys' pants did not have a hatch any longer and the legs were long. As woollen garments, the boys wore a sweater, pants, and socks that were worn on top of the pants. Woollen or leather mittens kept the little boys' hands warm.

The girls' winter headgear was made of woollen thread, fabric, or leather and usually had a lining. The boys wore a cap made of fur and leather. It had side flaps that could be tied on the top of their heads as well. 'Väinämöinen's' (an old Finnish mythic hero) cap was a sun hat used by both the girls and boys. In the summer, the girls wore headscarves or a narrow-brimmed sewed or crochet hat. The boys had different kinds of flat caps. Sometimes, they did not wear a cap at all.

A very important clothing accessory for boys was a sheath belt – a traditional masculine symbol – with its sheath knife and sheath. The girls showed off their handbags when going to fairs. The boys' hair was cut almost to the point of hairlessness at the beginning of the summer after which they let their hair grow. By the next spring, their hair was fixed if necessary. The girls wore plaits on both sides of their heads. In the 1930s, even the girls of Rautiosaari had their hair cut short.

The boys and girls walked and skied in the winter with shoes with a one-layered bottom. Their twisted top stayed in a ski binding well. Sometimes, the girls wore leather shoes that reached to the middle of their legs and had quite high heels and long laces. On the contrary, the boys wore shoes that had lower heels and wider toes. In the 1930s, boots with leather legs and rubber feet were in fashion. In the summer, they used small leather shoes or sneakers-like shoes if any.

Discussion

Clothing reflects human behaviour. The people remain unchanged, although clothes change. Indeed, Rudofsky (1972) talked about 'the unfashionable human body'. Both in the historical perspective of this research and at present, it is important to view a child and his/her clothing in that context where he/she lives and acts. The topicality of dressing, telesis that the clothes bring out, illustrates the pupils' life in Rautiosaari and the system for which and within which the clothes were purchased. A garment is born, lives, and dies at a specific time, place, and space. It meets its wearer in the countryside of Rautiosaari, in the cold climate of the North at the beginning of the twentieth century, and lives having a significant interaction with its wearer.

A pupil's garment services well when he/she likes to live with it. The 'good life' of a garment and a child is particularly connected to the surroundings; when a change in the surroundings occurs, the garment changes as well. When clothing is perfect, a dressmaker, its user, and environment are in unison. If a garment is designed and made by an adult and worn by a child, the functions of the garment do not always meet. In the light of the historical point of time on which this research is based, clothing was defined by the living conditions (see Buck, 1996; Collard, 1973; Huggett, 2006; Martin, 1978; Rose, 1989; Schimpky & Kalman, 1995; Sichel, 1983; Worrell, 1980).

In this research, clothing is introduced as one ordinary and necessary mechanism of human action (Johnson, Yoo, Kim, & Lennon, 2008). In this article, human existence is understood by the relationship with school clothes and children's opportunity to attend school. If a child did not have anything to wear, he/she could not go to school either. If a child had gone to school without proper warm clothes, it would have posed a threat to his/her health and existence. 'As we didn't have many pairs of shoes, we had to go to school in turn' (Olga's remembrance, Group interview, 1997). They had to adjust to the situation and act according to the prevailing conditions.

The relationship with an object – in this case, a piece of clothing – will not become concrete if the object or means does not exist, such as the shoes in Olga's case. How the children in Rautiosaari dressed in the period that was studied in this article can be seen as an interaction that took place within the conditions prevalent during that time. Dressing was a dynamic process where the pupils got their clothes bought, washed, and sewed up, and finally the worn clothes were used as materials for mats or patches. Clothing made the history that was studied at present (see Gurel & Gurel, 1979). A life span of a garment can be seen to end only at that point when, for example, it gives its last energy for the growth of new flax on being burnt. The ecological use of clothes was perfect.

The contribution of this article is to give a small glimpse into children's clothing in the past. The interviewees created children's culture at the beginning of the twentieth century and cultural history of clothing when reminiscing about the happenings and clothing during their school years. The photographs used are significant for understanding this research. Furthermore, realising the history of children's clothing reflects in a future scenario in cloth design and production. Research on the culture of children's clothing can help analysing significant junctions in order to make them serve industrial design and production of children's clothes.

In the future, children's dressing and the clothing industry (Gupta, 2009) will face new challenges that are expressed both by the future culture (Hodges, DeLong, Hegland, Thompson, & Williams, 2007) and by changing craft education at schools (O'Neal, 2007).

The research data and archives

RmlkA. The Archives of Rovaniemi rural municipality.
The Archives of the Elementary School of Rovaniemi Rural Municipality, III:I3:I
RmlkA III:I3:IEa; RmlkA III:I3:IBc.

Other documents

Decree on Elementary Education 11 May 1866.
Keisarillisen Majesteetin Armollinen julistus [The Merciful Declaration of Imperial Majesty] 7/3 1893.

Interviews and letters

Halvari Lempi, interview 1997.
Heikkilä Erkki, letter 1997.
Heikkilä Mirja, interview 1998.
Heikkilä Mirja, interview 2006.
Heikkilä Mirja, notification 2006.
Group interview, 1997 ($N = 10$ people).

Note

1. By middle school, we mean the school level between the lower level of the comprehensive school (or elementary school) and college or vocational school. This school level in contemporary Finland may also be thought as corresponding to the British upper level of comprehensive school.

References

Ahvenainen, J. (1970). *Rovaniemen historia II 1932–1960* [The History of Rovaniemi II 1932–1960]. Kuopio: Otava.

Barthes, R. (1985). *Valoisa huone* [A sunny room]. Jyväskylä: Gummerus.

Bigelow, M.S. (1970). *Fashion in history: Apparel in the Western World*. Minneapolis, MN: Burgess Pub.

Buck, A. (1996). *Clothes and the child: A handbook of children's dress in England, 1500–1900*. New York, NY: Holmes & Meier.

Collard, E. (1973). *From toddler to teens: An outline of children's clothing circa 1780–1930*. Burlington, ON: Author.

Enbuske, M. (1997). Tukkimiesten ja kauppiaiden kairoilla [In the steppes of log floaters and tradesmen]. In M. Embuske, S. Runtti, & T. Manninen (Eds.), *Rovaniemen historia 1721–1990: Jokivarsien kasvatit ja junantuomat* [The History of Rovaniemi in 1721–1990: The foster children of the riversides and emigrants] (pp. 87–169). Jyväskylä: Gummerus.

Evans, M. (1949). *Fundamentals of clothing and textiles*. New York, NY: Prentice Hall.

Ford, M., & Drake, F. (1982). Attitudes toward clothing, body, and self: A comparison of two groups. *Home Economics Research Journal, 11*(2), 189–196.

Furches, M.M., & Staley, H.K. (1963). *Trade fairs and their influence on textiles in Central Europe, 10th through 15th centuries*. Greensboro, NC: Woman's College of the University of North Carolina at Greensboro.

Ginzburg, C. (1996). *Johtolankoja. Kirjoituksia Mikrohistoriasta ja historiallisesta metodista* [Leads: Writings about micro-history and historical method]. Tampere: Tammer-Paino Ltd.

Gupta, S. (2009). Communication clothing design. *Journal of the American Society for Information Science and Technology, 60*(9), 1915–1919.

Gurel, L.M., & Gurel, L. (1979). Clothing interest: Conceptualization and measurement. *Home Economics Research Journal, 7*(5), 274–282.

Hannula, M., Gebhard, H., Ollonqvist, M., Harmaja, L., & Wiherheimo, A. (1932). *Emännän tietokirja III* [The housewife's manual III]. Porvoo: WSOY.

Heikkilä, A. (2008). *Vaate lapsen elämässä. Koululaisen pukeutuminen pohjoissuomalaisessa maalaiskylässä vuosina 1909–1939* [Clothes in the life a child. Clothing of a schoolchild in a countryside village in northern Finland during the years 1909–1939] (Acta Universitatis Lapponiensis, No. 132). Rovaniemi: University of Lapland.

Hodges, N.N., Delong, M., Hegland, J., Thompson, M., & Williams, G. (2007). Constructing knowledge for the future. Exploring alternative modes of inquiry from a philosophical perspective. *Clothing and Textiles Research Journal, 24*(4), 323–348.

Horridge, P., & Richards, L. (1984). Relationship of fashion awareness and clothing economic practices. *Home Economics Research Journal, 13*(2), 138–152.

Huggett, J. (2006). *Children's clothes: 1580–1660*. Bristol: Stuart Press.

Inomata, M., & Simizu, K. (1991). Ability of young children to button and unbutton clothes. *Journal of Human Ergology, 20*(2), 249–255.

Johnson, K., Yoo, J.-J., Kim, M., & Lennon, S.J. (2008). Dress and human behavior. A review and critique. *Clothing and Textiles Research Journal, 26*, 3–22.

Kerkkonen, K. (Ed.). (1923). Kansakoulu-käsikirja lisäyksineen. Järjestelmällinen kokoelma asetuksia, määräyksiä, kiertokirjeitä y.m. Suomen kansanopetuksen alalta [The manual of elementary school with annexes. A systematic collection of decrees, instructions, circulars, etc. from the field of Finnish folk education] (Decree of Elementary School 1866, 102§, 114§, 139§). Porvoo: WSOY.

Korkiakangas, P. (1996). *Muistoista rakentuva lapsuus. Agraarinen perintö lapsuuden työnteon ja leikkien muisteluissa* [Childhood built of memories. The agrarian heritage in the retrospection of childhood working and playing]. Vammala: Vammalan Kirjapaino Ltd.

Koski, M. (1999). Todellisuuden kuvia, kuvia todellisuudesta [The real pictures, the pictures of reality]. In J. Kukkonen & T.J. Vuorenmaa (Eds.), *Valoa Otteita suomalaisen valokuvan historiaan 1839–1999* [Light. Extracts from the history of Finnish photographing 1839–1999] (pp. 11–25). Helsinki: The Museum of Finnish Photographic Art.

Kwon, Y.-H., & Drayton, M.A. (2007). Factors affecting the selection of clothes on daily basis: Male and female differences. *Journal of Consumer Studies and Home Economics, 11*(1), 57–69.

Lapitsky, M., & Smith, C.M. (1981). Impact of clothing on impressions of personal characteristics and writing ability. *Home Economics Research Journal, 9*(4), 327–335.

Lee, J.S. (1953). *Elementary textiles.* New York, NY: Prentice Hall.

Lennon, S.J. (1990). Effects of clothing attractiveness on perceptions. *Home Economics Research Journal, 18*(4), 303–310.

Levi, G. (1992). *Aineeton perintö. Manaajapappi ja talonpoikaisyhteisö 1600-luvun Italiassa* [The immaterial heritage. An exorcist priest and agrarian community in Italy of the 17th century] (T. Seppä, Trans.). Helsinki: Like.

Mansfield, E.A. (1953). *Clothing construction.* Boston, MA: Houghton Miffin.

Martin, L. (1978). *The way we wore: Fashion illustrations of children's wear, 1870–1970.* New York, NY: Scribner.

McCullough, W.A., Miller, M.F., & Ford, I.M. (1977). Sexually attractive clothing: Attitudes and usage. *Home Economics Research Journal, 6*(2), 164–170.

Morganosky, M., & Creekmore, A.M. (1981). Clothing influence in adolescent leadership roles. *Home Economics Research Journal, 9*(4), 356–362.

Niemelä, M. (1997). *Menheiltä ajoilta* [From the past]. Rovaniemi: Pohjolan Painotuote Ltd.

O'Neal, G.S. (2007). Continents, cultures, curriculum. Some thoughts on the future of the profession. *Clothing and Textiles Research Journal, 25*(4), 375–379.

Peltonen, M. (1992). Esipuhe [Foreword]. In L. Giovanni (Ed.), *Aineeton perintö. Manaajapappi ja talonpoikaisyhteisö 1600-luvun Italiassa* [The immaterial heritage. An exorcist priest and agrarian community in Italy of the 17th century] (pp. 7–17). Helsinki: Like.

Peltonen, M. (1996). Carlo Ginzburg ja mikrohistorian ajatus [Foreword: Carlo Ginzburg and the idea of microhistory]. In C. Ginzburg (Ed.), *Johtolankoja* [Leads] (pp. 7–34). Helsinki: Gaudeamus.

Perry, M.O., Schutz, H.G., & Rucker, M.H. (1983). Clothing interest, self-actualization, and demographic variables. *Home Economics Research Journal, 11*(3), 280–288.

Rensselaer, M.V. (1972/1931). *The home and the child: Housing, furnishing, management, income, clothing: Report of the subcommittee on housing and home management.* New York, NY: Arno Press.

Rose, C. (1989). *Children's clothes since 1750.* New York, NY: Drama Book.

Rudofsky, B. (1972). *The unfashionable human body.* New York, NY: Doubleday.

Schimpky, D., & Kalman, B. (1995). *Children's clothing of the 1800s.* New York, NY: Crabtree Pub.

Seitz, K. (2003). The effect of changes in posture and clothing on the development of unfamiliar person recognition. *Applied Cognitive Psychology, 17*(7), 819–832.

Sichel, M. (1983). *History of children's costume.* London: London Batsford Academic and Educational Ltd.

Stone, J.F., & Sternweiss, L. (1994). *Consumer choices: Selecting clothes for school-age children, aged 6 to 9.* Ames, IA: Iowa State University, Extension.

Tuomaala, S. (2004). *Työtätekevistä käsistä puhtaiksi ja kirjoittaviksi. Suomalaisen oppivelvollisuuskoulun ja maalaislasten kohtaaminen 1921–1939* [From workers' hands into clean and writing hands. The confrontation between Finnish compulsory education and county people 1921–1939] (Bibliotheca Historica No. 89). Helsinki: Finnish Literature Society.

Uotila, M. (1995). *Pukeutumisen kuvaus. Kuvia kulttuurin merkeistä* [A description of dress. Pictures of cultural signs]. Helsinki: Helsinki University Press.

Workman, J.E. (2009). Fashion consumer groups, gender, and need for touch. *Clothing and Textiles Research Journal, 28*(2), 126–139.

Worrell, E.A. (1980). *Children's costumes in America, 1607–1910.* New York, NY: Scribner.

The child diary as a research tool

Tiina Lämsä, Anna Rönkä, Pirjo-Liisa Poikonen and Kaisa Malinen

The aim of this article is to introduce the use of the child diary as a method in daily diary research. By describing the research process and detailing its structure, a child diary, a structured booklet in which children's parents and day-care personnel ($N = 54$ children) reported their observations, was evaluated. The participants reported the use of the diary to be an interesting but time-consuming experience. The main ethical challenges were related to power positions, confidentiality, consequences and motivation. With respect to adults' observations of children's emotions, the results indicated that the child diary is valuable in providing information about individual differences and daily dynamics and that the diary reveals some of the conventions in child-related everyday interactions in home and in day-care environments. In addition to its use as a research method for capturing situation-specific information in the family and day-care contexts, the child diary also serves as a tool in collaboration between parents and day-care personnel aimed at enhancing children's well-being.

Introduction

This article examines the diary method as a systematic tool for observation of the daily life of children in family and day-care settings. We demonstrate and evaluate such a diary methodologically and empirically and discuss its possibilities in pedagogical applications and in home–day-care cooperation. Methodologically, the article focuses on the development and use of a child diary in research with young children, their parents and day-care personnel. The diary's methodological value is evaluated by utilising feedback received from the participants. Ethical issues are also discussed. Empirically, the interest in this study lies in describing how children are seen in daily interaction at home and in the day-care centre in terms of their daily moods. The child diary proposed here is innovative in that it is designed to capture adults' observations in everyday life situations through structured questions that take into account the daily rhythm of family life and day-care schedules.

The child diary focuses on the home and day-care environments. Both are major arenas of children's everyday life and the continuity and social relations between and within them are seen as important for children's well-being. The home, with parents and siblings, and the day-care context, with adults and other children, are very different arenas of actions and emotions. The day-care environment includes negotiated relationships; the adult contacts may change and the possibilities for peer-group relations may vary. Home, in turn, provides a possibility for private space (Kyrönlampi-Kylmänen & Määttä, 2012) and, according to its most common definitions, emotionally and genealogically bonded long-term relationships. Furthermore, the continuity between these contexts may be understood as something provided to the child by the environment, something that the child brings to the environment or a combination of both (Shpancer, 2002). Nevertheless, these environments are connected, as the child carries experiences from both across all contexts (e.g. Lahikainen & Strandell, 1988). By comparing and examining the home and the day-care environments and the conventions in them, we attempt to address the task (Darbyshire, Schiller, & MacDougall, 2005; Shpancer, 2002) of designing a tool which will shed light on the multiple dimensions of children's intercontextual relations. Hence, the purpose of this article is to explain the functionality of the child diary by reporting the results of a diary-based study of assessments by parents and day-care personnel of children's mood in the home and day-care settings. The article briefly describes the diary method in general and the Finnish Palette study within which the present child diary was developed.

Theoretical background

Daily diary approach

The diary, by definition, has long been used as a scientific tool. For example, Charles Darwin (1809–1882) kept a diary on infant behaviour when developing the theory of the evolution of species (see Poveda, 2009). The origins of the diary method as a research tool with children can be found in developmental psychology, particularly in the work of Jean Piaget (1896–1980). With Piaget's documentation of his own children's activities during the first half of the twentieth century, the diary achieved scientific recognition, and subsequently became a popular tool to study children and human development (Furth, 1970; Poveda, 2009). Childhood became a topic of interest in the human sciences (especially in psychology), since observations about human development were seen as important in addressing basic epistemological and theoretical questions. However, as psychology developed more firmly into a quantitative discipline and experimental procedures that used systematically selected samples of children became the preferred methodology, interest in child diaries and case studies declined (Poveda, 2009). Despite the shifting trends in research methodologies, diary methods and parental diaries for the study of children have been used for many decades in various disciplines and research traditions, for example family research (Hofferth & Sandberg, 2001), psychology (Bates, Viken, Alexander, Beyers, & Stocton, 2002; Beidel, Neal, & Lederer, 1991; Whalen et al., 2006), sociology (Sayer, Bianchi, & Robinson, 2004), pediatrics, medical and health research (Boddy & Smith, 2007; Hitchings & Moynihan, 1998), studies of language development (Baghban, 1984) and pedagogical research in schools (Armstrong, 1982). However, they have been less applied in early childhood education and pedagogy, although their value in pedagogical documentation has been noted (e.g. Blenkin & Kelly, 1992; Buldu, 2010; Lally, 1991).

The diaries used in research vary in form. The basic idea of the daily diary is to study the target phenomenon intensively for a limited time. One central reason for the use of daily diaries in research is to capture 'life as it is lived' (see Bolger, Davis, & Rafaeli, 2003). The diary method is an effective tool for gaining information about easily forgettable real life situations (e.g. how events are experienced) (Larson & Almeida, 1999; Matjasko & Feldman, 2006; Rönkä, Malinen, Kinnunen, Tolvanen, & Lämsä, 2010; Schulz et al., 2004; for reviews see also Laurenceau & Bolger, 2005).

Child diary: mood assessments

In this article, we focus on adult's interpretations of children's moods. Emotions have, during the last ten years, gained in importance in research in the social sciences (Duncombe & Marsden, 1993; Giddens, 1990; Jamieson, 1999; Layder, 2004; Thagaard, 1997), psychology and family studies (Koh, 2005; Larson & Gillman, 1999; Sonnentag & Kruel, 2006) and education, childhood and youth studies (Boler, 1999; Cole, Martin, & Dennis, 2004; Fox, 2001; Pfeifer et al., 2009). Emotions also exemplify the utility of daily diary data well, as one aim in using the method in the research context is to capture the variation in inconsistent and fluctuating emotions and their related interactions (Green, Rafaeli, Bolger, Shrout, & Reis, 2006). Family life and emotions are known to be strongly connected in terms of caring, responding to other family members' needs (Fisher & Tronto, 1990) and learning emotional skills (Daly, 2003; Perrez, Schoebi, & Wilhelm, 2000). Family relationships are saturated with emotions, including repeated hassles, routines and arguments when family members do family life together (Galinsky, 1999; Larson & Richards, 1994; Smart, 2007).

Although studies of emotions are widespread nowadays, little is known about the emotional lives of children in day-care settings. An exception are the studies of infant–mother attachment and children's experiences of stress (e.g. Ahnert, Gunnar, Lamb, & Barthel, 2004). We obtained some information related to this topic from our previous analyses (Lämsä, 2009), when we asked parents and day-care personnel to evaluate children's developmental stages. Although their evaluations of cognitive, physical and language skills were statistically significantly connected, their evaluations of social and emotional skills were not. The results indicate that observations of social and emotional skills might be more challenging due to their rather abstract nature, and hence more subject to adults' personal interpretations and impressions. On the other hand, differences in behaviour and self-expression in different contexts can appear more marked in these areas. The similarity observed in the assessments of cognitive, physical and language skills indicate convergence in the acquisition of these skills across contexts. These skills are also more concrete and therefore easier to observe (Lämsä, 2009). For the above reasons, our empirical examination focuses on evaluations of children's moods in everyday situations.

Aims

Our aim is to demonstrate the research benefits of the diary method. First, our data analysis shows parents' and caregivers' perceptions of children's mood in their daily interaction. Next, we evaluate the method by reference to the feedback received from the participants and highlighting the special ethical issues related to the present diary. We addressed the following questions: (1) How do parents and day-care personnel assess children's mood at home and in day-care environments? (2) How do parents and day-care personnel experience the use of the child diary as a research method? (3) What are the main ethical challenges related to the child diary?

Method

Study context. In Finland, all children have a subjective right to day care outside the family regardless of the family's economic situation or parents' employment status. All parents of children up to age 3 are also entitled to choose either to have a place for their child in day care provided by their local authority or to receive a child home care allowance (for more information, see Hännikäinen, 2010). Day-care centres are popular as slightly under a half of under school age children attend municipal or private day-care centres (National Institute for Health and Welfare, 2009). Day-care personnel in Finland are highly qualified with specialist training in early childhood education and child care. The child diary type of observation in its more general pedagogical sense is a familiar procedure in the day-care context. Every child has an individual early childhood education plan, which is drawn up by parents and day-care personnel together in an annual meeting focusing on the child's growth, development and well-being. Day-care personnel may also collect work done by the child (drawings, etc.) and add them into the document/folder. The plan forms the basis for cooperation between the day-care personnel and parents and is specified in the national curriculum guidelines on early childhood education and care (*National Curriculum Guidelines*, 2003; see also Ministry of Social Affairs and Health, 2004).

Participants and data collection

This study forms part of the Finnish research project Palette, funded by the Academy of Finland. The participants were recruited to the child diary study with the assistance of 32 local day-care centres. The research project as a whole involved 208 Finnish families from which all the participating adults (204 mothers, 161 fathers) completed a questionnaire related to family life. Three types of diaries were used to study daily family dynamics and everyday family situations. The diary study, in which parents kept their own paper-and-pencil diaries, involved 107 families, from which 45 dual-earner couples also kept electronic diaries (using mobile phones) reporting their moods and interactions.

The child diary concerned 54 children aged 1–6. Of these families, 37 also participated in all the other methods mentioned above and 17 participated in some of those methods. The parents in 54 families (one child/family) and day-care personnel in 34 day-care groups (one to three children/group) kept a child diary, and thus there were two separate diary booklets for each child: one for home and one for day-care observations. Thus, the data comprise 108 diaries. The paper-and-pencil type of diary was completed during one week (week 46 in 2006) for 7 days at home and 5 days at the day-care centre.

Of the participating families, 85.2% were nuclear families, 5.6% reconstituted families and 9.3% single-parent families (with mother and children). The participating parents were relatively highly educated: 55.5% of mothers and 46.7% of fathers had an academic degree (bachelor's/master's/doctoral degree). The average number of children in a family was 2.06, which is slightly above the national average of 1.83 (Statistics Finland, 2007). Mean parental ages were 35.5 for mothers and 37.1 years for fathers. Among the children, 70% were over 3 years old ($n = 38$) and 30% ($n = 16$) 3 years and under. There were the same number ($n = 27$) of girls as boys (Rönkä, Malinen, & Lämsä, 2009).

Diary questions

Empirically, the child diary data comprise observations reported in the diary booklets about the child's moods and daily activities and everyday situations. We operationalised everyday situations by detailing some common routines, practices and situations (e.g. Morgan, 2004) at home and in the day-care centre. The diaries shared some questions while others were context-specific. Both diaries were structured, meaning that they contained specific questions and fixed response scales. Checklist-type questions were used to obtain data on a large number of daily issues in a limited space and open-ended questions to allow participants to express themselves more openly (Rönkä et al., 2009). The diary contained pages for children's own comments and drawings, and these were collected every day if the children so wished. A box of crayons for doing drawings was sent with the materials. The aim of involving children was to investigate what kind of content adults and children produce collaboratively and to catch a glimpse of the children's world through their own contributions. The drawings can be analysed separately or as supportive data.

The child diary design comprised three parts: the first part gave detailed instructions on how to make observations and fill in the booklet. The second part contained background questions which parents and day-care personnel answered once only, before the diary week commenced. The third part contained the actual daily questions, which were to be answered twice a day during the observation week. On the last page of the diary booklet, the informants were asked to give feedback on the diary. Some of the questions (e.g. moods) were also designed to match those in the parents' own electronic and paper-and-pencil diaries (see Rönkä et al., 2010). The use of structured scales enables comparison between the home and day-care diaries.

Background questions

The background section contained questions on demographics and the adults' views on child development and behaviour. We also mapped the child's earlier life (e.g. what events/changes, if any, in the child's life) and the flow of daily life in general (e.g. what interaction situation the child enjoys most; particular everyday challenges, if any). The types and content of the background questions are presented in Table 1.

Daily questions

These questions were the same every day and were ordered according to the daily rhythms of family and day-care life. The types and content of these are presented in Table 2. To enable the informants to answer as quickly as possible, and to facilitate the marking of the observations, we developed an observation matrix consisting of a checklist on which the answers that best described the situation were ticked (yes/no options). In developing the matrix, we focused on daily behaviour and action, and we consulted the research literature on the evaluation of child behaviour (e.g. Goodman, 1997), play (Hampton & Fantuzzo, 2003; Strandell, 1997) and peer group behaviour and conflicts in children's relations (Crick, Casas, & Mosher, 1997). The matrix included claims about interaction situations and daily doings. We also included questions on transition situations, as these are known to be 'key moments' in everyday life situations with young children (e.g. Jung, 2011).

Table 1. The background questions in the diary.

Question types and content	Structured questions	Semi-structured/open questions
Background questions: home and day-care diary combined		
Child's growth and development	Scales of child's development, basic skills in different areas and child's temperament (Buss & Plomin, 1984)	Descriptions of child's temperament, development and skills
Child's behaviour and social relations	Behaviour scale (modified from Goodman, 1997)	Descriptions of typical situations of interaction and play (e.g. when argues, how maintains the play situation)
Child's everyday life in context of day care and home	Assessment of child's well-being in daily environments (e.g. how often child can do his/her favourite things, does the child have opportunities to participate in decision-making).	Descriptions of social relations, habits, routines and main strengths/challenges (modified from Heinämäki, 2005; Wilson, Mott, & Batman, 2004)
Co-operation between parents and day-care personnel	Assessment of co-operation (e.g. have there been disagreements related to child's behaviour; is there mutual consent about practices)	Focus on the transitions between home and day care

We used a separate scale for measuring daily mood. The mood assessment scale was modified from PANAS-C (Laurent et al., 1999), which is a version for use with children of the Positive and Negative Affect Schedule PANAS (Watson, Clark, & Tellegen, 1988). Overall, the PANAS-C is a brief measure originally designed to identify childhood anxiety and depression, but the PANAS scales and modifications are used in many research areas (e.g. fathering behaviours; see Jain, Belsky, & Crnic, 1996). We modified it to measure positive and negative mood of children: of the 14 items of our scale, 7 measured negative mood (e.g. sad, jittery, angry) and 7 positive mood (e.g. happy, attentive, energetic). Parents and day-care personnel were asked to rate the extent to which the 14 characteristics describe the child's mood and appearance during the occasion in question. The answers were given on a seven-point likert scale (1 = not at all, 7 = very well). Space was also provided for open commentary and answering more detailed questions (e.g. 'If something special happened during this morning, please describe what and how').

Findings

Assessments by parents and day-care personnel of children's expressions of mood in the home and day-care environments

The focus in this study is on adults' perceptions of children's positive and negative mood and the possible effects on these assessments of day of the week, time of the day and child's gender. Children's daily moods were assessed in the diaries by parents and day-care personnel altogether four times per day for five days (the day-care centres were open Monday to Friday). Parents assessed their child's mood in the morning before going to the day-care centre and also in the evening. Day-care

Table 2. The daily questions in the diary.

Question types and content	Structured questions	Semi-structured/open questions
Daily questions: home and day-care diary combined		
Morning at Home	Assessment of how the child slept during the night	Descriptions of child's awakening and assessment of the reasons for the quality of sleep
Transition between home and day care	Assessment of the child's willingness to go to day care	Descriptions of getting ready and leaving to go to and from day care (e.g. dressing up situation; what the child was doing before leaving)
Activities during morning/forenoon, midday/afternoon/ evening	The matrix includes claims about whether the following happened (e.g. the child played with computer or watched television; the child was willing to do the tasks; the child seemed to be restless and stressed)	Descriptions of the basic activities during the observation period (e.g. breakfast, outdoor activities). Descriptions of the types of play or games the child was involved in
Mood and behaviour	Mood assessment scale and evaluations of how the child's mood changed during certain occasions (e.g. time between arriving at day care and after parents left). Evaluation of child's tiredness during the day	Assessment of the reasons for child's moods
Discussions between adults	Free descriptions of discussions between parents, child and day-care personnel	
The dynamics between adults and the child	Paying attention to situations when the child was not willing to participate in the activities in day care group by describing the situation and its resolution	Focus in situations (if occurred) when child would have wanted do something or get something that adult could not allow
Childs own pages	Double page for child's own pictures and stories in both diaries	

personnel rated the child's mood twice, in the forenoon before lunch and afternoon. We choose to obtain assessments from both parents and day-care personnel as this allows comparison between observations made in two contexts and by separate observers. General linear modelling (GLM) for repeated measurements was used to analyse main and interaction effects of gender, day and time of the day for children's positive and negative mood. Because the sphericity assumption was not met, Greenhouse-Geisser-corrected degrees of freedom were used to ensure the correct p-values.

The number of missing values concerning the mood assessments was greater in the day-care data than home data: the mean for missing values in the day-care data was 18.43% per child (range 0–80%), compared with 1.94% (range 0–80%) in the home data. For 18 children, we had mood assessments without missing values for both home and day care. Because for some children there were very few assessments by day-care personnel, we removed the evaluations of five children from the analysis.

After this ($n = 49$), the mean of missing values per child was 1.73% (range 0–20%) at home and 13.78% (0–50%) in day care. Thus, the data used in this analysis contain evaluations of 49 children from the original sample of 54 children. Because GLM uses a listwise method, the missing values were imputed using the expectation–maximisation algorithm in SPSS.

Positive mood and effects of day of the week, time of day and gender

Statistically significant main effects of day ($F[3.16, 148.55] = 6.26, p < 0.001$), time of day ($F[1.94, 91.14] = 8.95, p < 0.001$) and gender ($F[1,47] = 5.02, p = 0.03$) were found for positive mood. No interaction effects were found. As Figure 1 shows, children's mood was assessed as most positive on Friday; the difference between this day and all the other days was statistically significant. Children's mood was also assessed as more positive on Tuesday than on Monday. In addition, children were seen as less positive in the mornings than at the other evaluation times (forenoon, afternoon and evening). No statistically significant differences were observed between the other evaluation times. Finally, girls were evaluated as exhibiting more positive mood than boys.

Negative mood and effects of day of the week, time of day and gender

A statistically significant main effect ($F[2.14, 100.39] = 14.05, p < 0.001$) of time of the day was found for children's negative mood. The most negative times for children were reported to be mornings and evenings at home (the difference between these two was not significant), followed by forenoons, while the least negative time of day was reported to be afternoon in the day-care centre. One interesting finding related to the time of day was the great difference between the afternoon and evening evaluations (the most and least negative assessments in direct succession). Gender did not have a significant effect, although boys' mood tended ($p = 0.075$) to be evaluated as more negative. No interaction effects were found for negative mood (Figure 2).

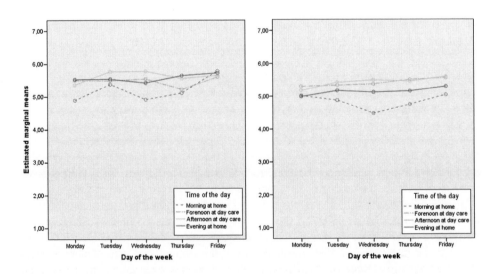

Figure 1. Daily assessments of positive mood of children (girls: left; boys: right).

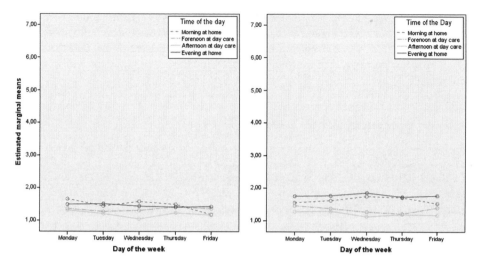

Figure 2.   Daily assessments of negative mood of children (girls, left; boys: right).

In general, children's mood was evaluated as rather positive, with a low level of negative mood. In sum, the evaluations of positive and negative mood complemented each other in portraying the children's emotional state. Girls' mood was appraised as more favourable than boys' mood. The most positive combination for mood was *girl, Friday* and *afternoons in the day-care centre*. In addition, children were evaluated as displaying more negative mood during *mornings* and *evenings at home*.

Parents' and day-care personnel's experiences about the use of the child diary as a research method

We were interested in examining the participants' experiences of the use of the diary. On the last page of the diary booklet, we asked the participants to paraphrase the diary process. Our aim was to gain more information about the use of this new method, piloted here for the first time. We received feedback from 43 diary participants (18 parents, 25 day-care personnel) out of the total of 108 diaries. We analysed the written feedback by inductive analysis (see, e.g. Johnson & Christensen, 2004), classifying the content on the basis of issues emerging from the data. Three main categories summarising the participants' experiences were identified: *content and usability, the effects of participation on one's own life* and *proposals for improvement*.

Content and usability

Most often the comments concerning the content concerned single questions – what worked well, what was difficult. The criticism from day-care personnel focused on the length of the diary; they felt it was burdensome and time-consuming (for all participants). Generally, lack of time was the most negative experience in both contexts. The use of repeated questions daily in the diary booklet made answering easier by the end of the week, but also monotonous and frustrating in both contexts. Some parents complained about the timing of the diary week that it was exceptional in some way. They also commented that there were easy questions and answering was easier than expected. Then again, some parents felt that there were unclear, difficult and confusing questions. They also commented that answering in the morning was difficult and that sometimes the child was not willing to draw. Day-care personnel felt that the scales and scope were adequate but complained that the study was more demanding than expected.

The effects of participation on own life

The parents reported that the participation was an awakening, pleasant, educative and interesting experience and reported learning much from the diary week. They had noticed that child enjoyed participating and expressed gratitude to the researchers for undertaking an important study. The diary week motivated the participants to pay closer attention to the child in everyday situations and, in the day-care context, also enabled them to concentrate on the child's play and doings, including when play was fluent and an adult's presence unnecessary. Some participants noticed that they gained much more detailed information about the child's day than was normally the case. In particular, the diary helped day-care personnel to understand the importance of making observations of children. They reported participation as interesting and providing new information. In some cases, making diary observations in large day-care groups was mentioned as very challenging, especially where personnel were few. In both contexts, participants wondered about the possibility of finding more time and resources for keeping diaries.

Proposals for improvement

Based on their experiences, some participants suggested improvements. These suggestions have encouraged us to consider how to make this new method more flexible and less time consuming. For the day-care context, the fixed response alternatives and structured checklist questions appeared to be the most efficient data collection alternatives. However, they would like quicker ways of answering (lists etc.), separate questions for outdoor play and more focused and age-oriented questions. They also commented that older children would be easier to observe. Parents, in turn, asked for more options to choose from, more open-ended questions and a focus on evenings, which they considered the best time for answering. In addition, to encourage children to draw or tell something about their day, the participants had noticed that it is important that the adults involved are also motivated and sensitive to when the child is showing willingness to cooperate.

The main ethical challenges related to the child diary

The focus in this examination is on special dilemmas regarding this observational child diary in the context of a large research project. We consider four main ethical challenges: *power positions, confidentiality, consequences* and *motivation*.

Power positions

Although the main informants in the study were adults, the data gathering concerned children's lives as well. Hence, the main ethical challenge was to ensure that the child had the freedom to choose whether to participate or not. The recruitment of day-care personnel and families for our study was not easy and used up time and other resources. The willingness of the whole family (both parents and the child) and day-care personnel to participate is also a quite strong criterion. To ensure the willingness of all our participants and to compensate for the imbalance (dominating positions of adults), we designed an information leaflet, especially for children. The adults at home and in the day-care centres were asked to read the leaflet with the child and inform the child about the study and what participation in it means. The leaflet consisted information about the data gathering, for example who is gathering the data (including a photograph of the researchers') and that participation was voluntary.

As Johansson and Emilson (2010) state, a child is both vulnerable and competent, which is an issue that needs to be addressed by researchers. Although we advised the adult participants not to pressure the children in any ways, the same issues, for example how to confirm voluntariness in very young children or how to define the boundaries so that the research is not burdensome to them, are present in this study as in other studies involving children.

Confidentiality

The second challenge was to decide who would be allowed to see the observations made. In this type of research involving interrelated people, participants might reveal information concerning other participants or show their answers to each other accidentally or advisedly, as Margolin et al. (2005) also point out. We recommended no discussing of the observations before the diary week was over, although the parents had the right to read the evaluations on their own child when the day-care data were returned to the researchers. However, no one used that possibility. The day-care personnel knew about the parents' rights to the research materials, and this might have affected their reporting. In this connection, it should also be remembered that parents or others in close relations with children, frequently face ethical and role conflicts in deciding what events are public and therefore permissible to be recorded as data versus what events are private and confined to the parental (or caregivers') role (Corsaro, 2005, p. 57; Poveda, 2009).

Consequences

The third ethical challenge is linked to the study's possible effects on the children's and other participants' lives. Although previous diary research (Merrilees, Goeke-Morey, & Cummings, 2008) has noted that participation *per se* in diary studies has not greatly affected participants' lives, it is known that diary studies are commonly used as intervention studies with the aim of achieving positive outcomes. The research group made efforts to construct research materials that respected the participants, and a resource-oriented rather than problem-centred approach was adopted. Although our participants' responses showed some positive outcomes, it should be remembered that by involving children, even if only as subjects of observation', researchers are creating a whole new social arena for them, with unpredictable long-term effects.

Motivation

The last challenge is connected to the recruitment process. Based on our experiences (e.g. missing data values) and the feedback received from participants, the recruiting process and the information given before participants commit themselves to the study are essential parts of the diary research process. The research group organised several information sessions for both day-care personnel and parents in which the research project was described and the different data gathering methods were demonstrated. Because not all the participants (especially from day-care centres) attended the information sessions, it was harder for absentees to obtain a realistic picture of the study as a whole. The lack of motivation and commitment observed in keeping the diary might be caused by such gaps in the information flow.

Discussion

The present study examined the diary method as a systematic tool for making daily observations in everyday life situations and critically addressed the special issues related to it. We chose adults as informants and co-researchers because we were interested in adult's assessments of children. The results need to be interpreted in this light: the researchers designed the questions and the informants observed the children through their own personalities and in the contexts of day-care practices and parenting. The results are discussed from a methodological viewpoint.

Main findings

The method used enabled study of perceptions of children's daily life by their parents and day-care personnel that reflect adults' readings of the situation present in the observation moment. The diary method allowed us to combine two separate contexts and the views of different informants. The results shed light on weekly and daily rhythms which cannot be captured by other methods, for example interviewing. Home was the place for the emotional expression of negative mood, supporting Galinsky (1999), who noted that during the so-called rush hour in the afternoon or in the morning the home atmosphere may be emotionally laden (see also Schulz, Cowan, Cowan, & Brennan, 2004). Apart from differences in the expression of mood by the children, the differences in the weekday evaluations – Friday being the most positive, and the clear difference reported between Monday and Tuesday – might also be due to the time needed for the observers to gain familiarity with the diary as a tool. Then again, the present data concerned only five working days (Monday to Friday), and since the days where the differences were found were also those immediately before and after the weekend, they might be different from the other weekdays.

The consistency found in the mood assessments indicates that certain events and situations were particularly challenging at both the individual and contextual levels. One of the most interesting findings, gender differences (boys' mood assessments less positive than girls'), might reflect individual and gender differences between the children, and the dynamics between the child and the observer, although a resemblance to predictable views (boys as rough and girls as nice) is also visible. On the other hand, boys may be more sensitive to environmental influences in general and exhibit more aggressive behaviour in a broad sense (e.g. externalising problems) than girls (Chen, 2010; DiLalla, 1998; Shpancer, 2002; Wachs, 1992). The present diary tool does not reveal whether these results are due to generalisations made by observers or other factors, but it does render the phenomenon more visible. This might be considered as one of the main empirical findings of this study.

This study also concerned research ethics about which much has been published on the involvement of children in research (e.g. Christensen & James, 2000; Greene & Hogan, 2005; Mayall, 1994; Punch, 2002). The challenges especially related to the child diary concern power positions, confidentiality, consequences and motivation, which was linked to the recruiting process. Some effects on participant's lives emerged from the feedback. Our results revealed that while the diary was considered too time-consuming, participation was an awakening and positive experience that helped the adults to notice the importance observing children.

Limitations

Although the method has potential, it has few limitations that should be taken into account. These are related to the recruitment process, the optimal duration of the diary period and the optimal amount and content of diary questions.

One limitation of the study was the challenge of participant recruitment, which affected the number, selection and commitment of the participants. Due to the demanding nature of the study and its partial interest in dual earner families, the participating families were selected. Although we managed to recruit enough participants, the parents represented a relatively highly educated population. However, recruiting families is a particular problem in diary research and family studies in general, and not confined to our study (see Rönkä et al., 2010). Furthermore, participants' commitment to the study is linked to the adequacy of the information given beforehand. We did not perhaps succeed in providing a realistic picture of the full extent of the study and as a result the data have missing values. It is also worth considering whether participation on the part of the day-care personnel might be taken as a professional obligation. Finally, the children's willingness to participate (being observed or contributing themselves) might be difficult to ascertain due to the adult–child power relation. This challenge in research involving children and the use of participatory methods has been rigorously discussed in many research fields (e.g. Gallacher & Gallagher, 2008).

The data collection lasted only for one week, which might also have affected reliability; a longer diary period would yield a more reliable picture. We noticed, for example, that some families reported the diary week as exceptional, which could have influenced their responses. The main consideration regarding the optimal length of the diary period is, however, related to the familiarity of the tool. For example, if the participants had performed the mood assessments for a longer period, they would have become accustomed to filling in the diary at the beginning of the week (note: the difference between Mondays and Tuesdays). While it is possible that the mood assessments would not have changed, the assessments can also be explained by reference to familiarity with the observation tool.

Furthermore, the method is time-consuming and possibly burdensome for participants, because making observations demands undivided attention by the observer. The documentation process required time and effort, a challenge faced not only in other diary studies (e.g. Bolger et al., 2003) but also in research concerning pedagogical documentation in kindergarten settings (Buldu, 2010). The number of diary items is a validity issue that should be addressed when developing the diary further. Another limitation of our method concerns the broad age range of the participating children. The content could have been more age-focused in terms of diary questions and children's own contributions, as drawing and other possible ways for children to fill their own pages required skills better possessed by older children.

Implications

The present child diary gives valuable information about individual children and daily life in the family and day-care contexts. As a research method, the diary can be used to study weekly and daily rhythms and quickly changing emotions and experiences. It enables all the participants (e.g. family members) to be studied simultaneously and, to some extent, their individual points of view taken into account. The diary described here is currently being used as a basis for developing electronic diaries in a research project focusing on challenging family situations (Jokinen, 2009).

The diary provides information both about individual children and the observational context. Hence, it may be inferred that the child diary also has potential in pedagogical applications. Our results indicate that the diary might motivate adults to pay closer attention to the child and child-related everyday interactions. Because it is daily, structured, situation-specific and detailed, this diary type of tool makes a novel contribution to the early childhood education literature on pedagogical documentation (e.g. Buldu, 2010). From the child's viewpoint significant others' views, or to be more precise, how the child thinks they view him/her (i.e. reflected appraisals, Hoelter, 1984) in everyday life situations is the basis of how the child defines and evaluates him/herself. The development of such a pedagogical tool which provides a possibility for teachers to focus on the interpretations made in micro-scale situations (through which social interaction is modified, e.g. Hergovich, Sirsch, & Felinger, 2002; Mead, 1934) could be beneficial. By means of systematic observations of daily situations, personal opinions (e.g. that the child is *always* such a good eater; that the child is *always* tired) can be disentangled from the actual details in daily situations. That is important at home, but even more so in institutional contexts. Furthermore, besides providing a possibility to learn more about the individual child's growth, development and his/her behaviour in different contexts, such a tool can help to identify the conventions and societal structures built around childhood (see James, 1998). The itemised documentation of everyday life using a simplified version of the child diary, even over a short period of time, might reveal information otherwise unobtainable in the contexts which form the child's daily environment.

The child diary has also features that can be utilised in strengthening the partnership between parents and day-care personnel. The child's well-being can be promoted by supporting the connections between the home and day-care environments, as such supportive links may facilitate continuity between the contexts (Bronfenbrenner, 1979; Shpancer, 2002). The diary could be used to promote that continuity by observing children's daily life so as to enhance every-day practices in home–day-care cooperation. The diary can also generate information about children's lives across contexts: children's experiences in one context influence their behaviour and experience in another, and they apply their individual characteristics and skills (i.e. gender, temperament) to the demands and affordances of their different environments (see Scarr, 1992; Shpancer, 2002). These applications can be used worldwide, but in Finland the use of detailed observations can supplement the existing documentation and teamwork concept, as individual early childhood education plans are made collaboratively by parents and day-care personnel. Based on the opinions of our participants, an improved version of the observational diary/supplement for use in constructing the individual early childhood education plan could be more context-specific, more age-oriented and less time-consuming. By following the footsteps of a long-established, in some ways traditional, method, new information can be produced on the relations between the family and day-care settings with the aim of helping children to navigate between these central areas of life.

Acknowledgement

This research was supported by a grant from the Academy of Finland (grant number 7110192).

References

Ahnert, L., Gunnar, M.R., Lamb, M.E., & Barthel, M. (2004). Transition to child care: Associations with infant–mother attachment, infant negative emotion, and cortisol elevations. *Child Development, 75*(3), 639–650.

Armstrong, M. (1982). *Closely observed children: The diary of a primary classroom.* London: Writers and Readers.

Baghban, M. (1984). *Our daughter learns to read and write: A case study from birth to three.* Newark, DE: International Reading Association.

Bates, J.E., Viken, R.J., Alexander, D.B., Beyers, J., & Stocton, L. (2002). Sleep and adjustment in preschool children: Sleep diary reports by mothers relate to behavior reports by teachers. *Child Development, 73*(1), 62–75.

Beidel, D.C., Neal, A.M., & Lederer, A.S. (1991). The feasibility and validity of a daily diary for the assessment of anxiety in children. *Behavior Therapy, 22*(4), 505–517.

Blenkin, G.M., & Kelly, A.V. (Eds.). (1992). *Assessment in early childhood education.* London: Sage.

Boddy, J., & Smith, M. (2007). Asking the experts. Developing and validating parental diaries to assess children's minor injuries. *International Journal of Social Research Methodology, 11*(1), 63–77.

Boler, M. (1999). *Feeling power: Emotions and education.* New York, NY: Routledge.

Bolger, N., Davis, A., & Rafaeli, E. (2003). Diary methods: Capturing life as it is lived. *Annual Review of Psychology, 54*(1), 579–616.

Bronfenbrenner, U. (1979). *The ecology of human development: Experiments by nature and design.* Cambridge, MA: Harvard University Press.

Buldu, M. (2010). Making learning visible in kindergarten classrooms: Pedagogical documentation as a formative assessment technique. *Teaching and Teacher Education, 26*(7), 1439–1449.

Buss, A., & Plomin, R. (1984). *Temperament: Early developing personality traits*. Hillsdale, NJ: Erlbaum.

Chen, J. (2010). Gender differences in externalising problems among preschool children: Implications for early childhood educators. *Early Child Development and Care, 180*(4), 463–474.

Christensen, P., & James, A. (2000). *Research with children: Perspectives and practices*. London: Falmer Press.

Cole, P., Martin, S., & Dennis, T.A. (2004). Emotion regulation as a scientific construct: Methodological challenges and directions for child development research. *Child Development, 75*(2), 317–333.

Corsaro, W. (2005). *The sociology of childhood* (2nd ed.). London: Pine Forge Press.

Crick, N.R., Casas, J.F., & Mosher, M. (1997). Relational and overt aggression in preschool. *Developmental Psychology, 33*(4), 579–588.

Daly, K. (2003). Family theory versus the theories families live by. *Journal of Marriage and Family, 65*(4), 771–784.

Darbyshire, P., Schiller, W., & MacDougall, C. (2005). Extending new paradigm childhood research: Meeting the challenges of including younger children. *Early Child Development and Care, 175*(6), 467–472.

DiLalla, L.F. (1998). Daycare, child and family influences on preschoolers' social behavior in a peer play setting. *Child Study Journal, 28*(3), 223–244.

Duncombe, J., & Marsden, D. (1993). Love and intimacy: The gender division of emotion and 'emotion work': A neglected aspect of sociological discussion of heterosexual relationships. *Sociology, 27*(2), 221–241.

Fisher, B., & Tronto, J. (1990). Toward a feminist theory of caring. In E.K. Abel & M.K. Nelson (Eds.), *Circles of care. Work and identity in women's lives*. Albany, NY: State University of New York Press.

Fox, B. (2001). The formative years: How parenthood creates gender. *Canadian Review of Sociology & Anthropology, 38*(4), 373–390.

Furth, H.G. (1970). *Piaget for teachers*. Englewood Cliffs: Prentice-Hall.

Galinsky, E. (1999). *Ask the children. What America's children really think about working parents*. New York, NY: William Morrow.

Gallacher, L.-A., & Gallagher, M. (2008). Methodological immaturity in childhood research? Thinking through 'participatory methods'. *Childhood, 15*(4), 499–516.

Giddens, A. (1990). *The consequences of modernity*. Cambridge: Polity.

Goodman, R. (1997). The strengths and difficulties questionnaire: A research note. *Journal of Child Psychology and Psychiatry, 38*(5), 581–586.

Green, A.S., Rafaeli, E., Bolger, N., Shrout, P.E., & Reis, H.T. (2006). Paper or plastic? Data equivalence in paper and electronic diaries. *Psychological Methods, 11*(1), 87–105.

Greene, S., & Hogan, D. (2005). *Researching children's experience. Methods and approaches*. London: Sage.

Hampton, V.R., & Fantuzzo, J.W. (2003). The validity of the Penn Interactive peer Play Scale with urban, low-income kindergarten children. *School Psychology Review, 32*(1), 77–91.

Hännikäinen, M. (2010). 1 to 3-year-old children in day care centres in Finland: An overview of eight doctoral dissertations. *International Journal of Early Childhood, 42*(2), 101–115.

Heinämäki, L. (2005). *Varhaista tukea lapselle – työvälineenä kehittämisvalikko* (Oppaita 62). Helsinki: Stakes.

Hergovich, A., Sirsch, U., & Felinger, M. (2002). Self-appraisals, actual appraisals and reflected appraisals of preadolescent children. *Social Behavior & Personality: An International Journal, 30*(6), 603–611.

Hitchings, E., & Moynihan, P.J. (1998). The relationship between television food advertisements recalled and actual foods consumed by children. *Journal of Human Nutrition and Dietetics, 11*(6), 511–517.

Hoelter, J.W. (1984). Relative effects of significant others on self-evaluation. *Social Psychology Quarterly, 47*(3), 255–262.

Hofferth, S.L., & Sandberg, J.F. (2001). How American children spend their time. *Journal of Marriage and Family, 63*(2), 295–308.

Jain, A., Belsky, J., & Crnic, K. (1996). Beyond fathering behaviors: Types of dads. *Journal of Family Psychology, 10*(4), 431–442.

James, A. (1998). Foreword. In I. Hutchby & J. Moran-Ellis (Eds.), *Children and social competence. Arenas of action* (pp. vii–x). London: The Falmer Press.

Jamieson, L. (1999). Intimacy transformed? A critical look at the 'pure relationship'. *Sociology, 33*(3), 477–494.

Johansson, E., & Emilson, A. (2010). Toddlers' life in Swedish preschool. *International Journal of Early Childhood, 42*(2), 165–179.

Johnson, B., & Christensen, L. (2004). *Educational research: Quantitative, qualitative, and mixed approaches* (2nd ed.). Boston, MA: Pearson Education Inc.

Jokinen, K. (2009). Research plan for research project 'Children's emotional security in multiple family relations (EMSE) 2010–2013'. Retrieved December 22, 2011, from https://www.jyu.fi/ytk/laitokset/perhetutkimus/en/research

Jung, J. (2011). Caregivers' playfulness and infants' emotional stress during transitional time. *Early Child Development and Care, 181*(10), 1397–1407.

Koh, C.-Y. (2005). The everyday emotional experiences of husbands and wives. In B. Schneider & L.J. Waite (Eds.), *Being together, working apart. Dual-career families and the work–life balance* (pp. 169–189). Cambridge: Cambridge University Press.

Kyrönlampi-Kylmänen, T., & Määttä, K. (2012). What is it like to be at home: The experiences of five- to seven-year-old Finnish children. *Early Child Development and Care, 182*(1), 71–86.

Lahikainen, A.-L., & Strandell, H. (1988). *Lapsen kasvuehdot Suomessa*. Helsinki: Gaudeamus.

Lally, M. (1991). *The nursery teacher in action*. London: Paul Chapman.

Lämsä, T. (2009). Monta ikkunaa lapsen maailmaan: Lapsitietämys aikuisten havaintoina ja lasten kertomuksina. In A. Rönkä, K. Malinen, & T. Lämsä (Eds.), *Perhe-elämän paletti. Vanhempana ja puolisona vaihtelevassa arjessa* (pp. 89–124). Jyväskylä: PS-kustannus.

Larson, R.W., & Almeida, D.M. (1999). Emotional transmission in the daily lives of families: A new paradigm for studying family process. *Journal of Marriage and the Family, 61*(1), 5–20.

Larson, R.W., & Gillman, S. (1999). Transmission of emotions in the daily interactions of single-mother families. *Journal of Marriage and the Family, 61,* 21–39.

Larson, R., & Richards, M.H. (1994). *Divergent realities. The emotional lives of mothers, fathers, and adolescents*. New York, NY: Basic Books.

Laurenceau, J., & Bolger, N. (2005). Using diary methods to study marital and family processes. *Journal of Family Psychology, 19*(1), 86–97.

Laurent, J., Catanzaro, S.J., Joiner, T.E. Jr., Rudolph, K.D., Potter, K.I., Lambert, S., …, Gathright, T. (1999). A measure of positive and negative affect for children: Scale development and preliminary validation. *Psychological Assessment, 11*(3), 326–338.

Layder, D. (2004). *Emotion in social life: The lost heart of society*. London: Sage.

Margolin, G., Chien, D., Duman, S.E., Fauchier, A., Gordis, E.B., Ramos, M.C., …, Oliver, P.H. (2005). Ethical issues in couple and family research. *Journal of Family Psychology, 19*(1), 157–167.

Matjasko, J., & Feldman, A.F. (2006). Bringing work home: The emotional experiences of mothers and fathers. *Journal of Family Psychology, 20,* 40–46.

Mayall, B. (1994). *Children's childhoods: Observed and experienced*. London: Routledge.

Mead, G.H. (1934). *Mind, self & society from the standpoint of a social behaviorist*, with introduction, by Charles W. Morris. Chicago, IL: University of Chicago Press.

Merrilees, C.E., Goeke-Morey, M., & Cummings, E.M. (2008). Do event-contingent diaries about marital conflict change marital interactions? *Behaviour Research and Therapy, 46*(2), 253–262.

Ministry of Social Affairs and Health. (2004). *Early childhood education and care in Finland*, Brochures 2004:14. Helsinki: Ministry of Social Affairs and Health. Retrieved January 1, 2011, from http://pre20090115.stm.fi/cd1106216815326/passthru.pdf

Morgan, D. (2004). Everyday family life and family practices. In E.S. Suilva & T. Bennett (Eds.), *Contemporary culture and everyday life* (pp. 37–51). Durhan: Sociology Press.

National Curriculum Guidelines on Early Childhood Education and Care in Finland. (2003). Helsinki: STAKES. Retrieved January 1, 2011 from http://www.thl.fi/thl-client/pdfs/267671cb-0ec0-4039-b97b-7ac6ce6b9c10

National Institute for Health and Welfare (THL). (2009). *Lasten päivähoito 2009, tilastora-portti*. Retrieved January 1, 2011 from http://www.stakes.fi/tilastot/tilastotiedotteet/2010/Tr32_10.pdf

Perrez, M., Schoebi, D., & Wilhelm, P. (2000). How to assess social regulation of stress and emotions in daily family life? A computer-assisted family self-monitoring system (FASEM-C). *Clinical Psychology & Psychotherapy, 7*(4), 326–339.

Pfeifer, J.H., Masten, C.L., Borofsky, L.A., Dapretto, M., Fuligni, A.J., & Lieberman, M.D. (2009). Neural correlates of direct and reflected self-appraisals in adolescents and adults: When social perspective-taking informs self-perception. *Child Development, 80*(4), 1016–1038.

Poveda, D. (2009). Parent and ethnographer of other children. *Anthropology Matters Journal, 11*(1), 1–10.

Punch, S. (2002). Research with children. The same or different from research with adults? *Childhood, 9*(3), 321–341.

Rönkä, A., Malinen, K., Kinnunen, U., Tolvanen, A., & Lämsä, T. (2010). Capturing daily family dynamics via text messages: A development of a mobile diary. *Community, Work & Family, 13*(1), 5–21.

Rönkä, A., Malinen, K., & Lämsä, T. (Eds.). (2009). *Perhe-elämän paletti: Vanhempana ja puolisona vaihtelevassa arjessa* [The palette of family life: As a parent and as a spouse in fluctuating daily life]. Jyväskylä: PS-Kustannus.

Sayer, L.C., Bianchi, S.M., & Robinson, J.P. (2004). Are parents investing less in children? Trends in mother's and fathers' time with children. *The American Journal of Sociology, 110*(1), 1–43.

Scarr, S. (1992). Developmental theories for the 1990s: Development and individual differences. *Child Development, 63*(1), 1–19.

Schulz, M.S., Cowan, P.A., Cowan, C.P., & Brennan, R.T. (2004). Coming home upset: Gender, marital satisfaction, and the daily spillover of workday experience into couple interactions. *Journal of Family Psychology, 18*(1), 250–263.

Shpancer, N. (2002). The home-daycare link: Mapping children's new world order. *Early Childhood Research Quarterly, 17*(3), 374–392.

Smart, C. (2007). *Personal life: New directions in sociological thinking*. Cambridge: Polity Press.

Sonnentag, S., & Kruel, U. (2006). Psychological detachment from work during off-job time: The role of job stressors, job involvement, and recovery-related self-efficacy. *European Journal of Work and Organizational Psychology, 15*(2), 197–217.

Statistics Finland. (2007). *Perheet 2006*. Helsinki: Tilastokeskus.

Strandell, H. (1997). Doing reality with play. Play as a children's resource in organizing every-day life in day care centres. *Childhood, 4*(4), 445–464.

Thagaard, T. (1997). Gender, power, and love: A study of interaction between spouses. *Acta Sociologica, 40*(4), 357–376.

Wachs, T.D. (1992). *The nature of nurture*. Newbury Park: Sage.

Watson, D., Clark, L.A., & Tellegen, A. (1988). Development and validation of brief measures of positive and negative affect: The PANAS scales. *Journal of Personality and Social Psychology, 54*(6), 1063–1070.

Whalen, C.K., Henker, B., Jamner, L.D., Ishikawa, S.S., Floro, J.N., Swindle, R., ..., Johnston, J.A. (2006). Toward mapping daily challenges of living with ADHD: Maternal and child perspectives using electronic diaries. *Journal of Abnormal Child Psychology, 34*(1), 115–13.

Wilson, L., Mott, D., & Batman, D. (2004). The asset-based context matrix: A tool for assessing children's learning opportunities and participation in natural environments. *Topics in Early Childhood Special Education, 24*(2), 110–120.

Experts or good educators – or both? The development of early childhood educators' expertise in Finland

Iiris Happo, Kaarina Määttä and Satu Uusiautti

Well-educated staff consists of multidimensional experts, and this staff is one of the strengths of the Finnish day-care system. The aim of this article is to clarify the development of the expertise of those early childhood educators who have qualified as kindergarten teachers. The data consisted of the early educators' stories ($n = 80$) of their growth towards expertise. The analysis was carried out as content analysis. As the results, four key factors in the process of growth towards expertise were created. According to the informants, personal life history, education, work experience and personal attitudes towards work had been the most influential factors in the process of growth towards their expertise. The working environment both facilitated and hindered the growth of the expert. It is possible to foster educators' professional growth with an individual development plan.

Introduction

Early childhood education and care can be seen as educational interaction taking place in young children's different living environments. As every preschool age child in Finland has the right to day-care, its different forms are the most important area of early childhood activities (Act on Children's Day Care, 1973/36; National Curriculum Guidelines on Early Childhood Education and Care in Finland, 2003). In order to develop these activities, it is important to consider early childhood educators' expertise and their professional development. The purpose of this article is to clarify how the expertise of early childhood educators develops, especially in the Finnish context.

Well-educated staff is one of the strengths of the Finnish day-care system. In the day-care centres, the term 'educator' refers to the staff responsible for care, education, and teaching. In Finland, day-care centres have multi-professional staff and therefore the level of education varies among the staff. The legislation sets out clear requirements for staff qualification. At least one-third of the staff must have a post-secondary level degree: Bachelor of Education, Master of Education, or Bachelor of Social Sciences

(Decree on Children's Day-care, 239/1973; National Curriculum Guidelines on Early Childhood Education and Care in Finland, 2003; OECD, 2006). This is the foundation for early childhood educators' qualification provided by law. What about their expertise?

It has been noted that (Wood & Bennett, 2000, p. 647), in the context of early childhood education, there is increasing emphasis on multi-professional and inter-agency collaboration, and on liaison with parents and practitioners in different settings. Therefore, there is a need for greater professionalism amongst early childhood educators to enable them to function as change agents, to articulate the theories that guide their practice, to provide models of skilled, expert practice, and establish discourse and research communities.

In this article, we dissect Finnish early childhood educators' expertise and what factors promote or hinder its development. We will also further the analysis by discussing who a good early childhood educator is and how to become one.

How to define early childhood educators' expertise?

Expertise is a concept which is used in many different connections (Ericsson, Chairness, Feltovich, & Hoffman, 2006). Generally, it refers to the special know-how which is related to different professions (Burnard, 1992; Carter, Sabers, Cushing, Pinnegar, & Berliner, 1987; Disch, 2002; Sim & Kim, 2010; Walker et al., 2010). A certain amount of education and work experience is usually needed for the development into the expert (see also Adelson, 1984).

Experts are people who have the ultimate skills and knowledge of their own field. They usually have a long working experience and they are able to use their professional ability in practice. (Selinger & Crease, 2006; Woods & Bennett, 2000). Pedagogical know-how is the early childhood educator's core competence as it represents the educators' substance field. In Finland, early childhood educators are professionals in the pedagogical field, working mainly in the various forms of day-care sector (National Curriculum Guidelines on Early Childhood Education and Care in Finland, 2003).

Finnish early childhood education covers care, education, and instruction. However, expertise included in these areas can also be examined as the separate fields of competences. Early childhood educators' instructional knowledge includes curriculum, content, and pedagogical knowledge. Curriculum knowledge directs an educator to utilise appropriate contents and structure of teaching young children. In addition to a subject to be taught, content knowledge contains the competence of knowing how to teach young children. Pedagogical knowledge contains the choices made in the teaching situation as well as practical action. A pedagogically skilful teacher has excellent interaction skills. She/he understands what makes learning easy or difficult and can choose developmentally appropriate practices flexibly during a teaching situation (Guskey, 1986; Saracho & Spodek, 2003). The implementation of early childhood education is a multidimensional phenomenon that consists of, for example, planning, carrying out, and evaluating learning processes. Educators should be able to consider many aspects: managing appropriate teaching and guiding methods, organising learning environment, and perceiving the children with special needs among other things. (See, e.g. Bredekamp & Willer, 1992; Guskey, 1986; Happo, 2006; Olson, 1994; Puckett & Diffily, 1999; Saracho & Spodek, 2003; Ylitapio-Mäntylä, Uusiautti, & Määttä, submitted)

The expertise of an early childhood educator is apparently versatile and this phenomenon contains skills and competences of different kinds to be reviewed. According to Karila and Nummenmaa (2001), early childhood educators' competences are contextual knowledge, interaction and cooperation skills, and pedagogical knowledge. In order to improve as an educator, critical reflection skills are needed as well. (See also Happo, 2006; Happo & Määttä, 2011).

Contextual knowledge contains understanding about culture and society. Early childhood educators have to be aware of children's and families' living environment and take this into account in their educational work. Interaction and cooperation skills are needed in cooperation with children, families, and partners. A good relationship between parents and educators is an essential part of children's well-being and these social skills are inseparable part of educators' work (Karila & Nummenmaa, 2001; National Curriculum Guidelines on Early Childhood Education and Care in Finland, 2003).

Early childhood educators' core competence is pedagogical knowledge. In order to be able to improve children's well-being and development, early childhood educators should be aware of the values and goals of education as well as the concept of learning. They should understand the meaning of supporting interaction. However, the understanding of education and concept of learning constantly develops (Happo, 2006; Happo & Määttä, 2011; Karila & Nummenmaa, 2001).

Ryan and Cooper (2004) suggest that teachers' self-knowledge and enthusiasm have a significant implication for successful educating and teaching. Successful educational work requires a positive attitude towards children, colleagues, and parents. Especially, children are sensitive in perceiving adults' behaviour and emotions (Ryan & Cooper, 2004). Also Van Manen (1991) emphasises interaction as a part of a good pedagogical process.

The development of expertise

Becoming an expert is a manifold process in which experiences and knowledge gathered along with education and career have a central role. According to Bereiter and Scardamalia (1993), true experts can be distinguished from non-experts by their gradually proceeding way of working and progressive problem-solving process. Besides automatised actions, a true expert defines his/her tasks and action over and over again at higher and higher levels (Lajoie, 2003).

Those factors that essentially contribute to expertise can be called the builders of expertise (Karila, 1997). These factors relate to societal and cultural structures and in Finland, they are, for example, the legislative solutions that regulate children's day-care. They affect the idea of day-care which, for its part, has an influence on the foci and organisation of the day-care system.

Furthermore, early childhood educators' personal life history is one important dimension in the development of their expertise. According to Raymond, Butt, and Townsend (1992), teachers' early personal experiences strongly affect their development as teachers. Therefore, early childhood educators' development appears as a manifold process and the paths towards expertise may vary greatly (Goodfellow & Sumsion, 2003).

Ryan and Cooper (2004) describe teachers' professional development with a three-level model. At the first level, teachers pay attention mostly to outer factors in teaching situations, such as discipline and the number of tasks. At the second level, teachers are already able to evaluate their own action in teaching situations and notice children as individuals. However, in surprising situations, teachers may have difficulties in moulding their action in a functional manner. At the third level, teachers are creative and effective. They have extensive substance knowledge and are capable of noticing children individually even in unexpected situations.

Ryan and Cooper (2004) call the examination and evaluation of one's own work as reflective thinking and emphasise its importance for vocational development. A deep reflection on work helps educators to perceive and evaluate their educational action. According to Wood and Bennett (2000), teachers who are engaged in the reflection process of their everyday practical problem-solving strategies and pedagogical interactions are able to articulate their professional knowledge and obtain a deeper understanding about their theories and practice. Similarly Costigan and Crocco (2004) stress the significance of reflection for teachers' development. Furthermore, it would be important to use reflective thinking at work starting immediately from the first work year. However, vocational development should continue over the whole career (Costigan & Crocco, 2004).

Katz (1977) has described teachers' professional action as a four-phased development process. Newly graduated teachers have to survive from the initial struggle when they have to be responsible for rearing in reality. This phase is followed by the phase of consolidation that begins at the end of the first or at the beginning of second work year. During consolidation, teachers can pay attention to children's individual needs for the first time. After three to four years of work experience, the renewal phase takes place. Teachers' development needs may vary but a common need is to acquire new skills to improve and complement one's own teaching and rearing practices. The overall development progresses towards maturity that can be only achieved through survival, consolidation, and renewal (Katz, 1977; see also Jalongo & Isenberg, 2004).

The nature of the teacher's profession changes and develops constantly and it is not possible to define it in future (e.g. Bullough & Baughman, 1995; Starkey et al., 2009). However, it seems clear that keeping up professional competence necessitates continuous seeking for new information and education. Teacher's work has also changed more and more towards collegial activity. Learning from others and solving problems together have become more and more common. Mentoring can help beginning teachers' development significantly at the initial phase of careers (Bartell, 2004).

Although development into an expert is an individual process, common features in that process are the pursuit of employing topical information about how to develop one's own work, a reflective approach to work, strong self-direction and self-assessment (Knowles, 1975; see also Jalongo & Isenberg, 2004).

Research questions

The purpose of this article is to study early childhood educators' expertise and what factors promote or hinder its development in the day-care context in Finland.

The key questions of this research are:

(1) What factors affect the development of early childhood educators' expertise the most in Finland?
(2) What is the importance of the working environment for the development of early childhood educators' expertise?

In conclusion, we will discuss the nature of good early childhood educator's expertise: what it consists of and how to develop into a good educator.

Research method, data, and analysis

The research was conducted in the province of Lapland in Finland. The target group ($n = 346$) comprised the early childhood educators who worked with children in day-care and had at least a post-secondary degree from the field. Because early childhood education is closely connected to pedagogy, the target group consisted of those who had the widest pedagogical education. They were working as kindergarten teachers, special kindergarten teachers, or early childhood educators.

The material was collected by using a questionnaire which consisted of background information questions and a composition assignment about 'The story of my growth toward expertise in early childhood education'. The questionnaire was sent to the whole target group ($n = 346$). The data were gathered during the years 2003 and 2004.

Eighty early childhood educators participated in the study and sent their story by mail. Seventy-seven of them were women and three men. The participants were aged between 25 and 55 years. 45–49-year-old participants formed the biggest group ($n = 24$). The youngest participants were 25–29 years old ($n = 6$) and the oldest ones over 55 years old ($n = 9$). Seven of them were 30–34 years old, twelve 35–39 years old, twelve 40–44 years old, and ten 50–54 years old.

The basic population ($n = 346$) of the research covered persons who work daily with children at a day-care and who are qualified according to the decree (804/1992) on the conditions of qualification of social welfare personnel. The actual degrees that qualify one as early childhood educators among the participants ($n = 80$) were early childhood education teacher's degree ($n = 56$) of whom three had also the degree of a special teacher or special early childhood education teacher, social educator's degree ($n = 13$), bachelor's degree in social services ($n = 9$), and bachelor's degree in education ($n = 2$). In addition, two participants had master's degree and four had bachelor's degree or vocational degree.

62.5% ($n = 50$) had taken studies (between 10 and 80 study weeks, one study week equals to 40 h of studying) at universities or universities of applied sciences as in-service training. 49.2% ($n = 39$) of the participants had performed specialised studies in early childhood education and/or elementary education (15–20 study weeks).

The study had a qualitative approach. The data collection method consisted of the early childhood educators' stories of their growth towards expertise. Altogether, the data comprised 311 sheets of written text. The analysis was carried out by the methods of content analysis which entailed a systematic reading of the body of texts. The analysis of the research data began by searching the elements of their knowledge related to their own work from the early childhood educators' own descriptions.

According to Guba and Lincoln (1981), content analysis should progress systematically and regularly. The aim is to generalise about the studied phenomenon. The analysis proceeded in a data-driven or inductive manner: first with the reduction of data and next by clustering. The analysis units were selected according to the purpose of the research and research questions. At the first phase of analysis, quotations that described the development of expertise were selected from the participants' stories. This data reduction meant dividing the data into pieces. The second phase of analysis consisted of clustering the quotation by common nominators (Guba & Lincoln, 1981; Holloway, 2011; Huberman & Miles, 1994; Tuomi & Sarajärvi, 2002).

When considering the reliability of qualitative research, the demand for truthfulness and objectivity is crucial (Whittemore, Chase, & Mandle, 2001). Of epistemological theories about truth, the one that is based on consensus emphasises that people can create a consensual 'truth'. Indeed, we can talk about a consensus-based perspective in this research (Tuomi & Sarajärvi, 2002). The research participants wrote about their own expertise and its development in a free form and defined those factors that related to expertise in their own action. There is not just one truth about the development and manifestation of expertise. Each participant's personal experience on their own expertise forms its own truth; however, it is possible to find some common and consistent factors that are commonalities among participants (Buchbinder, 2011).

Results

Factors that affected the development of early childhood educators' expertise

Participants described the development of their expertise in various ways. Based on data reduction and clustering, it was possible to recognise four main factors: the participants' own history, education, work experience, and personal attitude to work.

One's own life history and background

Early childhood educators describe the meaning of their own family and children as well as the happenings – both hardships and happy events – that had taken place in their life. Of those participants who had children ($n = 72$), 47% said that their own child had contributed to the development of their expertise. According to their stories, the experience gained after having one's own child helped to understand families and improved collaboration with parents.

> After my own child was born, I think I changed the most as an early childhood education teacher. It provided me with a totally new dimension in my work: the parent's perspective.

The most important partners in cooperation in day-care are children's parents. Educational partnership with parents requires good cooperation and interaction skills. Happenings in one's own history were considered as affecting development in this field as well. It made empathising parents' position easier.

> When I had my own children, my way of thinking changed a lot, immediately into more realistic one, and I didn't demand too much on parents anymore. I understood parents' fatigue better and the difficulty of setting limits to a child.

Knowledge acquired from education, work experience, and life events (e.g. one's own child) improved the participants' understanding about child development and growth and the meaning of childhood. Along with having their own children, the participants' became more aware of the fact that the educational interaction relationship has to be created with each child separately. Furthermore, their pedagogical proficiency developed, awareness of rearing became more structured, and their reflection of educational goals, purposes, and methods increased. The early childhood educators stated that they have started to observe critically – to reflect – their own action as educators and their rearing principles, and how their work community functions as well.

> Noticing such a thing that children are individuals, they cannot be raised according to the same pattern, has been an important thing.

My own children changed my principles. Previously, I was often quite strict in certain circumstances; now I notice myself being flexible when necessary and questioning things. The question 'Why' comes to my mind more often.

The participants named also hardships, such as a divorce, bullying at work, the experience of failing in challenging educational tasks or in cooperation with parents that enhanced the development of their expertise. These kinds of events increased their appreciation of early childhood education work.

I have taken two degrees in adulthood. In my private life, I have traveled 'a long and difficult route'. All these things have made me understand the great value and responsibility of my work.

Education

Education and new information about their own professional field were considered the most important factor for the development of expertise. An extensive theoretical knowledge base is needed when working in early childhood education and this appeared in the participants' education. The early childhood educators had studied the science of education, special education, social policy, psychology, adult education, and cultural history at the university. Through education, they had also acquired knowledge about work methods and other relevant skills. Furthermore, they had strengthened their pedagogical proficiency by studying drama, physical exercise, art and culture and other studies that support work in the field of early childhood education. Besides university studies, they had improved their competence by taking studies provided by other institutions as well.

The early childhood educators described the significance of education for the development of their expertise in three ways:

Firstly, *an individual course or information acquired by oneself* could be seen as a crucial factor. Professional development can follow various paths: it is not necessarily steady progress but can include steady phases and insights that further development in leaps and bounds. The early childhood educators had had insights that had emerged along with a singular training day or reading a book.

'Could something be done differently in day-care' research in the 1980s was crucial for my professional development.

The participants also named certain wider post-graduation educational entities significant for the development of their expertise.

Secondly, education was regarded as a *moving force and support for the change*. The early childhood educators in this research had a positive attitude towards education. Over half of them (62.5%) had acquired relatively wide supplementary education. They described certain in-service education periods as moving forces: education encouraged them to develop themselves and their work and thus, could start a long-term period of professional development. They could, for example, acquire new means and methods which were put to test and developed at work.

In-service education periods have been the key word; they have started 'the process'.

Thirdly, education was perceived as 'walking by one's side' *in the process of developing into an expert*. Some of the participants said that they participated regularly either in voluntary education or one organised by the employer in order to keep updated or develop one's own expertise. Education was considered a crucial part of an early childhood educator's work. One's own activeness in seeking for new information occurred in many participants' stories. They followed current literature and research of their own field.

> I have constantly kept myself updated about early childhood education and that's my strength.

The participants described their responsibility in searching information and keeping up-to-date. According to the early childhood educators' writings, basic education, in-service and supplementary education, voluntary studying and the improved facilities of finding information developed especially their pedagogical proficiency. For example, they could improve their upbringing skills among children who need special support. Constant development concerning early childhood education methods was considered important as was deepening one's theoretical thinking. Also their decision-making skills improved (see also Bredekamp, 1997; Calderhead, 1984).

> Along experience and supplementary education, my ability to make careful observations and reflect them in theoretical knowledge has improved.

> Due to various studies, I have gotten new viewpoints or strengthened the old ones, my confidence in work increases (e.g. when it comes to child welfare issues).

Work experience

Career development is always an individual process and it is not always bound to work years (Collins & Evans, 2002). Therefore, it can be analysed from quite different points of view. The participants in this research had worked for three months to 37 years. They named *the amount of work experience* as a factor that increases their expertise.

> Time certainly (21-year-old educator's experience base is not very wide yet) does it.

Furthermore, the quality of work experience (e.g. in the form of versatile work tasks) affected the development of early childhood educators' expertise.

> ... different kinds of work experiences (working as a special teacher, kindergarten teacher, head of the day-care center, supervisor ...)

The confidence that resulted from work experience was seen as enhancing development but also giving courage to rise to the new challenges. Therefore, also *the challenges in work experience* had affected the participants' expertise.

> Probably problem situations and solving them. If I have found a functional solution to problems, I have been able to adapt the solutions afterwards as well of course. One only has to remember that the same solution does not necessarily work always.

Furthermore, *other people at the work community* can affect the development of expertise because interaction and collaboration were named as furthering factors.

> I have learned much from her during the last years. The lack of one's own proficiency or skills in some sector is not a disaster but a motive to acquire information and education or pass those tasks to someone else who can do them better.

Personal attitude towards work

Studies about expertise (Eisenhart, 2006; Engeström, 1992; Reilly, 2008; Tynjälä, 1999; Valkeavaara, 1999) have proved that not all those people who are highly educated and long work experience act in their work tasks similarly. Also in this research, those early childhood educators who are at the same phase in their careers described their personal attitude towards work and approach in many different ways. Those features that had affected the development of their expertise were their own personal characteristics, their way they look at new things and their interests.

I am dutiful in my work and want to do it as well as I can.

The motivation to learn and new desire to develop and seize challenges were apparent in the participants' stories when they described their development.

Therefore, I have kept my senses alert for the past 10-15 years.

Early childhood educators' personal characteristics can be also analysed as if they were professional skills or super-professional qualifications. The constant societal change requires of employees willingness and readiness to change – as do children who develop and grow constantly and the change in the nature of day-care. To be able to change one's own action demands reflection skills. When describing their personal features, the participants emphasised their reflective approach that was considered meaningful to the development of their professional competence and expertise (see also Ryan & Cooper, 2004).

Reflectivity as a factor that supported the participants' expertise could be perceived two ways. On the one hand, the participants thought that they developed personally through the reflective approach to work. They evaluated their own work regularly, closely connected to everyday work.

Stocktaking and evaluation of my own work – even daily – have widened my understanding about early childhood education teacher's work in the long run.

On the other hand, they described joint activities. Indeed, according to Kupila (2001), the development of expertise also demands analysing one's own thoughts and experiences together with others in a collegial manner.

Along the way, the support, encouragement, and even friendship by my co-workers have been significant. It has been important to evaluate my own functions together and even question them.

The early childhood educators said that their work was constantly changing. Therefore, reflection was considered an important part of work because outer circumstances, children and families, change all the time in early childhood education. The participants had noticed needs for change in their work community and in addition to personal action, the work practices of the work community needed to be changed.

I pursue to develop myself as an educator all the time.

The significance of working environment for the development of expertise

The working environment of the early childhood educators who participated in this research was the day-care system in Finland. Physical working environments varied, among other things, by the sizes of day-care centres, working hours, and facilities as well as the stability of position. There were less than 20 children in the smallest day-care centres and over a hundred in the largest ones. Some day-care centres also offered 24/7 care. Some early childhood educators could change their working environments during a week as they worked, for example, as special early childhood education teachers or as itinerants. Child groups varied as well. Most of the participants worked in child groups that were divided into age groups. Some were responsible for the preschool education group of six-year-old children, while others worked in sibling groups that consisted of children of various ages. Most of the educators reported that there are children who need special assistance in their group.

According to the participants' descriptions, facilities and equipment varied greatly as well. Most of them worked in premises that were 'proper', some described them as 'magnificent for day-care use', while some worked in 'inadequate' premises. Yet, the physical settings as such were not considered important to one's own professional development. Instead, mental working environment appeared significant.

Enabling and developing factors in work environment

In this research, early childhood educators named enabling and developing factors that relate to work environment, work content, and work community. When it came to *work environment*, the early childhood educators thought that change in the environment provided them with new perspectives on work.

> The beginning of my career involves several changes of residence and along with them, the changes of work places. It has probably been richness when considering my professional expertise.

The new environment and working in various situations require that early childhood educators are capable of adjusting their own action in new situations. Adaptive expertise develops due to constant challenging tasks (see Hatano & Inagaki, 1986, 1992).

> In addition, the large and changing circle of coworkers has introduced plenty of models and I have been able to compare myself with various people and approaches.

> Also changing work place from normal day-care center into round-the-clock day-care has introduced a lot of new perspectives.

Certainly, a constantly changing work environment may also be a drain but perceiving it as a positive resource illustrates a specific attitude towards work (see also Uusiautti & Määttä, 2010). The development of expertise does indeed necessitate *work tasks* that are both challenging and provide one with experiences of surviving the challenges. Also, responsibility was considered as one factor that enhances development.

> I have developed the most in my work when I was given a variety of responsibilities where I was allowed to make self-reliant solutions and when I have noticed the meaning of group work and how it works well in practice.

The dynamic nature of work was regarded as motivating and promoting. The participants said that they engage keenly in interesting, challenging, and varying work tasks. Work experience as such will not promote expertise if work tasks are monotonous or workmanlike.

> I have had to (been able to) contemplate my work, education, knowledge and skills, values and the goals and contents of (primary) education as I belong to the municipal planning and steering group and curriculum planning group.

Expertise develops within the interaction between an individual and environment – *in the work community*. In this research, the early childhood educators described that their expertise had developed if the work community gave space to it by providing a confidential and safe atmosphere where employees dare and want to express their thoughts and test new kinds of ways of action and practices.

> We could fulfill ourselves and we were encouraged to creative solutions. During that time, I learned a lot.

Support was considered motivating and encouraged the participants to try new things. Several early childhood educators brought out the significance of feedback for the development of expertise. Feedback from customers and co-workers was found to be inspiring and gave more confidence in working. Getting feedback from children and parents was considered a significant resource and promoting development.

> Feedback from children and parents have been encouraging and given confidence that you are on track.

The participants' ages and time spent at work varied greatly. This kind of heterogeneity at the work community was seen as promoting professional development both by novices and those educators who had worked for a long time.

> To me, it has been rewarding to work as almost the youngest one in my work community. I can give and get a lot from older employees.

The factors that hinder the development of expertise in work environment

Work environment and work community can also inhibit expertise from developing (see Turner, 2001). Societal setting reflects in the day-care system, regulating the work environment, which appeared worrying and partly also hindered the development of expertise. Economic resources were considered insufficient. The quality of early childhood education was contemplated. Some of the early childhood educators belonged to work groups that are supposed to improve quality. This quality work was seen as important for professional development in day-care; on the other hand however, it was not seen as very effective when it comes to daily work.

> Day-care is evaluated but crucial factors (group sizes, work load, etc.) are ignored or people invoke the legislation.

Although the work environment at the day-care sector was said to have changed greatly since the 1980s, some of the participants considered day-care relatively stable and conservative, not enabling or even inhibiting the development of expertise.

Workmanlike expertise seemed to be a dominant form of expertise in some work communities and, therefore, testing new ideas caused resistance.

> Introducing new ways of action has demanded risk-taking and resistance on myself and the work community.

People create the atmosphere in the work environment. Some of the early childhood educators stated that they had managed to affect the atmosphere positively. In some cases, the participants had been even able to remove factors that prevent expertise from developing. At its worst, the atmosphere in the work community was considered even discouraging and thus acting as an expert remained flawed or totally missing (see also Starkey et al., 2009).

> People's voices are silenced, support and spur are missing.

> It is easier to be a new employee in a big day-care center than a small one. A small work community tends to be 'clannish'. It is hard to become a member if the work community has already started to function as a home.

Conclusions

Many factors affect the development of early childhood educators' expertise. Early childhood educators can affect some factors with their own choices but some factors are inevitable and unpredictable ones that are related to the course of life. According to the participants, their own life history, education, work experience, and personal characteristics had influenced the development of their expertise. The development process was seen as personal and resulting from the synergy of the above-mentioned factors. Work environment either enabled or promoted the development of expertise or hindered the development process. Based on the participants' stories, changes and flux in work environment, work tasks, and co-workers enhanced the development of expertise. Respectively, immutability was seen as inhibiting development.

The early childhood educators considered feedback given by children, parents, and co-workers important. However, based on their descriptions, the feedback systems were informal, but if giving and receiving feedback were fundamental parts of work, its role in the development of expertise would be considered significant.

Acting as an expert is especially demanding in the field of education because every rearing situation is different. There is not any universal solution or just one way of action. In educational situations, early childhood educators use several various sources in order to confirm the fairness and appropriateness of their solution. (See also Bredekamp, 1997.)

The path of professional development may vary greatly individually (e.g. Inkson & Amundson, 2002; Uusiautti & Määttä, 2011). According to early childhood educators' stories, education and working life are important parts of this path and supporting the development of expertise appears challenging.

Results of this research showed that various factors can advance or hinder the development of early childhood educators' expertise. What are, then, the core features of a good early childhood educator? In the next section, we highlight some issues that modern early childhood educators and teachers should consider in their work.

Discussion: a good early childhood educator

Good teacherhood or educatorship has been characterised in several ways (e.g. Korthagen, 2004; Määttä & Uusiautti, 2011; Marcos, Sanchez, & Tillema, 2011; Van Manen, 1991). In addition to teachers' personality and individual characteristics, leadership skills, collaboration and social skills as well as substance knowledge have been considered important (e.g. Elliott, Isaacs, & Chugani, 2010; Jakku-Sihvonen, 2005; Taylor, Yates, Meyer, & Kinsella, 2011; Wall & McAleer, 2000). Indeed, interaction, cooperation, and group work skills are needed in human relationship work and service trades, but the ability to work autonomously is crucial in early childhood educators' work as well (see Evers, Rush, & Berdrow, 1998).

Professional competence is a dynamic concept. It can be used, developed, and changed with time and thus, it forms one phase of professional development from a novice into an expert. Competence is seen as an inevitable prerequisite for successful or at least satisfactory professional performance (Luukkainen, 2004). Professional competence develops the best in a learning process where people participate in developing their own work, in other words, are developers of the work and not just executors (Drexel, 2003). Many illustrations on work competence consider it as a result of various interconnected factors, such as cognitive skills, personality, work performance that occur and affect it in a certain situation and context (see, e.g. Kanfer & Ackerman, 2005) or as a result of several developmental stages (see, e.g. Dreyfus and Dreyfus's (1986) model from Novice to Expert).

Competence is an important part of expertise as competence consists of the mastery of substance and experience gathered through working. According to the present study, knowledge about the substance, for example, child development or pedagogical issues, is not enough. Nor can expertise be measured or developed just by work experience: 'Research in the field of expertise has demonstrated that "experienced" does not equal "expert"' (Dunn & Shriner, 1999, p. 648) although in teaching and educational professions practical experience is crucial (Palmer, Stough, Burdenski, & Gonzales, 2005).

Today's early childhood educators have to adopt a reflective approach in their work. In most educational research, reflection is defined as a useful and necessary method for teachers helping to analyse both a teacher's own and others' teaching critically and thus leads to better action in teaching (e.g. Artzt & Armour-Thomas, 2002; Mayall, 2000; Swain, 1998). One way of becoming a better educator is through observing and reflecting on one's own teaching, and using observation and reflection as a way of bringing about change – in other words 'Reflective Teaching' (Taggart, 2005).

According to Blay and Ireson (2009), there is a link between teachers' pedagogical beliefs and their classroom practices. That is why reflection should take place at every level of early childhood education daily. However, educators' work has become more and more collegial. Co-workers learn from each other and joint problem-solving in the work community is increasing. It is necessary to expand the notion of individual expertise in the realm of collaborative and socially shared expertise. Expertise can be collectively created through the processes of reflective dialogue (Allen & Casbergue, 1997). Beginning educators need support especially to solve pedagogical problems at every level and in order to develop the work community; experienced colleagues should mentor novices (Bartell, 2004; Reilly, 2008; Tochon & Munby, 1993).

Reflection makes an educator become aware of his/her practices and prejudices and ways of thinking. Yet, we claim that reflection can be carried out in a special manner, namely through love. Love cannot be ignored when reflecting good teacherhood or educatorship – regardless of educational level. Pedagogical love concerns early childhood educators as well. Today's expertise also necessitates a new kind of approach in all teaching and education (see Happo, 2006; Määttä & Uusiautti, 2011). Also in this research, love, genuine caring, and tenderness were described as a significant part of early childhood education and their meaning to a child was recognised. Indeed, many participants said that they used their 'lap, love, and limits' in their educational work and that they had 'their bosom and soul with them; plenty of love and caring'.

Love appears in teaching as guidance towards disciplined work but also as patience, trust, and forgiveness. The purpose is to create a setting for learning where children can use and develop their own resources, eventually proceeding at the maximum of their own abilities. An early childhood educator's expertise is manifested by the ability to look at things from a child's point of view (e.g. Zombylas, 2007).

All in all, an early childhood educator's expertise results from versatile mastery of the content in teaching (Davis, 1993; Hansen, 2009). However, even this mastery does not seem to be enough, but in order to develop into a good early childhood educator, we have to have a reflective and loving attitude towards our work and our children. Indeed, it would be important to study how to turn educators' personal attitude into initiative and reflection already during their basic education and later on in the work community.

References

Act on Children's Day Care. (1973/36). Retrieved February 6, 2011, from Finlex database http://www.finlex.fi/fi/laki/ajantasa/1973/19730036?search%5Btype%5D=pika&search% 5Bpika%5D=laki%20lasten%20p%C3%A4iv%C3%A4hoidosta

Adelson, B. (1984). When novices surpass experts: The difficulty of a task may increase with expertise. *Journal of Experimental Psychology: Learning, Memory, and Cognition, 10*(3), 483–495.

Allen, R.M., & Casbergue, R.M. (1997). Evolution of novice through expert teachers' recall: Implications for effective reflection on practice. *Teaching and Teacher Education, 13*(7), 741–755.

Artzt, A.F., & Armour-Thomas, E. (2002). *Becoming a reflective mathematics teacher: A guide for observations and self assessment.* Mahwah, NJ: Lawrence Erlbaum Associates.

Bartell, C.A. (2004). *Cultivating high-quality teaching through induction and mentoring.* Thousand Oaks, CA: Sage.

Bereiter, C., & Scardamalia, M. (1993). *Surpassing ourselves. An inquiry into the nature and implications of expertise.* Chicago, IL: Open Court.

Blay, J.A., & Ireson, J. (2009). Pedagogical beliefs, activity choice and structure, and adult–child interaction in nursery classrooms. *Teaching and Teacher Education, 25*(8), 1105–1116.

Bredekamp, S. (1997). Developmentally appropriate practice: The early childhood teacher as decisionmaker. In S. Bredekamp & C. Copple (Eds.), *Developmentally appropriate practice in early childhood programs* (pp. 33–52). Washington, DC: National Association for the Education of Young Children.

Bredekamp, S., & Willer, B. (1992). Of ladders and lattices, cores and cones: Conceptualizing an early childhood professional development system. *Young Children National Association for the Education of Young Children, 47*(3), 47–50.

Buchbinder, E. (2011). Beyond checking. Experiences of the validation interview. *Qualitative Social Work, 10*(1), 106–122.

Bullough, R.V., Jr., & Baughman, K. (1995). Changing contexts and expertise in teaching: First-year teacher after seven years. *Teaching & Teacher Education, 11*(5), 461–477.

Burnard, P. (1992). Expert to novice. *Nurse Education Today, 12*(5), 321–322.

Calderhead, J. (1984). *Teachers' classroom decision-making.* Worcester: Billing & Sons.

Carter, K., Sabers, D., Cushing, K., Pinnegar, S., & Berliner, D.C. (1987). Processing and using information about students: A study of expert, novice, and postulant teachers. *Teaching and Teacher Education, 3*(2), 147–157.

Collins, H.M., & Evans, R. (2002). The third wave of social studies: Studies of expertise and experience. *Social Studies of Science, 32*(2), 235–296.

Costigan, A.T., & Crocco, M.S. (2004). *Learning to teach in an age of accountability.* New Jersey: Lawrence Erlbaum Associates.

Davis, B.G. (1993). *Tools for teaching.* San Francisco, CA: Jossey-Bass.

Decree on Children's Day-care. (239/1973). Retrieved February 6, 2011, from Finlex database http://www.finlex.fi/fi/laki/ajantasa/1973/19730239?search%5Btype%5D=pika&search%5Bpika%5D=asetus%20lasten%20p%C3%A4iv%C3%A4hoidosta

Disch, J. (2002). From expert to novice. *Journal of Professional Nursing, 18*(6), 310.

Drexel, I. (2003). *The concept of competence – an instrument of social and political change,* (Working Paper No. 26). Retrieved June 18, 2011, from http://www.ub.uib.no/elpub/rokkan/N/N26-03.pdf

Dreyfus, H.L., & Dreyfus, S.E. (1986). *Mind over machine: The power of human intuition and expertise in the age of computer.* Oxford: Basil Blackwell.

Dunn, T.G., & Shriner, C. (1999). Deliberate practice in teaching: What teachers do for self-improvement. *Teaching and Teacher Education, 15,* 631–651.

Eisenhart, C. (2006). The humanist scholar as public expert. *Written Communication, 23*(2), 150–172.

Elliott, E.M., Isaacs, M.L., & Chugani, C.D. (2010). Promoting self-efficacy in early career teachers: A principal's guide for differentiated mentoring and supervision. *Florida Journal of Educational Administration & Policy, 4*(1), 131–146.

Engeström, Y. (1992). *Interactive expertise: Studies in distributed working intelligence.* Helsinki: University of Helsinki.

Ericsson, K., Chairness, N., Feltovich, P.J., & Hoffman, R.R. (2006). *The Cambridge handbook of expertise and expert performance.* Cambridge: Cambridge University Press.

Evers, F.T., Rush, J.C., & Berdrow, I. (1998). *The bases of competence: Skills for lifelong learning and employability.* San Francisco, CA: Jossey-Bass.

Goodfellow, J., & Sumsion, J. (2003). Transformative pathways in becoming an early childhood teacher. In O.N. Saracho & B. Spodek (Eds.), *Studying teachers in early childhood settings* (pp. 59–77). Greenwich, CT: Information Age Publishing.

Guba, E.G., & Lincoln, Y.S. (1981). *Effective evaluation. Improving the usefulness of evaluation results through responsive and naturalistic approaches.* San Francisco, CA: Jossey-Bass.

Guskey, T.R. (1986). Staff development and the process of teacher change. *Educational Researchers, 15*(5), 5–12.

Hansen, K. (2009). Strategies for developing effective teaching skills in the affective domain. *Journal for Physical and Sport Education, 23*(1), 14–19.

Happo, I. (2006). *Varhaiskasvattajan asiantuntijuus. Asiantuntijaksi kehittyminen Lapin läänissä* [Expertise of early childhood educators. Growth of expertise in early childhood educators in the Province of Lapland]. Acta Universitatis Lapponiensis 98. Rovaniemi: University of Lapland.

Happo, I., & Määttä, K. (2011). Expertise of early childhood educators. *International Education Studies*, *4*(3), 91–99.

Hatano, G., & Inagaki, K. (1986). Two courses of expertise. In H. Stevenson, H. Azuma, & K. Hakuta (Eds.), *Child development and education in Japan* (pp. 262–272). New York, NY: W.H. Freeman.

Hatano, G., & Inagaki, K. (1992). Desituating cognition through the construction of conceptual knowledge. In P. Light & G. Butterworth (Eds.), *Context and cognition: Ways of knowing and learning* (pp. 115–133). New York, NY: Harvester Wheatsheaf.

Holloway, I. (2011). Being a qualitative researcher. *Qualitative Health Research*, *21*(7), 968–975.

Huberman, A.M., & Miles, M.B. (1994). Data management and analysis methods. In N.K. Denzin & Y.S. Lincoln (Eds.), *Handbook of qualitative research* (pp. 428–444). Thousand Oaks, CA: Sage.

Inkson, K., & Amundson, N.E. (2002). Career metaphors and their application in theory and counseling practice. *Journal of Employment Counseling*, *39*, 98–108.

Jakku-Sihvonen, R. (2005). Kasvatustieteiden opetus ja asiantuntijan arkipätevyys [Education of the educational sciences and expert's everyday competence]. In J.-S. Ritva (Ed.), *Uudenlaisia maistereita. Kasvatusalan koulutuksen kehittämislinjoja* [New kinds of masters: Developmental guidelines of education of the educational sciences] (pp. 125–150). Jyväskylä: PS-kustannus.

Jalongo, M.R., & Isenberg, J.P. (2004). *Exploring your role: A practitioner's introduction to early childhood education* (2nd ed.). Upper Saddle River, NJ: Merrill/Prentice-Hall.

Kanfer, R., & Ackerman, P.L. (2005). Work competence: A person-oriented perspective. In A.J. Elliot & C.S. Dweck (Eds.), *Handbook of competence and motivation* (pp. 336–353). New York and London: The Guilford Press.

Karila, K. (1997). *Lastentarhanopettajan kehittyvä asiantuntijuus – Lapsirakkaasta opiskelijasta kasvatuksen asiantuntijaksi* [An early childhood education teacher's developing expertise – from a child-loving student into an educational expert] (PhD Thesis). Helsinki: Edita.

Karila, K., & Nummenmaa, A.R. (2001). *Matkalla moniammatillisuuteen Kuvauskohteena päiväkoti* [A the way toward multiprofessionalism: day-care centre as the target of depiction]. Helsinki: WSOY.

Katz, L.K. (1977). *Talks with teachers. Reflections on early childhood education.* Washington, DC: National Association for the Education of Young Children.

Knowles, M.S. (1975). *Self-directed learning. A guide for learners and teachers.* Chicago: Follett.

Korthagen, F.A.J. (2004). In search of the essence of a good teacher: Toward a more holistic approach in teacher education. *Teaching and Teacher Education*, *20*(1), 77–97.

Kupila, P. (2001). 'Peilaan omaa asiantuntijuuttani toiseen' – yhteinen reflektio oppimisen tukena ['I reflect my own expertise in the other' – common reflection as a support for learning]. *Pedaforum. Yliopistopedagoginen tiedotuslehti*, *8*(2), 35–37.

Lajoie, S. (2003). Transitions and trajectoris for studies of expertise. *Education Researcher*, *32*(8), 21–25.

Luukkainen, O. (2004). *Opettajuus - Ajassa elämistä vai suunnan näyttämistä?* [Teachership - living in time or leading the way] (Acta Universitatis Tamperensis No. 986.). Tampere: University of Tampere. Retrieved July 25, 2011, from http://acta.uta.fi/pdf/951-44-5885-0.pdf

Marcos, J.M., Sanchez, E., & Tillema, H.H. (2011). Promoting teacher reflection: What is said to be done. *Journal of Education for Teaching*, *37*(1), 21–36.

Mayall, B. (2000). The sociology of childhood in relation to children's rights. *The International Journal of Children's Rights*, *8*, 243–259.

Määttä, K., & Uusiautti, S. (2011). Pedagogical love and good teacherhood. *In Education*, *17*(2). Retrieved from http://ineducation.ca/article/pedagogical-love-and-good-teacherhood

National Curriculum Guidelines on Early Childhood Education and Care in Finland. (2003). *Guidelines 56.* Helsinki: Statistics Finland. Retrieved February 6, 2011, from http://kasvunkumppanit.thl.fi/thl-client/pdfs/267671cb-0ec0-4039-b97b-7ac6ce6b9c10

Organisation for Economic Co-operation and Development (OECD). (2006). *Starting strong II:* *Early childhood education and care*. Retrieved February 14, 2011, from http://www.oecd. org/document/56/0,3746,en_2649_39263231_37416703_1_1_1_1,00.html#ES

Olson, G. (1994). Preparing early childhood educators for constructivist teaching. In S.G. Goffin & D.E. Day (Eds.), *New perspectives in early childhood teacher education: Bringing practitioners into the debate* (pp. 37–47). New York, NY: Teachers College Press.

Palmer, D.J., Stough, L.M., Burdenski, T.K., Jr., & Gonzales, M. (2005). Identifying teacher expertise: An examination of researchers' decision making. *Educational Psychologist, 40*(1), 13–25.

Puckett, M.B., & Diffily, D. (1999). *Teaching young children: An introduction to the early childhood profession*. Orlando, FL: Harcourt Brace & Company.

Raymond, D., Butt, R., & Townsend, D. (1992). Contexts for teacher development: Insight from teachers' stories. In A. Hargreaves & M.G. Fullan (Eds.), *Understanding teacher development* (pp. 143–167). Columbia, NY: Teachers College Press.

Reilly, R.C. (2008). Is expertise a necessary precondition for creativity? A case of four novice learning group facilitators. *Thinking Skills and Creativity, 3*, 59–76.

Ryan, K., & Cooper, J.M. (2004). *Those who can, teach* (10th ed.). Boston, MA: Houghton Mifflin.

Saracho, O.N., & Spodek, B. (2003). The preparation of teachers for the profession in early childhood education. In O.N. Saracho & B. Spodek (Eds.), *Studying teachers in early childhood settings* (pp. 1–28). Greenwich, CT: Information Age Publishing.

Selinger, E., & Crease, R.P. (2006). *The philosophy of expertise*. New York, NY: Columbia University Press.

Sim, M., & Kim, J.-U. (2010). Differences between experts and novices in kinematics and accuracy of golf putting. *Human Movement Science, 29*(6), 932–946.

Starkey, L., Yates, A., Meyer, L.H., Hall, C., Taylor, M., Stevens, S., & Toia, R. (2009). Professional development design: Embedding educational reform in New Zealand. *Teaching and Teacher Education, 25*, 181–189.

Swain, J. (1998). Studying teachers' transformations: Reflections as methodology. *The Clearing House, 72*(1), 29–34.

Taggart, G. (2005). *Promoting reflective thinking in teachers: 50 action strategies*. Thousand Oaks, CA: Corwin Press.

Taylor, M., Yates, A., Meyer, L.H., & Kinsella, P. (2011). Teacher professional leadership in support of teacher professional development. *Teaching and Teacher Education, 27*, 85–94.

Tochon, F., & Munby, H. (1993). Novice and expert teachers' time epistemology: A wave function from didactics ton pedagogy. *Teaching and Teacher Education, 9*(2), 205–218.

Tuomi, J., & Sarajärvi, A. (2002). *Laadullinen tutkimus ja sisällönanalyysi* [Qualitative research and content analysis]. Helsinki: Tammi.

Turner, S. (2001). What is the problem with experts? *Social Studies in Science, 31*(1), 123–149.

Tynjälä, P. (1999). Konstruktivistinen oppimiskäsitys ja asiantuntijuuden edellytysten rakentaminen koulutuksessa [The constructivist idea of learning and creating the prerequisites of expertise in education]. In A. Eteläpelto & P. Tynjälä (Eds.), *Oppiminen ja asiantuntijuus. Työelämän ja koulutuksen näkökulmia* [Learning and expertise. Perspectives of working life and education] (pp. 160–179). Porvoo: WSOY.

Uusiautti, S., & Määttä, K. (2010). What kind of employees become awarded as employees of the year in Finland. *Enterprise and Work Innovation Studies, 6*, 53–73. Retrieved July 25, 2011, from http://hdl.handle.net/10362/5725

Uusiautti, S., & Määttä, K. (2011). The process of becoming a top worker. *International Education Studies, 4*(4), 69–79.

Valkeavaara, T. (1999). Ongelmien kauttako asiantuntijaksi? – Henkilöstön kehittäjien kokemuksia työnsä ongelmallisista tilanteista [Through problems into an experts? – The experiences of personnel coaches about the problematic situations in their work]. In A. Eteläpelto & P. Tynjälä (Eds.), *Oppiminen ja asiantuntijuus. Työelämän ja koulutuksen näkökulmia* [Learning and expertise: Perspectives of working life and education] (pp. 102–124). Porvoo: WSOY.

Van Manen, M. (1991). *The tact of teaching. The meaning of pedagogical thoughtfulness*. Albany, NY: State University of New York Press.

Walker, G.H., Stanton, N.A., Salmon, P.M., Jenkins, D.P., Rafferty, L., & Ladva, D. (2010). Same or different? Generalism from novices to experts in military command and control studies. *International Journal of Industrial Ergonomics, 40*(5), 473–483.

Wall, D., & McAleer, S. (2000). Teaching the consult teachers: Identifying the core content. *Medical Education, 34*(2), 131–138.

Whittemore, R., Chase, S.K., & Mandle, C.L. (2001). Validity in qualitative research. *Qualitative Health Research, 11*(4), 522–537.

Wood, E., & Bennett, N. (2000). Changing theories, changing practice: Exploring early childhood teachers' professional learning. *Teaching and Teacher Education, 16*(5–6), 635–647.

Ylitapio-Mäntylä, O., Uusiautti, S., & Määttä, K. (submitted). Critical viewpoint to early childhood education teachers' wellbeing at work.

Zombylas, N. (2007). Emotional ecology: The intersection of emotional knowledge and pedagogical content knowledge in teaching. *Teaching and Teacher Education, 23,* 355–367.

Index

Printed in Great Britain
by Amazon

60769055R00133